TO

MY OLD FRIENDS OF THE CITY TEMPLE
AND
THE SUNDAY MORNING CONGREGATION
OF CHRIST CHURCH, WESTMINSTER,
THIS BOOK IS INSCRIBED

Read 1922 - Feb.
Fine. See last chaps for
full opinion.

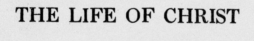

THE LIFE OF CHRIST

THE LIFE OF CHRIST

By R. J. CAMPBELL, D.D., OXONIAN
VICAR OF CHRIST CHURCH, WESTMINSTER
FORMERLY ❧ ❧ ❧ ❧ ❧ ❧ ❧ ❧ ❧
MINISTER OF THE CITY TEMPLE, LONDON
AUTHOR OF A SPIRITUAL PILGRIMAGE

D. APPLETON AND COMPANY
NEW YORK ❧ ❧ ❧ MCMXXI

PREFACE

This book requires some explanation. Six years ago, at the request of Messrs. Cassell, the author undertook to write a life of Christ which should meet the needs of the ordinary churchgoer in regard to the devout study of the subject without ignoring the accepted conclusions of scholarship. The difficulty, foreseen from the first, in executing this commission was that of compressing the material into manageable one-volume space, and it was a difficulty which became accentuated as time went on, especially with the rapidly rising cost of book production in consequence of the war. The work grew under the writer's hands to such proportions that he asked the publishers to allow him to divide it into a short series of smaller volumes instead of presenting it whole and entire in one. This they could not see their way to do—at any rate not at present—so the course has had to be adopted of cutting down the matter to the dimensions available. It is hoped that at some future time this short outline of a great subject may be supplemented by a homiletical commentary on the gospels.

For this is essentially a preacher's life of Christ in so far as it is a life of Christ at all. There is no life of Christ, nor ever will be, with our present

knowledge of the brief earthly story of Jesus of
Nazareth. A problem it is, a problem it must remain. But in this book the author has endeavored
to commend a special point of view, the point of
view of Christian experience, as being of first importance for the study of the gospel records; and
he has never lost sight of his congregation. This
book has been preached almost in its entirety—in
part to the City Temple congregation, and the re-
mainder to the Sunday morning congregation
which the author addresses week by week in Christ
Church, Westminster. Hence the homiletical
method predominates in the treatment of the contents and the principles governing their selection.
Should any reader be disposed to complain of a
lack of proportion in the discussion of one aspect
of the general subject as compared with another,
he will now understand the reason. It was impossible to give adequate space to all, so a choice had
to be made. The omissions will be obvious. To
examine the parables in detail, for instance, would
require an extra volume.

Perhaps it may be worth while to mention that
the principle has been followed herein of putting
capitals only when a word has some claim to stand
for a unique idea. Thus the Church universal is
spelt with a capital, any local church with a small
initial letter; the Kingdom of God with a capital,
any kingdom of this world with a small initial letter; the word Gospel itself should represent the
Christian evangel as a whole, while any one of the
four gospels may be written without a capital.

In view of the fact also that this book is intended for the use of the average man or woman who is in the habit of attending public worship, a careful selection has been made of literature cited in the text or wherewith to continue the study. It is to be regretted that not all of this is obtainable in English, though the greater part of it is. The titles are given in English throughout.

CONTENTS

xi

CONTENTS

CONTENTS

THE LIFE OF CHRIST

CHAPTER I

INTRODUCTORY

RELIGION IN HISTORY

THE period of recorded human history is but short compared with the unnumbered ages which lie behind. Science tells us that our world has been millions of years in preparation for the advent of humanity; there may even have been organic life on this planet millions of years ago; but man himself, man as clearly distinguished from the brute creation, is only of yesterday. And of that yesterday what a small portion is thoroughly known! History, properly speaking, begins a few generations back, and beyond that is a far longer stretch of time concerning which we know almost nothing. Primeval man has left many traces behind him, principally implements of war and the chase, but how he thought and felt about the great mystery that we call life is completely hidden from us. Perhaps he did not think and feel much; perhaps the

1

fierce necessities of existence forbade the contemplation of abstract questions; perhaps he had no more inclination or capacity for these than an Australian aborigine has at the present day. Still there is this to be said about the matter, that what specially differentiates man from all other living creatures is that he does ask questions, he does wonder and worship, he does seek to know how he stands related to the power or powers partially revealed in the phenomenal universe. A savage might not put the case to himself in this way, nor have the capacity for doing so, but even in animism this is what is dimly present to his mind. He is ever conscious of a beyond, a veiled presence, a greater than himself, with which (or whom) he has to do whether he will or no. This may not be a very lofty experience in its initial stages, but such as it is it is the root of all religion. For religion is essentially a reaching out to what is above and beyond ourselves, above and beyond all that we can see and know of the material order of things. It is our attempt to enter into relations with our cause; and man in the mass has never yet been persuaded that that cause is itself material. We instinctively feel it to be spiritual—that is, self-conscious as we are self-conscious, and capable of willing and acting as we will and act. Nay, more— it is that whence we derive these qualities and capacities.

Let it be recognized as aforesaid that it is highly improbable that primitive man reasoned in this way; but if we are to judge from the psychology of undeveloped races in the world to-day, he went straight to the mark and took it all for granted, as it were. He could not help investing the forces of nature with the kind of intelligence he himself possessed, and assuming that those forces were directed by thought and purpose; and where you get that you get religion. We have no good ground for thinking that any other earthly creature is capable of so much; man is the being with the upward look; we might almost say that the capacity for religion is the dividing line between the human and sub-human kingdoms. Nowhere do we find man without religion; it is that which constitutes him man. This statement may be gainsaid, but only by citing the most degraded and abnormal types of humanity. The history of man is the history of religion. Every achievement that stands to his credit in his long and arduous upward climb is directly or indirectly associated with his religious consciousness.

Short as is the period of recorded history, it is longer than we used to think. We have now good reason for believing that civilization reaches back as far as 10,000 B.C. and even farther. Religion has succeeded to religion in that vast period of time, race to race, society to society. But one thing is certain throughout, and that is that man has ever been deeply impressed by the mystery of his being and his dependence upon superhuman power. The instinct of worship has always made itself felt within him, together with the ineradicable belief that his sources are in the unseen, that his nature is fundamentally spiritual and therefore not wholly to be interpreted in terms of his fleshly constitution.

Nevertheless, it must be admitted that on the whole the religious systems of the world have not been very elevating. In many instances they can only be classed as degrading and cruel superstitions; not a few were and are morally licentious. It cannot be maintained that religion has invariably and necessarily had a lofty or inspiring influence upon the ideals and conduct of mankind; too frequently it has had quite the reverse. Even such a marvelously developed civilization as that of classical Greece was from the religious point of view in many ways anything but admirable; [1] the gods and goddesses of the Greek pantheon were credited with being rather worse in their behavior than their votaries. No one could pretend that Greek religion stood for idealism in belief and practice, though this is a statement which may require to be modified if we have regard to the products of Greek philosophy which assimilated itself very readily later in certain ways to the Christian religion.[2] We also need to take account of the fact that the various Greek mystery-cults which came into existence near to the Christian era seem, as far as we can gather—for we have not much reliable information about them—to have laid stress upon ideas which we now think of as specifically Christian. The idea of sacrifice is one of these—the sacrifice of God for man. Bound up with this is another, that of the dying and rising

[1] But for a balanced and illuminating view of this subject *vide* Prof. Gilbert Murray's *Four Stages of Greek Religion.*
[2] *Vide* Lewis Campbell: *Religion in Greek Literature,* chap. xiii to end; T. R. Glover: *Conflict of Religions in Early Roman Empire,* p. 106 *ff;* Lecky: *History of European Morals,* Vol. I, chap. ii, p. 161 *ff.*

savior.[3] And behind both is the thought of a world needing to be redeemed from its evil.

But the most noteworthy fact relating to religion in the ancient world is the rise of the Israelitish prophets. It should be understood by modern readers that these were primarily preachers, not merely soothsayers or foretellers of events.[4] And they rendered one inestimable service to all the ages that followed them, ours as much as any, and that was their welding of religion and morality. Believing themselves to be divinely inspired, they taught that their God, the God of Israel, must be worshiped in righteousness. Hence Israelitish religion is a unique fact in history; it stands by itself both in the purity of its lofty monotheism and in the wonderful influence it has exerted upon the rest of the world. It would be more correct to say Jewish religion, for it is only the tribe of Judah that has persisted right through the ages and given its name to the faith from which Christianity sprang. The other tribes which constituted the ancient kingdom of Israel have for the most part, through successive conquests and apostasies, been scattered and merged in surrounding kindred peoples. The Jews alone, through all the vicissitudes of their national existence, have preserved their consciousness of identity and their ancient faith; they have been, as they still

[3] It may be new to some readers that this was ever a Greek idea or in fact any other than a Christian idea; but the knowledge is of value as showing that the preparation in history for the Christian faith was wider and deeper than is often supposed.

[4] Hamilton: *People of God*, Vol. I, chap. v, and Marti's excellent chapter on this subject in his *Religion of Old Testament* (Williams & Norgate).

are, a peculiar people in more ways than one.

It need hardly be said that Judaism was not always the clear-cut ethical and monotheistic system that it is to-day or that it was in later Old Testament times. Originally Jehovah (Yahweh) was regarded by the people of Israel as only one God among many, their own particular tribal deity as distinguished from the deities of other nations. And the righteousness insisted upon by the earlier prophets as acceptable to Jehovah was often grim and terrible, far removed indeed from the Christian standard with which we are familiar to-day. But at least it can be said that the religious ideal and the ethical ideal were held to imply each other; the prophets would not suffer them to be considered apart. This was why the prophets strove so hard throughout the history of Israel, while it remained one, and not a very large one, of the number of Semitic nations inhabiting hither Asia, to preserve the national worship from contamination from foreign sources. Elijah's fierce battle against the Baalim, for instance, was not a mere question of names; all the future of the race was at stake. Had Baal worship prevailed it would have meant a permanent lowering of the whole standard of moral and religious belief and practice; Israel would have become assimilated in manners and conduct to the rest of the Canaanitish peoples, and probably like these would ultimately have perished from the earth. It is a very impressive fact in the providential order, when we come to consider it, that this did not happen, but that Israel—or at least Judaism—survived to maintain a constant witness to the unity and righteousness of God, the power behind phenomena, the Creator and sustainer of all that is. For gradually the God of Israel came to be thought of as the God of the whole earth, the one and only God; and the idea of righteousness was slowly clarified and ennobled until the fuller and higher Christian revelation became possible.[5]

This is one fact then to be specially noted: the religion of Israel is a unique phenomenon in the pre-Christian world.[6] The claim made for it is fully justified, that it represents a special divine revelation, a preparation for a true world-religion when the time should be ripe. Its very narrowness and exclusiveness, which we must note later, and its determination to arrogate to itself a position of privilege in relation to the things of God, may actually have helped up to a point to preserve the content of this revelation; but those bonds had to be burst in the end to give room for the ampler life which had sprung up within the old Jewish environment.[7]

THE TWO PLANES OF BEING

Now for a space let us turn away from the historical standpoint and consider another. Instead of going back into the past to learn how things have come to be what they are in the present, we may

[5] Marti, *ut sup.* p. 4 *et seq.* Hamilton: *ut sup.*, Vol. I, chaps. iii, iv.

[6] This view has been challenged, but is surely demonstrable from the facts of history.

[7] Addis: *Hebrew Religion* (Williams & Norgate), pp. 76, 138, 152 *ff*. Loisy: *Religion of Israel*, v, vi, Judaism and Messianism. *Cf*. Montefiore: *Religion of the Ancient Hebrews,* concluding Lect.

view the whole subject in an equally important but entirely different way: we may examine the structure of existence itself.

In modern times science has been familiarizing us with a view of the constitution of the universe which at first sight might seem to leave little room for religion. We find the universe to be vaster than the ancients ever knew, the particular star on which we live being one of the smallest out of untold myriads. It is wonderful, amazing beyond words, to the imagination inconceivable in its immensity, this universe of universes in a comparatively tiny speck of which we dwell and are whirled through space with a velocity all but immeasurable. This stupendous whole of things is said by some to be self-contained and self-sufficient. Out of the boundless ocean of ether, which forms its basis, solar systems continually arise, evolve, pursue their course for an indefinite number of ages, disintegrate and sink back into their primordial elements only to begin the same process all over again; there is no cessation to it. At this moment in the heaven above us we can observe planetary aggregations at every stage of the cosmic integration and dissolution through which the particular group of worlds to which our mother earth belongs has passed, is passing, and will pass from the beginning to the end of the life of a sun and his satellites.

As far as the planet earth is concerned the details of the process up to the present have been fairly well laid bare. We have learned from what lowly beginnings organic life took its rise, and how slowly and painfully it has developed through species after species till its culmination in man. Some authorities maintain that it is going on farther, and will by and by produce a superman. That may be; religion need have no quarrel with the thought; but so far man represents nature's supreme achievement. We need not argue the question whether any outside agency was required for making him what he is, or whether the slow and gradual operation of natural forces and material conditions was sufficient for the purpose. Here he is, and there is that in him which is not to be accounted for on material grounds alone. He can wonder, love, plan, achieve; he can probe nature's secrets and make use of nature's powers to his own ends; he may be comparatively puny in face of nature's colossal energies and terrific catastrophes, but he knows, and he knows that he knows, whereas nature does neither. This one impressive fact that here is a being that knows, a being that can think and plan, that can look before and after, is not to be explained by evolution or natural selection or any other theory of existence which takes account of the material and phenomenal only. It belongs to another order of things altogether. Man is a being belonging to the visible universe in his body and the conditions under which it has to be kept alive; but he belongs to something superphysical in what is most really himself, his thinking part, that of him which knows, and feels, and aspires.

This consideration throws us back upon a thought implied in all which has been said hitherto, namely,

that religion is primarily the assertion of a supernatural order as contrasted with the natural.[8] This
is the most important thing to grasp at this stage
of our inquiry. The world that lies open to us
through the five senses represents an order of things
complete and coherent in itself. It is an order
wherein are certain observable sequences which we
call laws. These sequences are both of time and
space, and, constituted as we now are, we cannot
think without them. If we press our analysis of
them far enough we find that they tend to disappear or to result in hopeless mental tangles and con-
tradictions, but we cannot get outside them. For
instance, let us say, it is twenty minutes to seven
by the clock as you read these words, but it was
about twenty-five minutes past six when you first
began to do so. No one could convince the ordinary plain man that that lapse of time has not
meant a real and lasting change; when an hour is
gone, it is gone never to return. We live so many
years, and we too pass away, never to return. Generation succeeds to generation, life to life, age to
age. We live all our days in time-relations, and
we cannot conceive what a state would be like in
which there was no time. It is the same with space
—in fact the two imply each other. Form, color,
mobility, distinguishing characteristics—all these
depend upon our constant experience of an order
of things in which we are governed by the ideas of
space and time. It takes us so long to walk across

[8] Employing neither term in the strict theological sense as defined,
e.g., by Fr. Sollier in *Catholic Encyclopædia* (Caxton Publishing Co.).

INTRODUCTORY

the room, so much longer to journey from London to Edinburgh by train, and so much longer still to travel from the cradle to the grave. We are born, grow up, marry and are given in marriage, struggle, suffer, grow old, decay, and die—unless we are cut off before our time. Everything else follows much the same course, be it long or short. The sun rises and sets, flowers bloom, rivers flow, all in conformity with certain observable sequences bound up with space and time. Within limits we can depend upon these absolutely. "While the earth remaineth, seed-time and harvest, and cold and heat, and summer and winter, and day and night shall not cease." [9]

Such is the natural order. We cannot imagine any other. Try to picture any other, and at once you are at fault. Do what you will, the order you picture will have three dimensions—length, breadth, and height. You may draw a fearsome dragon for your little boy, such a dragon as the world never saw and never will see, but you will have to give it the same kind of organs as you possess yourself in common with the rest of creation. The limbs with which you invest it may be such as no creature has ever walked about on, but they will be limbs. Its eyes may dart flames of fire or scintillate with all the hues of the rainbow, but they will be eyes; and so on with all the rest of it. We cannot even in imagination escape the dominion of the natural order, although, as has already been indicated, the fact that we can conceive of and direct our conduct by such values as love, truth, honor, and the like,

[9] Gen. viii. 22.

11

shows that we have affinities with something not wholly to be expressed in terms of the natural order.[10]

Is there then a higher order of being than this natural order with which we are so well acquainted? Yes, all religion affirms it; all goodness declares it. What is it like? We do not know, and by our own unaided faculties have no means of knowing. "Eye hath not seen, nor ear heard, neither have entered into the heart of man the things which God hath prepared for them that love him." [11] But this much we know about it on the testimony of divine revelation and of our own finer instincts, a witness attested by the highest spiritual experience, that it is all-perfect. No one needs to be told that the natural order is very far from being perfect. Things seem to have gone wrong somewhere; the conditions of earthly life are very unideal indeed; the world is a scene of strife and trouble. For the lowest of created things to the highest every species has to fight for its life and lives by killing. Man is the worst of all in this respect, for he kills most ruthlessly. The higher we rise in the scale of being the more our capacity for pain increases; we have more to fear, and have to add care and sorrow to the physical terrors to which our humbler kinsfolk are subject. It is no wonder that idealists in all ages have dreamed of a state wherein the wicked cease from troubling and the weary are at rest. Clearly this is not it, nor from the evidence of his-

[10] Bushnell: *Nature and the Supernatural* (Dickinson, 1887), chap. ii. Erskine of Linlathen: *The Spiritual Order,* chap. i, p. 11.
[11] I Cor. ii. 9.

tory is this ever likely to be made even approximately like it; and supposing this could be made like it, what of the unnumbered multitude of human beings of past and present who would have no share in the grand result?

Let us not be misled here. The difference between the two planes of being is not a mere matter of geography; we do not pass out of the one into the other as we pass out of one room into another; the two interpenetrate, or rather the higher to a certain extent interpenetrates the lower though we are only dimly conscious of it. Further, the Christian hope is that one day the higher will fully invade and possess the lower and transform its whole character.

We must lay firm hold upon this one grand conception: There is a supernatural order wherein everything is already perfect, just what it ought to be. It is that which is, that which abides, as opposed to all that appears to be and passes away. Nothing needs to be added to it, nothing can be taken from it. It is a state of perfect harmony, perfect bliss, perfect good will, a state wherein all noblest hopes are fulfilled and all beautiful dreams have already come true. We cannot perceive that state, for it is not revealed to flesh and blood; it is not cognizable by the five senses; it is not governed by natural laws; nor is it confined within the categories of space and time. Nevertheless we cannot say that it has nothing to do with us at all. The natural order is not without evidence of the supernatural wherever the material is the vehicle of the spiritual. All gracious and uplifting things that enter into our experience are tokens of the supernatural order. The two stand related to each other as a glorious landscape to its blurred and broken reflection in the waters of a lake.[12] In some degree heaven is continually present, and in special ways is continually breaking through into the darkness and disorder of earth.[13]

There have been many of these special invasions, no doubt. Tokens abound of the nearness and potency of that invisible order whence we derive and towards which all our highest aspirations are consistently directed. Visions and revelations of the Lord have been vouchsafed to the spiritually susceptible from age to age. In spite of all denials and all secularity of temper, the supernatural is constantly reasserting itself in the experience of mankind. Celestial beings have revealed themselves to terrestrial observers occasionally in times of special stress or urgent need; intimations have never been wanting of the fact that heaven takes a vivid interest in the affairs of earth and is ever ready to help. The story of the angels of Mons, whether true or imaginary, does not stand by itself; there are many like it, and their frequency and persistence are a standing proof, if proof were needed,

[12] Rendel Harris: *Sidelights on New Testament Research*, p. 220. The primitive Christians under Platonic influence "had perhaps heard that the visible world was connected with an ideal world of which it was the outward stamp or expression."

[13] Eucken: *Life of the Spirit* (Williams & Norgate), chaps. ii and iii, and *Truth of Religion* (Dr. Tudor Jones' translation) has much suggestive matter on this point. *Also* Wicksteed's striking essay on the "Religion of Time and the Religion of Eternity" in *Studies in Theology* (J. M. Dent), 1903.

that a more or less continuous commerce is maintained between the hither and the yonder, the higher and the lower, the natural and the supernatural.

But there is no need to lay stress upon quasi-miraculous visitations in support of the statement that these two planes of being can and do communicate with each other to a certain extent: it is better to appeal to the testimony of spiritual life itself. Messengers of God have generally declared themselves to be conscious of special divine inspiration in preparation for their work, and often this preparation has been preceded or accompanied by something supernormal, some opening of the eyes to the presence of what is ordinarily hidden from human apprehension. As examples of this we might cite Isaiah's vision in the Temple at Jerusalem and that of Saul of Tarsus on the road to Damascus. In each case we have the sudden unveiling of supersensuous realities in such a way that the percipient found it impossible to doubt his vocation or the overwhelming importance of the spiritual order as contrasted with the material. Abundance of similar testimony exists even to-day. And every saintly soul knows and would be prepared to maintain that faith, goodness, humility can at any time contact the spiritual plane and receive assurance of help and strengthening. These are they whose conversation is in heaven, who are already living with greater or less success the life eternal in the midst of the things of time.[14]

Beyond all reasonable question, however, the

[14] Von Hügel: *Eternal Life.*

greatest invasion of the natural order by the supernatural that has ever been made took place about nineteen centuries ago when a little child was born in Palestine whose name has since become to the whole civilized world what Mr. Gladstone called "the one central hope of our poor wayward race." If there be a supernatural at all—and upon that postulate, as we have seen, all idealism truly rests—then the coming of Jesus Christ into the world is the strongest evidence of it that has ever been given. It need hardly be pointed out here that the word "supernatural" as thus employed does not relate wholly or principally to what are commonly regarded as miraculous events: it means that plane of being which transcends all that we at present know as the natural world; and nearly everyone would admit that the person and influence of Jesus, whoever He may be, are indissolubly associated in our minds with the conception of the supernatural order and all that it implies. What we have to learn if we can is how His life relates itself to history on the one hand and to eternal reality on the other.

THE PROBLEM OF THE LIFE OF JESUS

There are two ways of approaching the study of this unique life. The first is that which has been in vogue ever since Strauss published his *Leben Jesu* in the middle of the nineteenth century; that is, the assumption that it can be explained on purely naturalistic hypotheses. This is or used to be the confessed or unconfessed prepossession of most of the modern advanced critics of the gospel sources. They start with the bias that the historical Jesus, if He can be found, will be discovered to be a person of extraordinary religious genius perhaps, but in all essentials like other persons who have left their mark upon history. At the very outset they tacitly rule out the possibility that He may belong to a different category altogether. They look for an ordinary human being of more than ordinary endowments, and then try to reconcile what they find in the New Testament with this theory. Even when they admit the presence of certain supernormal elements in His nature and work they discuss these throughout from the naturalistic standpoint. They explain away as much as they can of the miraculous and exceptional in the records that exist concerning Him. No one can read their works without perceiving that the problem before these experts is that of smoothing away the abnormalities in the life of Jesus as compared with other lives. By some of them the abnormalities are frankly regarded as incredible; and what such inquirers seek to do is to get behind these in some way and come upon what they believe to be the real Jesus, the Jesus who did not work miracles or make staggering claims in regard to His own person and its special relation both to God and man. The fact that in so doing they would not have much left has all along been felt to be a very real difficulty in the scientific examination of what is to be known about Jesus.[15] It presents us with an insoluble problem.

[15] As e.g. in Schmiedel's much discussed article on the gospels in *Encyclopædia Biblica*.

To believe that Jesus actually lived, and yet refuse to believe in the supernatural portents that attended His birth and His public ministry, or that He ever used the language that has been put into His mouth about His Messiahship, His second coming, and the like, is to be landed in a maze of critical questions to which no answers are forthcoming.

The outstanding fact to which we have thus drawn attention should be definitely recognized for what it is or our study is marred at the outset. We cannot study the life of Jesus as we should study that of Mahomet or John Wesley: the subject before us is of another kind, and that is why so much of the criticism of Christian origins has gone wide of the mark. The Church of Jesus is as unique as the being to whom it owes its origin and claims to owe its present existence. It is not like any other society and no other can be placed in comparison with it. In making this statement we do not beg the question of the true constitution of the Church or whether Jesus ever intended to found a Church; these questions do not govern the issue. The Church is a fact in history, a fact which bulks large, and we cannot rightly dissever the life that gave it birth from the experience of that life which has been developed and maintained within the Church through many generations. If we could place any other society in the wide world alongside of the Christian Church and compare the two our task would be easier. But we cannot; we have no analogue for it.[16] Here we have a great international

[16] Swete: *Holy Catholic Church,* pp. 30, 142.

organization or group of organizations with laws of its own and a life of its own distinct from that of the world around it. Its aims and standards are not those of other associations of human beings, whether political, scientific, literary, or commercial. It claims to be a supernatural society and to be sustained and directed from a higher world. The claim may be admitted or rejected but cannot be ignored. Much fault is being found with the Church at the present time among all classes and in nearly all countries; it has obvious defects and partakes greatly of the evils and disabilities of the secular communities within which it carries on a corporate existence. Many of the attacks upon it are justified up to a point by the weakness and ineptitude, not to use a stronger term, of its members; but when its friends fear and its foes exultantly proclaim that its day is done they forget that Jesus is said to have definitely prophesied that this should not be, and that He Himself would remain with it to the end of time. The Church cannot perish and Jesus live.

This suggests the second point of view alluded to above from which to approach the study of the life of Jesus. It is the Jesus presented to us in the continuous experience of the living Church with whom we have acquaintance, not a Jesus disinterred from written records. If the Church could have been blotted out of existence, and all knowledge of its teachings and institutions have disappeared as completely as, say, the religion of Mithras, and we were rediscovering the New Testament and reading its contents, there would be little need to discuss the person of Jesus: He would have no reality for us. It may be questioned whether many people realize how true this is or how little dependent we are upon the printed page after all for what we know of Jesus. We know him mainly and immediately through the life of the Church and then we go to the printed page with that conception of Him in our minds and find it there also; in fact the Jesus of the gospels and epistles is the projection of the experience of the apostolic Church. That experience has been passed on from age to age and life to life up to the present hour; it is that which we are really investigating when we inquire into Christian origins and the verdict of criticism upon the New Testament writings and their various affinities. Let us not lose sight of this truth. When all is said and done the living tradition counts for more than the written word, or rather, the written word only yields up its true meaning and value when interpreted in the light of the living tradition. We know Jesus in the New Testament because we already know Him in the Church which gave us the New Testament. The Church was in existence before the New Testament, in a sense was itself the New Testament from the first, the embodiment of a new life, a new spiritual idea, and the presentation of a new hope for mankind. There is no break in its continuity; it is the same Church to-day as in the apostolic age, and its witness to the Savior it proclaims is the same. Theologies may come and go, but the Jesus of

Christian faith and worship possesses an immediacy independent of all theorizing about its nature, an immediacy indissolubly one with the life of the Church He indwells.

Every reader knows the impossibility of conveying a complete pen picture of any personality whatsoever. You may describe minutely the appearance, manners, voice, and other peculiarities of a new acquaintance, but you do not succeed in giving to any one at a distance your own impression of the man himself, his spiritual idiom, so to speak; the thing which constitutes that man's special individuality and differentiates him from all the rest of the world is the indescribable. No matter how much you may have heard beforehand about a person or read of him and his doings, it is only when you come into actual contact with him that you receive a true idea of what he is. It is the present writer's conviction that this has been largely overlooked in recent years in the criticisms of New Testament literature. The only right method of approach to the Jesus of the New Testament is through the living witness, the witness of His continued presence with His Church. No other method can yield any but misleading results.

Again, be it understood that this does not necessarily mean the discussion of dogma. One can gain a psychological impression of a personality without knowing anything of its antecedents or associations. And many simple-hearted folk have this kind of impression of Jesus without being able to define His relation to the Godhead or to expound a single

clause of the creed. They know Him in Himself,
are conscious of His quality, respond to His spirit,
lie close to His heart, without being able in any
way to explain to a third party how much this relationship implies. Such devotional knowledge of
Jesus, which is of the very essence of all spiritual
communion with Him, has only been made possible
through the supernatural life inherent in the fellowship of the Christian Church. It is upon this
that we must chiefly rely if we are to study the life
of Jesus with profit. We may neglect as outside
the area of our present interest all purely dogmatic
questions and confine ourselves to examining what
is to be known about Jesus from the record of His
earthly ministry as viewed from the standpoint of
the Church to-day as in the days before the New
Testament was written.

In delimitating therefore the field within which
to work for the purposes of our present study we
must exclude from consideration all such subjects
as the combination of two natures in one person,
the Kenosis or self-emptying of the eternal Son in
taking upon Himself human flesh and living a human life, the doctrine of the Trinity and the procession of the Holy Ghost. These lie outside our
range though some might consider it impossible to
write about the life of Jesus without taking them
into account. We have nothing to do with the
divine plan of redemption as it is popularly called;
we shall not argue about the Atonement, nor is it
necessary to discuss at length whether Jesus believed in the Fall or not and how far the Christian

conception of immortality is governed by the assumption of some original catastrophe by which all creation has been vitiated and the course of human evolution deflected from its true path. We are not obliged to make any dogmatic assumptions at all. It is enough for us if we can obtain a firm grasp of the kind of person the Church has always affirmed Jesus to be and the kind of life which it derives from Him. What He was must inevitably precede any discussion of who He was. It was what He was that made those nearest to Him in the first instance realize His superhumanity. There is no need to describe this elaborately; everyone has a more or less accurate idea of the kind of person Christians believe Jesus to have been and the kind of character He required in His followers though few perhaps understand what a revolution these have effected in the moral standards of civilization. We cannot regard what Jesus was as an open question; we must assume that to be settled by nineteen centuries of Christian witness. Hence when critics of the gospel records of His ministry diverge from the accepted view of the Church on this point we can only reply that they are not in a position to determine it; we know Jesus, not from criticism of literary sources, but from the one unimpeachable fact that there is a continuity of Christian life which claims to derive historically from Him and to be immediately dependent upon fellowship with Him in the ordinances of the Church and the ministry of the word.

CHAPTER II

PRINCIPAL SOURCES FOR THE LIFE OF JESUS

THE APOSTOLIC STORY

BEARING in mind then that we can only rightly approach the study of the life of Jesus through the Church's continuous experience of Him, the question at once arises, Are we in a position to know what the Church thought and said about Him at first? and happily the answer is in the affirmative. The period of Church history of which we know least is not the very earliest but that which immediately succeeded it, not the apostolic but the sub-apostolic age. The first preachers of the Christian gospel and organizers of the original Christian society had a story to tell and they told it wherever they went. They made converts by that story which included the description of a new life which they themselves claimed to have received through their association with Jesus. The story has been preserved for us within the pages of a comparatively small book. Strictly speaking the New Testament is not a book at all but a collection of letters and tracts consisting mainly of versions of or comments upon one and the same apostolic story. Some part

24

of it, principally the Acts of the Apostles and the Apocalypse, relates more to the doings of the story-tellers themselves and the prospects of the new society they were forming and administering than to the subject matter of their message, but the story is not omitted even in these. It is the story of the Son of God who came down from heaven to give life unto the world, the story which in concentrated form constitutes the substance of the Christian creed to this day, for even the repetition of the creed is the telling of a story.

The earliest part of this story-telling to be put into literary form is probably the letters written by St. Paul to churches and individuals in whom he was specially interested. These do not tell us much about the earthly life of Jesus but they show that from the very beginning the person of Jesus was regarded in much the same way by His followers as it is regarded still—that is, at least, from the time of His final departure from the visible world. There may be an earlier document than any of St. Paul's letters, namely a collection of the sayings of Jesus embedded in the gospels of St. Matthew and St. Luke; but this is doubtful. It is the epistles, not the gospels, that come first in the order of time, broadly speaking, a valuable fact for the right interpretation of the latter; the gospels came into existence in the atmosphere of the epistles and tell in greater detail the story of the same person; it is impossible to suppose that the writers can have had any other standpoint than that of Christians in general at the time they wrote. It is important to realize this, for superficially there is a very great difference between the atmosphere of the epistles and that of the gospels, or at any rate that of the first three gospels. Had these gospels been written before the Pauline and other epistles appeared it might have been possible to argue with some show of reason that a remarkable human teacher, the theme of the former, had by the latter been exalted into a position he was never meant to occupy. But, as we see, it was just the reverse. The divine Savior was first preached, and then the little memoirs of His earthly life, with which the New Testament begins, were added to the apostolic record.

But here again care should be taken not to confuse the issues. The gospels tell us about a real person, not about an imaginary figure derived from the testimony of the epistles or the belief of the Church in which the epistles arose. The attempt made in recent years to suggest the opposite view has been generally rejected by New Testament scholars.[1] The truth is, as above mentioned, that the apostolic story was thoroughly familiar to the primitive Church.[2] There was no need at first to

[1] *Vide* the literature of the Christ Myth controversy, notably Drews' *Christ Myth* and Conybeare's trenchant criticism thereof (R.P.A.). Also J. M. Robertson: *Pagan Christs.* Principal Estlin Carpenter's *Historical Jesus and the Theological Christ* contains a temperate and scholarly criticism of the Christ Myth theories.

[2] *Vide* David Smith: *The Days of His Flesh*, Introd., wherein the author shows very convincingly that at first and throughout the apostolic age the oral Gospel, or "deposit" as it was called, was considered of vital importance and systematically memorized. It may be that present-day canons of criticism do not sufficiently allow for this.

On the other hand, Prof. Turner in his lecture on the present position of New Testament study says (p. 37): "To-day there is not, I suppose, a competent critic anywhere who assigns anything but a quite subordinate part to oral tradition."

make literature of it. Many persons were living when St. Paul was writing who had seen Jesus in the flesh and heard Him preach—if preach be the right word to employ of His public discourses. Most of His relatives were still living, perhaps even His mother, and there was plenty of authentic oral testimony concerning the details of His ministry. The special qualification of the apostles for their work was that they were eyewitnesses of what they had to tell; they had known Jesus in His capacity of teacher with an intimacy which no others possessed and were clothed with an authority derived directly from Himself; as long as they were alive and active there could be little need or demand for written narrative. Their story was the *Gospel,* the "good news" of the new dispensation. That was how the written gospels got their name.

No doubt there was a mass of floating tradition besides. Even a ministry of a few months' duration could cover more ground than is described for us in the very brief accounts of it which make up the bulk of the evangelical record. The greatest curiosity would prevail, especially among Gentile Christians, to know as much as possible about Jesus as He actually was in the days of His flesh, and by and by various writers set to work to satisfy it— indeed St. Luke expressly says so in the preface to his own gospel. What has become of these various efforts nobody knows; perhaps some of them may come to light as exploration proceeds, as fragments of them have already done; but we may fairly assume that the reason why our canoni-

cal gospels have lived on when the others perished
was that they were better and perhaps fuller; the
Church used them more and preserved them from
oblivion by the exercise of the same instinct as that
which has created the great literary classics of the
world. Not that these booklets can claim great
literary merit; their merit is of another and higher
order; they enshrine for us for all time an almost
contemporary portrait of the person who matters
more to mankind than all the men of letters who
have ever lived.

But, let it be understood, the Gospel was prior
to the gospels. There was, be it repeated, a great
story to tell, the story of the birth, work, words,
aims, superearthly significance, passion, death,
resurrection, and return to heaven of One the like
of whom had never dwelt amongst men before. It
was a wonderful story and those who listened to it
wanted to hear more; hence with the object of meeting this very natural desire a gradually increasing
literature came into existence, mostly imaginative,
part of which has come down to us under the designation of the apocryphal gospels. In the present
writer's opinion we may be mistaking the purpose
with which some of these were written; they may
not have been written as serious contributions to our
historical knowledge of the subject of which they
treat; it is more likely that they were, or most of
them were, produced with a view to pleasing or edi-
fying their readers and in much the same spirit as
religious fiction at the present day. Works are not
unknown in our own time in which the person of

our Lord is introduced as the central figure, but
no one supposes for a moment that these are meant
as statements of sober fact or to be regarded as reliable in the same way as the New Testament is
reliable. Perhaps this distinction explains much
that is puzzling in the quality of the apocryphal
gospels as contrasted with the canonical; the canonical derive directly from the apostolic tradition and
the apocryphal do not; the latter are a proof of the
widespread interest existing in Christian circles
from the earliest time in all that pertained to Jesus.
It was a loving interest, an interest that delighted
to magnify the miraculous and exceptional in His
doings without necessarily taking these extracanonical accounts of them very seriously. In no
other way can we explain the fact that the sound
judgment of the Church was never deceived as to
which gospels were the really authentic and trust-
worthy ones. The drop down from the exalted
moral level and dignified tone of the New Testament to the extravagances of the apocryphal narratives is very marked. It does not follow that all
the apocryphal matter is false; some element of
genuine tradition may have been incorporated
therewith. Some very beautiful stories and sayings
are to be found only within the apocryphal books,
and even of those which are obviously imaginative
we may justly say that a considerable proportion
is susceptible of charmingly suggestive spiritual interpretation.

In seeking then for the historical sources of our
knowledge of Jesus we get first the apostolic tra-

dition, which has been perpetuated in the very life of the Church in so far as its view of its founder is concerned; then comes the New Testament literature in which the substance of the apostolic tradition is enshrined, a literature which is itself a selection made by the mind of the Church from a much larger mass of material which existed at the close of the apostolic age and fragments of which have come down to us; and lastly we have an amount of extracanonical literature, most, if not all, of which came into existence after the New Testament was written, and which professes to give details of the life of Jesus not included in the New Testament. We may follow the example of the ancient Church in rejecting these as, for the most part, spurious, save and except that they illustrate the belief in the superhuman status of Jesus which was held in Christian circles from the very first. Let this once be grasped by the modern reader and a great deal else becomes plain. The farther back we push our inquiry into Christian origins the more certain it becomes that Jesus never was regarded by His followers—unquestionably not after His resurrection and ascension, however these events are to be explained—as a human person in the ordinary sense of the term. He was worshipped as superhuman, as a being from a higher world, as in some sense divine. We are on the wrong track if we attempt to begin with a human person who was gradually deified by the devout imagination of the Church after the apostles had passed away. Nothing could be farther from the truth. The apostles' doctrine concerning the person they had to proclaim to the world was substantially the same as that of the Church to-day; if there were any danger of exaggeration in what was said and thought about Jesus in the earlier period of the Church's life, as is abundantly evident from the contents of the apocryphal gospels, it was that of losing sight of our Lord's true humanity altogether; it was this that at first the Church had to struggle hardest to conserve in faith and worship—belief in the real manhood of the wondrous being who had lived and taught in little Palestine for a few short years and then been put to death, only, as every Christian earnestly maintained, to rise triumphant over death and reign from the eternal throne.[3] We cannot be too careful about getting hold of the main strand of testimony from the beginning; whether it accord with our present-day conceptions of what is inherently probable or not.

It is worth reiterating that the problem of the life of Jesus is not in the main a literary problem; we do not need to dig and delve amongst the meager records of the past in order to discover what it is important to know concerning Him; we must interrogate the living present and compare it with the testimony of the sacred page, sacred because of the associations of nineteen centuries. Christianity is not primarily the religion of a book but of a person, a person interpreted through a society. It may be seriously questioned whether the critical

[3] *Vide* Dorner: *Development of the Doctrine of the Person of Christ,* Vol. I (1st Division), chap. ii, pp. 184-252, more especially the section on the Gnosis (229 ff.).

problems of a literary character which beset New Testament study would have assumed their present magnitude if this principle had been kept consistently in view. It is not possible to discuss any New Testament problem rightly, much less solve it, without allowing for the fact that the New Testament itself is only the crystallized Christian witness of the first century and that that witness has been continuous in the Church with or without the New Testament to support it. The written word is of enormous value but it is not indispensable whereas the unwritten tradition is: it is the persistence of the unwritten tradition that has sent us back to study the New Testament afresh; it is safe to say that the New Testament would have had no interest for us apart from the fact that Jesus is still the greatest spiritual force to be reckoned with in the affairs of mankind. But to study the New Testament as we should study Homer is futile. Homer is dead and gone; we can ignore the intervening centuries when we bring higher and lower criticism to bear upon his work. Jesus is not dead and gone, or the Church claims that He is not, and there is just the difference. To treat a New Testament problem as though it had no relation to the living faith of Christendom is to ignore the right perspective in which to encounter it with any hope of success.

CRITICAL THEORIES

The problem of New Testament criticisms as a whole is not one with which we can concern ourselves here in detail but it is requisite that we understand its bearing upon the main question before us. The casual reader should be made aware of the scope and extent of that problem and how much it signifies for Christian faith. Its importance has been exaggerated as we have seen, nevertheless it cannot be neglected; there are certain assured results of criticism of which we may avail ourselves without misgiving; no research into historical records is ever likely to upset the settled conviction of Christendom in relation to what is to be known of Jesus. Nor should the mistake be made of assuming that the effect of scientific inquiry into Christian origins has been to weaken our confidence in the transcendent worth of the revelation of Jesus for mankind. On the contrary we owe an incalculable debt of gratitude to the body of experts who in every Christian country have toiled hard for the last few generations to place before us a clear picture of the period in which Jesus lived and the conditions under which His work was done; if they have been less successful in disposing of the difficulties and perplexities which confront us on every page of the New Testament that is not their fault; at least they have made us aware of what those difficulties and perplexities are. On the whole we have more to hope from the spade and mattock, from actual exploration in the Bible lands themselves, than we have from theorizing scrutiny of the New Testament as it stands. We now know fairly well what Palestine and the world around it were like in our Savior's time; we have

been minutely informed of the factors in history
which went to the making of the society in which
Jesus was born and brought up; there is little that
is new to say on any of these points. What we
should like to know is more about the psychology
of the men and women with whom He associated
and those for whom the New Testament was written; we want to know their mental idiom as compared with our own—how they thought and felt,
what life looked like to them, what mattered most
to the mind of the ordinary person and how he
viewed his duty in relation to God and man. This
is a complex subject still comparatively obscure.
It is plain that the mental climate of the gospels
is not like ours if for no other reason than that
the miraculous is taken for granted throughout.
Does the experience thus evinced correspond to
actualities or does it merely represent a way of
speaking? We wish we knew for certain. The
caution needs to be given to present-day readers of
the gospels that perhaps it is we and not the contemporaries of Jesus whose outlook is limited by
habit and training in relation to the supernormal.
To put the issue at the very lowest we ought to be
prepared to admit that our mentality may lack
something which the men and women of the New
Testament possessed if theirs be wanting in much
that abounds in ours. This is really the great problem of criticism, to know how to translate the mental dialect of the New Testament into that in which
we are accustomed to express ourselves to-day, and
any attempt at a satisfactory solution will mean the

shedding of some of our most obstinate prepossessions. There seems no point, for instance, in a critical bias against miracles when Jesus is Himself the one great miracle that we have to try to explain. How does it come that He occupies such a dominating place in the history of civilization during the past fifteen or sixteen hundred years? What was His secret? How far was He, if at all, the author of the Church; and what mysterious inherent force was it that enabled the Church, not only to survive the overthrow of the ancient social order which may almost be said to have come to an end with the advent of Jesus, but to substitute another for it which, however unlike the ideal put forward in the name of Jesus, shows no signs of passing away but on the contrary of covering the whole earth? It was with the object of discovering a solution of this many-sided problem that scientific investigation of the sources of the New Testament came into existence.

Strauss may be said to have begun it with his myth theory which is hardly yet superseded in many quarters though now generally admitted to have gone much too far and to have failed to discriminate adequately between the various historical strata discernible in the several narratives of the four evangelists.[4] Then came Renan with his fascinating life of Jesus[5] which was mainly the author's own subjective impression, charmingly told, of what

[4] *Leben Jesu* (1835-36), an epoch-making work, itself the product of a reaction on the part of the author against the supernaturalism of Schleiermacher, on the one hand, and the extreme rationalists who rejected the gospels as historical sources, on the other.

[5] Written 1860.

Jesus was and what He aimed at and how He met His end. The author explains away or ignores the supernatural, treats the gospels as on much the same level with the legendary lore of monkish chronicles and as possessing much the same intrinsic value for purposes of biography; he shows a certain preference for the fourth as being more intimate than the others in its portraiture of the Master. He thinks he discerns a certain deterioration in the temper and pure moral quality of Jesus towards the end, that under stress of opposition and slander His vision becomes clouded and He Himself fiercer and more fanatical as His troubles accumulate. The resurrection story this writer credits to the hysteria of Mary Magdalene and the deathless loyalty of the little group of Galilean fisher-folk who clutched at any straw of hope that their beloved teacher could not be wholly taken from them nor be wrong in His declaration that He would rise from the dead and return to earth in power and great glory to confound His enemies and usher in the long and wistfully expected golden age. Needless to say in view of the critical work of the last fifty years this general conception is utterly inadequate to explain the facts with which it deals. Seeley's *Ecce Homo*,[6] published in our own country, and written with some of the same literary charm as Renan's study—a charm which the successive works of Strauss conspicuously lack —gave a humanitarian picture of Jesus, true enough in its main outlines as far as it went but hampered

[6] First issued anonymously in 1865.

by the same endeavor, that of keeping the supernatural out of due consideration. To the latter half of the nineteenth century belong a multitude of lives of Jesus, mostly written from the same standpoint, the standpoint which viewed Him as a great religious genius, a wonderful spiritual teacher, ages in advance of His time and put to death on that account as the waymakers of the race have usually been since time began. The cry "Back to Christ" was raised and for a long time exercised a controlling influence over theologian and preacher alike and later over the general reader also in ever-growing degree. It had more than one meaning, to be sure. In one sense it was an appeal from an outworn ecclesiasticism to the God-man in whom are the springs of the life of the Church; but in another and more widely understood sense it meant a reaction against the Christ of dogma as presented by the Church and an attempt if possible to discover the real Jesus of history, the Jesus who it was supposed had been overlaid and buried out of sight by the divine official of the theologians. So criticism of the sacred text went to work hand in hand with exploration of the sacred soil once trodden by the foot of the Son of Man, together with examination of every historical authority which might by any chance be able to throw light upon the life He lived and the deeds He did, in the hope of coming upon a Christ more acceptable to the modern mind than the supernatural Christ of the inspired record as of the creeds.

We now know what happened. It fully expected

to succeed in its quest. The presumption seemed a reasonable one that if we could only get back to the fountainhead of Christianity we should come upon a supremely great man, great in His very lowliness and simplicity, of pure and lofty character and gifted with a spiritual intuition possessed by none of His contemporaries and few if any of His successors. He would behave more or less as a modern religious teacher would behave, would look upon life much as we look upon it, and be too wise as well as too modest to make astounding claims to divine authority such as were later made for Him. His teaching would be as simple as Himself—a few great principles, a number of imperishable aphorisms of universal application would constitute it all; its excellence would consist mainly in the fact that it was so spontaneous, so unfettered by tradition or prejudice. Naturally such a person would put forth no pretension to be a worker of marvels —did He not refuse to produce "signs" for those who wanted Him to attest His credentials thus?— and He would do His utmost to persuade His hearers to regard God as their Father and all men, including Himself, as their brothers; anything more than this would be superfluous and He would want to free men from the burdens of ritual and tradition, not add to them.

But ere long it became evident that this Christ was not to be found. Most unwillingly advanced criticism was compelled to admit that He was never there to be found; the only Christ of which either the New Testament or subapostolic, extracanonical literature had any knowledge was anything but a nineteenth century ethical teacher, an apostle of sweet reasonableness many centuries before His time. His thought was not nineteenth century thought, His ways were not nineteenth century ways, the world He knew and the problems He faced were not of a nineteenth century cast—not western, not utilitarian, not even practical in the sense ordinarily understood by western civilization. His outlook on life was not ours, His presuppositions were essentially different from those with which we are most familiar. These are facts largely concealed from modern western readers of the New Testament because we read our own ideas and modes of thought and feeling into the evangelic narrative. Above all it became plain that He was utterly unamenable to modern standards in regard to what is to be expected of a religious teacher who seeks a hearing amongst us. He made the most astounding personal claims, exacted a homage from His adherents such as no prophet had dared to exact before, and yet He did so with an entire absence of the egotism and self-assertion usual in the case of men whose heads have been turned by success; in Him it was perfectly natural, spontaneous, and unforced. If evidence goes for anything, the evidence of written word as well as of continuous tradition is that Jesus of Nazareth even went to the daring length of associating Himself with Deity in unique manner and degree. What was to be made of a person like this? He was as far as possible removed from the conception of a mere preacher of righteousness, the founder of a new ethical religion free from all burdensome and mystifying dogmas. The presumptions of the religions of the past were nothing to those henceforth bound up with His name. Was He then a mere visionary, or what? Had He a message to all time or had He not? Criticism was forced within the horns of a dilemma, and it is not too much to say that it is still there. The purely human Christ does not exist, never has existed. Either Jesus was superhuman, as He plainly said He was, or His personality is an utter enigma to which we possess no key. As stated above, the further alternative that the Jesus of history is either a myth or that He bears no relation to the Christ of the Church is not to be entertained by serious scholarship. We do know something about Him, and the only question that admits of discussion is how much it implies.

German criticism has led the way in attacking this problem, and it would be idle as well as ungracious to belittle what it has achieved, but reaction against its extreme conclusions may now be truly said to have begun. Everything has been adduced that could be adduced to account for Jesus on naturalistic hypotheses, and every such effort has failed—failed, that is, to give an adequate explanation of all the facts as furnished to us by the Christian experience of apostolic times; in other respects they have not failed; they have cleared the ground and brought into broad light many things that were previously obscure and unknown but that are now, of the greatest value for obtaining a true perspective upon the whole subject of the life of Jesus. Gradually the true sequence of the gospel tradition was ascertained, Mark's gospel being established as the earliest and John's as the latest. In this task Weisse [7] and Wilke [8] were the pioneers, the latter from the Roman standpoint. It was long, however, before New Testament scholarship in general was prepared to follow them in asserting the priority of the second evangelist. Bruno Bauer [9] anticipated the Christ Myth protagonists of the present day by insisting that the gospel tradition as a whole is not historical in any sense but that of reflecting the mind of the primitive Church, and that it gives us no glimpse of the real Jesus, supposing such a person ever lived; the real Jesus on this hypothesis has little or nothing to do with Christianity; the Church as a quasi-mystical cult or society, existing among many others in apostolic times, so idealized Jesus for purposes of worship as to sublimate Him away altogether. What we get in the gospels, Bauer and his school would contend, is a series of legends that arose within the Christian community, and neither have any biographical value nor are consistent with each other.

Not even Strauss was prepared to accept this. He insisted in his later works that Jesus was a personal force to be reckoned with, at the same time reiterating that the stories in the gospel tradition are in the main attempts to dramatize the new spir-

[7] *Critical Study of the Gospel History* (1838) and *Present Position of the Problem of the Gospels* (1856).
[8] *The Earliest Gospel* (1838).
[9] At first as developing the theories of Strauss, but later in his *Criticism of the Gospels* (1850-51) going far beyond them.

41

itual experiences which Jesus had brought into the
world. Naturally in this view of the subject the
fourth gospel as "the spiritual gospel" receives most
prominence and the others correspondingly recede
into the background. For a time under its influence there was a tendency to regard the gospels as
compositions of comparatively late date, well on
into the second century and, by some authorities,
even into the third. F. C. Baur [10] and the school
of which he was the most prominent master were
inclined to attribute the chief importance, not to
Jesus, but to St. Paul, in the work of establishing
Christianity and supplying its distinctive features.
This was not intended to belittle Jesus but rather to
show that the spiritual movement He had set going
soon became a very different thing when trans-
ferred from Jewish to Gentile soil and that the
greatest formative influence upon its early development, the real creator of the Church in fact, was
the mighty spiritual genius known to history as the
apostle of the Gentiles; the question soon arose and
was keenly debated whether Paul had really re-
flected or deflected the Gospel of Jesus. Keim [11]
and others restored the balance, declaring that Jesus
and not Paul must be considered as central for a
right understanding of the beginning of Christianity as a world religion; hence the gospels came increasingly to be regarded as genuine historical
sources, the fourth being separated from the other
three and placed in a category by itself. Bernhard

[10] In his second and greater period wherein he was probably stim-
ulated by Strauss, who had been his pupil in earlier days.
[11] *Jesus of Nazara* (Eng. tr. 1873-83).

Weiss [12] and Beyschlag,[13] following Holtzmann,[14] made elaborate studies of the life of Jesus in which the gospels were treated as historical documents of much the same character as the "Little Flowers of St. Francis." It is to Holtzmann more than to any man that we owe the elaboration of the synoptic problem—that is, the problem of accounting for the differences as well as the resemblances in the several versions of a narrative more or less common to the three earlier evangelists. He it was who first put forward the now generally accepted view that there are two main sources of the synoptic tradition— Mark for the history and a non-Marcan writing for the teaching.

Of Holtzmann's work Schweitzer [15] says: "Scarcely ever has a description of the life of Jesus exercised so irresistible an influence as that short life outline— it embraces scarcely twenty pages—with which Holtzmann closes his examination of the synoptic gospels. This chapter became the creed and catechism of all who handled the subject during the following decades," and gives it in summary thus: "That Jesus had endeavored in Galilee to found the Kingdom of God in an ideal sense; that He concealed His consciousness of being the Messiah, which was constantly growing more assured, until His followers should have attained by inner enlightenment to a higher view of the Kingdom of God and of the Messiah; that almost at the end of His Galilean

[12] *Life of Jesus* (Eng. tr. 1883).
[13] *Life of Jesus* (1885-86).
[14] H. J. Holtzmann, *The Synoptic Gospels* (1863).
[15] *Quest of the Historical Jesus* (Eng. tr.), pp. 203, 204.

ministry He declared Himself to them as the Messiah at Cæsarea Philippi; that on the same occasion He at once began to picture to them a suffering Messiah, whose lineaments gradually became more and more distinct in His mind amid the growing opposition which He encountered, until finally He communicated to His disciples His decision to put the Messianic cause to the test in the capital, and that they followed Him thither and saw how His fate fulfilled itself. It was this fundamental view which made the success of the hypothesis."

Alongside of Holtzmann, and in a sense deriving from him, we must place Ritschl [16] as emphasizing the value of the historical Jesus as presented in the synoptical gospels. That Jesus has for Christian experience "the religious value of God" is a fundamental tenet of this school but it will have nothing to say to the miraculous; in fact the general trend of criticism in Germany has been more and more unfavorable to admitting the supernatural in connection with the person and work of our Lord. Scientific theology for the most part rejects the apostolic authorship of the fourth gospel which is the most uncompromising in its insistence upon the supernatural dignity of Jesus; and the foremost exponent of New Testament theology in Germany at the present day, and in some respects the sanest and most conservative, Adolf von Harnack,[17] is no

[16] Essentially a systematic theologian rather than critic. His great work on justification has given rise to a vast literature.

[17] Perhaps the greatest living authority on Ante-Necene Christianity. Of late years has moved to a more conservative position in N. T. criticism. His *What Is Christianity?* leaves little room for the supernatural in religion. *Luke the Physician* and *Sayings of*

more disposed to speak of Jesus as a supernatural being than are the most radical of his contemporaries.

Last comes the eschatological school [18] which, while admitting the historicity of the person of Jesus and of the main outline of His career as set forth in the first three gospels, reduces Him to the status of a deluded visionary, if not a sheer madman. In this view Jesus is represented as influenced by current apocalyptic conceptions to such an extent as to come in time to persuade Himself that He was the long expected Man from heaven variously described in such writings as the Similitudes of Enoch, and that His work on earth was in some wise to inaugurate the entirely new order of dispensation which He, in common with many of His contemporaries of His own race, believed to be imminent and catastrophic in character. He had no other message, said nothing really original, had little or no interest in the improvement of existing temporal conditions, and was astounded when the consummation He announced did not take place according to program. He perished a martyr to His own dreams which never had any basis in reality, but the cult He created went on, gradually transforming its outlook with the postponement of the hope of His speedy return to put everything right for mankind at a stroke.

Now while it is too much to say that the eschato-

Jesus vindicate the third evangelist and his value as a first-hand authority, but the latter does not allow enough for the possibility that Mark may have known a version of the *Sayings*.

[18] Schweitzer: *Quest of the Historical Jesus.* The chief exponent.

logical school has already been discounted or has
failed to make out a case for its point of view, it
is undoubtedly true that Jesus as thus interpreted
becomes incoherent and fails to relate Himself
to the religious consciousness of any age. There
was, as we shall see, an important sense in which
the eschatological element in His utterances still
remains of indispensable value, but it is quite
absurd to suppose that it constitutes in itself the
whole sum and substance of the words and work
of Jesus. It is incredible that one whose name has
bulked so large in the spiritual history of the race
should have had no better title to His eminence
than that of making a tragic blunder at the outset,
assuming a grandiose function which had no basis
save in His own imagination, and declaring therewith an impending collapse of the world-order
which has not yet taken place and shows no likelihood of ever taking place in terms of His pre-
diction. The personality of Jesus must have possessed a greater significance than is thus evinced
or we should never have heard of it. There must
be some proportion between His achievements and
that which gave them birth. A great religious
movement is not initiated and sustained for nineteen
centuries on a tragic disillusionment. The eschatological bearings of the sayings of Jesus must therefore receive its due emphasis and no more; it must
not usurp the whole field of vision. It is curious to
note that the very rationalistic type of mind which
refuses credence to the miraculous aspects of the
Gospel story should be ready to affirm that the Gos-

pel itself arose out of the obstinate belief of a crazy wandering preacher and the group of followers He had gathered round Him in the most fantastic and stupendous miracle ever conceived by human brain. This is to strain at a gnat and swallow a camel with a vengeance. If people in any number were prepared to hold with such intensity to an expectation which involved the speedy and overwhelming destruction of the state of things which still continues, surely it is not unreasonable to conclude that they would be susceptible to the presence of the supernormal in their ordinary way of life and would generate the kind of mental atmosphere wherein what are commonly termed miracles could most readily take place or, to say the least, more readily than with us.

IMPORTANCE OF APOCALYPTIC

We cannot understand the New Testament without obtaining some idea of the mentality of contemporary apocalyptic literature, the literature which fills the gap between Old and New Testament religion and mode of thought.[19] No one can avoid seeing that this gap exists, and the only question that admits of much discussion in regard thereto is what best fills it. We want to know what people of serious religious mind, belonging to the race that gave us the Old Testament, and especially the peo-

[19] Charles: *Religious Development between the Old and New Testaments.* Burkitt: *Jewish and Christian Apocalypses.* Both of these distinguished scholars are inclined to attribute a little too much to the influence of Apocalyptic on the content of the teaching of Jesus, but their pioneer work has shed a flood of light on a hitherto obscure field.

ple inhabiting the land where Jesus was born and brought up, were thinking and feeling in the few generations intervening between the formation of the Old Testament Canon and the appearance of the New Testament writings; and the answer is supplied to a considerable extent by what we have been able to learn of certain remarkable literary productions, more or less of the character of the book of Daniel on the one hand and that of Revelation on the other, all possessing more or less the same features and general outlook. Here we have the key to much that is taken for granted without explanation in the New Testament; the same ideas and symbols are drawn upon, and much the same expectation is shown concerning the future. The two books of Enoch, the Syrian and Greek Baruch, the Sibylline Oracles, fourth Ezra, and the Assumption of Moses constitute part of what was probably a very much larger literature and illuminate for us much that would otherwise have to remain obscure in the gospels.[20] Their common features are obvious. They are all written in the same oracular style; they dwell upon the supernatural as contrasted with the natural order, and look forward to a crisis which is to come suddenly when the latter will be invaded and reconstituted by the former. There is to be a great upheaval, a series of fundamental cosmic changes, and a new beginning on better and purer lines. This is the main interest

[20] Such writings as the Psalms of Solomon and the Testaments of the Twelve Patriarchs are also valuable and illuminating, but their general standpoint is different from that of the above-mentioned. *Vide* excellent S.P.C.K. series.

of the writers; they have much to say about the two
ages of dispensations—the present and the better
one to follow—and their hopes are fixed upon the
imminence of the latter. They believe in the
struggle of good and evil powers which is to precede the grand consummation, and have much to
say about Antichrist, a personification of the forces
of evil, who appears again and again in their pages.
Generally speaking they take a larger world view
than that of Jewish nationalism; it is the whole human race, and not the Jews only, who enter into
the scheme of their anticipations and are to be
blessed by the fulfillment of the promises made
through Jewish religion, especially as concentrated
in the person of the Messiah. It is hard to determine who the Messiah is to these dreamers of a
distant past. There is no consistency in the pictures
of Him presented in these and other apocalypses
save that He is regarded in all of them as the hope
of the world. Sometimes He is presented as
simply an historic human figure, a man chosen for
the great work of acting as God's vicegerent on
earth and ushering in the heavenly kingdom; sometimes He is as plainly superhuman and belongs to
a higher than the temporal order of things, though
His relation to God is nowhere defined.

CHAPTER III

CONDITIONS IN THE TIME OF JESUS

RELIGION AND RACE

THERE is not much that needs to be said in addition to what has already been stated about the preparation in history for the advent of the greatest personal force that has ever come into the world. No race but one could have produced Jesus; in no other could He have found a spiritual setting; salvation was indeed of the Jews. Here was a nation whose specialty was religion and distinguished in no other direction—a small people inhabiting a small territory but preserved from the extinction which overtook surrounding and far more powerful empires and civilizations by the very intensity with which they held to their traditional faith. Political greatness was denied them; they contributed little to art and science; they produced no literature except the one imperishable record of their relations with God known as the Old Testament and the commentaries thereupon which have come down to us. Their thought and life were saturated through and through with religious feeling and a conception

of duty directly derived from their religious convictions. There is no need to doubt the substantial
truth of the story that their peculiarity in this respect arose from the conduct of a remote ancestor
whose conscience revolted against human sacrifices
and sensual orgies as associated with the practice
of religion, and that in obedience to the divine voice
within him he went forth from his kindred and his
father's house, "not knowing whither he went," in-
tent only upon the foundation of a purer form of
faith based on moral relations with the inscrutable
divine power that made and sustains heaven and
earth. This was the beginning of an age-long
process whereby a peculiar people was trained and
disciplined to be the repository of the oracles of
God to mankind. Who can question it who has an
eye for the manifestation of a divine purpose in human affairs? In its early stages Israelitish religion,
as noted above, was differentiated from that of surrounding peoples mainly by its ethical note and
the closeness of the relationship established between
the worshipers and their God. Its defeat was the
tendency of the worshipers to claim for Israel a
monopoly of the divine favor. They could not
easily rise above the assumption that the descend-
ants of Abraham were God's privileged children
in a sense and to a degree which no others could approach. Despite the efforts of the men of vision
who arose in their midst from time to time—most
of all perhaps the second Isaiah—they largely
failed to see that their peculiar eminence in the
world, their spiritual vocation, consisted in the wit-

ness they had to bear to the unity of the divine being and that He was to be worshiped in righteousness or not at all. Their very sufferings contributed to fitting them for this function, for no race has suffered more; they have been oppressed and afflicted, despised, persecuted, and scattered over the face of the earth, but nowhere have they gone without carrying this message with them as part of their very being: God is one, and God is just.

When we remember also the vicissitudes to which Israel had been exposed in its long history—or, more accurately, that remnant of Israel, principally the tribe of Judah, which still preserved a sense of national identity in our Lord's time—we can but marvel at the way in which God has wrought. This remnant came back from the great captivity no longer a nation but a church, or rather a church consisting entirely of the nation, a nation henceforth subject to the rule of a foreign power and soon to be deprived even of its own sacred soil and the spot on which its central shrine once stood. Yet from that barren rock whereon Jerusalem was built a stream of spiritual influence has gone forth which has blessed every other nation on the face of the globe. Judaism has given birth to two great world religions, Christianity and Mohammedanism, and still lives.

It was into a community with this already venerable record behind it that Jesus was born. Humanly speaking, He could not have been born anywhere else. He would have had to be a different being to be born of a Greek mother and in Athens or of a Roman mother and in Italy or Spain. All the impressive spiritual past of Israel went to the making of His human personality and the mental atmosphere in which His work was done. He could start from a certain moral and religious level in addressing His own countrymen which He could not have presumed in any other part of the world or with any other people; His message could have taken root on no other soil even though it were quickly to be transplanted to a new environment.

PALESTINE AND THE WORLD-EMPIRE

On the other hand He came at a moment when the civilized world had been unified under the scepter of the Roman Cæsars and lay at peace under Roman rule. It was a restless peace, a peace of domination rather than of good will, and destined ere long to be broken and pass into confusion and dismay. The advent of Jesus was the death-knell of the old world-order and the beginning of a new which has not yet reached its zenith; Cæsarism was not mistaken in descerning in Christianity its deadly and unrelenting foe. But there had been no time before, and there never has been a time since, wherein the world was quite so ready and ripe for a universal religion. It was the golden moment in the divine order.

It is hard to say just what the condition of Palestine was then. That it had been extensively Hellenized and Romanized would be inevitable,

just as the British occupation has set a deep mark
upon the life of India and Egypt to-day, yet there
is no evidence in the words of Jesus of His being
greatly influenced by Greek or Roman modes of
thought or speech. Not one single reference does
He make to the characteristic features, architec-
tural, literary, or philosophic, of the vast and complex civilization into whose orbit Israel had now
been drawn. But it would be impossible for Him
to remain wholly unaffected by the Gentile forces
which had everywhere penetrated Jewish society
and by the fact that Greek-speaking cities had
sprung up at various points on Palestinian soil.[1]
Galilee especially was saturated with Greek ideas
and modes of living, and contained many populous
Greek centers; it was prosperous and cultivated to
a degree almost unimaginable at the present day
after its exposure to centuries of Turkish misrule.
Renan may not be far wrong in describing it as at
that time one of the most fertile and beautiful
countries in the world.

Judea was different. Its inhabitants were
fiercer, more turbulent and fanatical than the Galileans and more resentful of Roman rule. They,
together with the Samaritans, were directly governed by a Roman procurator whereas the northern
province still preserved a sort of autonomy under
a local prince though of Edomite instead of Israelitish race. There was no friendship between Jews

[1] *Vide* Rendel Harris: *Sidelights on New Testament Research*—
concluding chapter, "Relation of Christianity to the Greek World"—
for an interesting discussion of the indebtedness of apostolic Christians to Greek ideas.

and Samaritans, and this fact operated with special discomfort at national festivals when pilgrims from Galilee had to pass through Samaria in order to get to the Temple at Jerusalem unless they were willing to go by the longer and more dangerous route through Perea. The Samaritans were a mixed race, partly Jewish and partly foreign. They had become paganized during the great captivity, and on the return of the exiles under Ezra and Nehemiah they were in consequence debarred from a share in the rebuilding of the Temple, a slight which they never forgave. They established a shrine of their own on Mount Gerizim, and on the whole their religious system approximated with some closeness to the Jewish, notwithstanding the repeated accusation that they were idolaters. They based their observances on the Pentateuch, practiced circumcision, and kept the feasts of Tabernacles, the Passover and Pentecost. The bitterness of the feud between them and the Jews was at its height in our Lord's time and often led to the shedding of blood. It is doubtful whether the name Samaritan should be extended to the inhabitants of the whole district bearing that name; it is more likely that only the sect which worshipped at Mount Gerizim was designated thereby. There is no reason to believe that the people of Samaria were either more or less of mixed origin than were the Galileans but the latter were strictly loyal to the religious system which centered in the Jewish Temple. The Jews proper regarded the Galileans half-contemptuously as rustics speaking a peculiar dialect. These appear to have been far more completely Hellenized than either Jews or Samaritans, much more tolerant of foreign ways and, like most of the Welsh to-day, bilingual. Indeed the difference of temper between Galileans and Jews is well illustrated by the contrast in the respective attitudes of Welsh and Irish towards the dominant English race. That Jews should admit Galileans to the fellowship of the Temple ordinances is one sign that Jewish religion was not so exclusive as is often supposed; in fact it was at this time to no small extent a proselytizing religion and might have become a world religion had it been content to cut itself free from legal obligations which weighed heavily upon converts of Gentile race as St. Paul and others were wise enough to see later in the case of Christianity.[2]

Judaism during this whole period may be described as a somewhat arid deism, tempered by the close personal and ethical relation in which the Jew was supposed to stand to God. Its greatest drawback was its slavish allegiance to the letter of the Mosaic Law which had now become a minutely elaborate and cumbersome system as interpreted by successive generations of authoritative commentators. Righteousness was looked upon as identical with keeping the Law and unrighteousness as failing to do this, with the sad result that formalism had largely taken the place of true godliness and men's consciences were sophisticated by the con-

[2] Illustrated in the epistle to the Galatians and contest with Judaizers, including even Peter for a time. *Cf.* latter's vision before visit to Cornelius, Acts x.

fusion existing between simple goodness and mere ritual precepts.

RELIGIOUS PARTIES

Of the various types of religious profession mentioned in the New Testament the Pharisees are the most prominent. The name means separatist, and the sect or party took its origin from the historic struggle of the Jews to maintain their nationality and their ancient faith against the efforts of their Syro-Greek masters to destroy both.[3] In a sense they were the Nonconformists of their age and had a similar honorable record of stiff-backed resistance to persecution and civil tyranny. Their great strength lay in the local synagogues as distinct from the Temple, and great as was their influence with the Jewish people at large it is doubtful if they were ever very numerous owing to the strictness of the standard they maintained. They laid the fullest stress upon the duty of rendering obedience to the Law in all its details. They prided themselves on doing this and held in contempt all who did not imitate their zeal. They studied nothing but the Law and regarded any other form of culture as unworthy the attention of a son of Abraham. Exclusive in the last degree in their religious outlook they were nevertheless eager to win adherents to their cause even from Gentile sources, a somewhat surprising fact; but their system was as simple as it was rigid in this respect: the Gentile

[3] B. C. 170 to 140.

convert must become a Jew. They insisted upon circumcision or its equivalent, and a form of baptism appears to have been usual for the admission of a Gentile into the fellowship of Judaism.

The officials of the Temple, drawn mainly from a few aristocratic priestly families, were very different from the Pharisees both in ideals and outlook. The centralization of national worship in the Temple had had the effect of accustoming the people to frequent the local synagogues for prayer and instruction and only to go up to Jerusalem for the greater feasts. The result was that the hierarchy dominated the situation in Jerusalem and the Pharisees elsewhere. The prominent figure in the synagogue was the scribe or doctor of the Law, the professional theologian who was supposed to be an expert commentator upon the sacred text. Naturally these were held in high honor, especially by the Pharisees whose rôle it was to inculcate the utmost reverence for the Law. Many scribes were Pharisees but not all Pharisees were scribes. Some of the scribes may have belonged to the priestly party called Sadducees, for originally, as the name implies, the principal function of the scribes was to make and preserve copies of the Law, and the duty of interpreting the Law was left mainly to the priests; but the very necessities of the case as created by the centralization of worship in one national temple extended the scope of the powers and responsibilities of the scribes. It is likely enough therefore that there may have been Sadducean scribes as well as Pharisaic. There were different schools of the scribes just as there are different schools of the theologians of to-day. The school of Hillel, for example, represented a more liberal tradition than the rival school of Shammai, hence the saying: "The law of Hillel loosens; the law of Shammai binds." But all parties among the scribes, like all the Pharisees, laid great stress upon oral tradition in interpreting the Law. The Law by this time had become a system so intricate, complex, and artificial that no one could really keep it in its entirety, and, as the gospel narrative shows, Jesus came into sharp conflict with the views of the Pharisaic party in regard to the nature of the distinctions they made between what was accounted meritorious in act and what was not. A burdensome series of ritual observances had usurped the place of true and simple piety and stifled the soul of religion. There was no spontaneity about it, no clear discrimination of ethical values, no freedom and freshness of spiritual life.

Nevertheless it would be a mistake to assume, as is so often done, that the Pharisees were all hypocrites or that the nation viewed them with indifference or contempt. As Mr. Montefiore has shown,[4] they were held in esteem by the populace who regarded them as examples of godliness and proper religious deportment.[5] For the most part they kept out of politics, though their sympathies were with the national aspiration for independence,

---

[4] *Synoptical Gospels*, Introd. 34.
[5] Yet the Baptist denounced them as scathingly as Jesus, a fact which shows that their pretensions were not universally accepted at their face value.

and there must have been many individuals among them of exemplary holiness of life; their reputation in this respect could not have been wholly undeserved. It is definitely stated in the gospels that although the party as a whole was opposed to Jesus there were some Pharisees among His followers. Nicodemus may have been a Pharisee, as certainly he was a person of special prominence in the Sanhedrin. Joseph of Arimathæa may have been another. There may have been some priests who adhered to the new teacher also; Simeon could scarcely have been the only one to perceive in the child or man Jesus the hope of Israel.

The Pharisees had their own idea of Messiahship, and we may assume that in the main it was that of the people at large. They did not think of the Messiah as a sin-bearer or perhaps a supernatural person at all but only as the deliverer of Israel and the restorer of the ancient kingdom, henceforth to be called the Kingdom of God. The party of the Zealots, Pharisaic in origin, differed from the main body in being ready to use violence to shake off the Roman yoke; they were the Sinn Feiners of their time and race; yet one of these was included in the apostolic band. It is not clear how far the Pharisees cherished a really definite Messianic hope; what they certainly did cherish was the hope of a reconstituted national life with world-wide consideration for the Jewish Law; they were indefatigable propagandists.

The Sadducees on the other hand partook of the characteristics of the priestly order from which they mainly derived.[6] The priests in contradistinction to the Pharisees had generally been willing to accommodate themselves to the secular rule of the period whatever it might be. They were a worldly-minded and exclusive caste, jealous of their privileges and unscrupulous in exercising them. The priestly order was aristocratic and hereditary, and there were as many grades therein as of Roman Catholic clergy at the present day. They were as cosmopolitan in outlook as the Pharisees were intensely national, and to maintain their own position had more than once shown themselves ready to assimilate the national religion to foreign models in conformity with the wishes of the ruler of the moment; they are even accused, not without some justification, of carrying their Hellenistic sympathies so far as to be willing to substitute the name of Zeus for that of Yahweh in the Temple devotions. No one but a scion of one of the priestly families could be a member of the party of the Sadducees. Like the Pharisees the Sadducees professed adherence to the Law but were not so scrupulous in keeping it, nor could they admit the addition of anything to it; they utterly rejected the unwritten traditions of which the Pharisees made so much. They were somewhat agnostic and materialistic in temper, would have nothing to say to aught that threatened their own official interests such as plots against the Roman power, and were

[6] The derivation of the name is not absolutely certain, but it may be equivalent to Zadokites or followers of Zadok, a teacher supposed to be a literalist in the interpretation of the Law, rejecting the oral traditions added thereto by the Pharisees.

largely cynical and time-serving in their methods of addressing themselves to the problems of the day. Hence when they united with the Pharisees to get rid of Jesus they did so from a different point of view. They had no fervor of devotion, and disbelieved in personal immortality, resurrection, and a future state, though there is no evidence that they doubted the existence of God. Jesus does not seem to have drawn any of His adherents from among the Sadducees. They had great influence in the Sanhedrin, which was the supreme council of the nation under the Roman power, an influence out of all proportion to their actual numbers, and it was owing chiefly to their antagonism that Jesus was put to death; the Pharisees alone could not have accomplished this end.

In addition to these two parties whose names appear so frequently in the New Testament, there was a third which is not mentioned at all, that of the Essenes.[7] Not very much is known of this peculiar sect but enough to make us wish to know more. There is no evidence that Jesus belonged to it or knew anything about it, or that it had any great influence on early Christianity. Its numbers could never have been large nor is it clear how far they were able to influence their contemporaries. They were an ascetic community organized very much in the manner of the monastic orders with which Christianity has familiarized us. Its members lived under a strict rule, observing apparently the vows of poverty, chastity, and obedience which

[7] *Vide* Josephus: *Wars of the Jews,* II. 8.

distinguish monastic communities in general. They had all their possessions in common and lived a simple and industrious life whose main object was the practice of piety. As those admitted to the order were under oath not to reveal what took place within it we cannot be sure of the view they took of the relations of the soul with God, but as they reverenced the Jewish Law we may assume that they were monotheists. On the other hand as they were excommunicated from all association with the Temple it is evident that their monotheism was suspect, and indeed there are some indications of an admixture of Persian dualism with their beliefs and of something akin to sun-worship.[8]

STATE OF THE PEOPLE

'As over against these comparatively small religious parties we have the great bulk of the people who belonged to none of them. What of these? We have seen that Palestine possessed a measure of self-government under Roman suzerainty, the south being directly administered by a Roman procurator and the north and east by local princes. For all ordinary affairs, civil and religious, the Sanhedrin was the supreme Judean court and preserved in its forms and composition a purely national character. How far it could really exercise jurisdiction it is

[8] F. C. Conybeare (Article on Essenes in Hastings Dictionary of the Bible) thinks Josephus reliable in the information he gives concerning this sect; but Josephus is not always reliable; and it is an arresting fact that the Essenes are not censured in the gospels as the other religious parties are.

impossible to say; probably the Roman authority took care to defer to it while retaining the right to override its decisions or anticipate them as might be expedient. As is illustrated in the case of Jesus the Sanhedrin had no power to pronounce sentence of death and the Roman procurator's word could have saved Him had that word been spoken.

How the people thought and felt about their religion we can only infer from their conduct. It is stated in the gospels that the Pharisees despised all who were unable or unwilling to maintain their own strict legalistic standards of piety, but it is not equally certain that these in their turn despised the Pharisees; in fact so far as we can judge the Pharisees were more popular than the priests. There was little if any religious indifference. The class of "sinners"—that is of persons who for one cause or another failed in paying outward respect to the observances of the Law though not necessarily of immoral life—must have been comparatively small.[9] Those of flagrantly vicious conduct would be fewer still, but all who were excluded from the synagogue, and therefore from ordinary social intercourse, were lumped together under the one designation, sinners. This category also included the body of men who farmed the revenues and collected the tribute for the Roman government. These publicans, as the New Testament styles them, were held in detestation as is easy to understand. They often waxed rich upon their profits so unpatriotically acquired, but that fact did not procure for them any consid-

[9] Montefiore: *Synoptical Gospels,* Introd. 34.

eration or respect; they were outsiders, and outsiders they had to remain.

Professor Glover thinks the Jewish people were
probably much disheartened by their long subjection to foreign masters and by the little comfort,
which their religion brought them, and this may be
true though there is not much direct evidence of
it.[10] It would rather appear that then, as now, the
burden of life pressed heavily upon the poorer
classes and that the conditions of their lot were
such as to produce in them a certain dullness of
mind, a sordid apathy, an obtuseness to all appeals
to their finer sensibilities. But they were more religious than now; everybody, or nearly everybody,
was religious as a matter of course. The people
loved the synagogue and the Temple as symbols
of their national identity and unique spiritual inheritance, and they clung passionately to both.
That they were disappointed with the nonrealiza-
tion of the high hopes entertained by their fathers
goes without saying, but one of the most pathetic
as well as almost inexplicable things about them at
this time is the intensity with which they went on
looking for a deliverance and a golden age which
never came. This at least is written in unmistak-
able characters on every page of the New Testament, and there would appear to have been a
reawakening of it at or near the moment when
Jesus was born, why we do not know. Certain it
is that the Jews chafed under their subjection to
the Roman power and were willing to revolt almost

[10] *Jesus of History.*

at any time; had a bold leader shown himself they would have responded to his call as spontaneously as their fathers had responded to that of the Maccabees. In fact large numbers of them did so respond from time to time when pseudo-Messiahs appeared upon the scene, and these local insurrections had to be strenuously suppressed. One single man of genius might have changed the whole face of affairs as did Mahomet in Arabia six hundred years later; as it was, all that happened were sporadic risings here and there under the leadership of guerrilla chiefs. These successive ebullitions of the national spirit more or less resemble what we have long been accustomed to in Ireland—a sullen, consistent, undying antagonism to the foreign imperial power and its garrison, shown by intermittent outbreaks captained by enthusiasts such as Robert Emmet, Edward Fitzgerald, and Smith O'Brien. And the point is worth making that Jesus Himself might have been proclaimed the hope of Israel in this sense with or without the countenance of priests and Pharisees, and there are indications that many wished Him to do so and would have given Him support in the enterprise. But priests and Pharisees although no lovers of Roman rule were not as a body prepared to jeopardize such national autonomy as they still possessed by committing themselves to an organized rebellion against Rome. When that rebellion finally did come it made an end of Jewish nationalistic hopes.

That the population of Palestine was not wholly of this character is well known. It also contained those whom we should now call saints, spiritually-minded men and women whose thoughts were centered on higher things than mere political independence or the meticulous observance of an ancient tradition. There are some hints in the New Testament that little groups or fraternities of these were accustomed to meet for prayer and converse concerning the hope of Israel. That hope as we see from the apocalyptic literature centered on the expectation that God would somehow intervene to deliver His people from all their ills. But it was not enough for individuals like the aged Simeon and Anna, or later like Nathanael of Cana in Galilee, that the kingdom of Israel should be restored in its temporal prosperity, but rather that Israel, and through Israel the world, should turn to God with regenerate heart and mind and seek to realize His will on earth. They believed in the new age, the new dispensation to come, as earnestly as any patriot of the time, but whereas the popular view was that the Jewish people would be supreme in the new world-order which was to accompany the change whenever it might come to pass, the saint thought chiefly of the universal blessing which the Jew was to be privileged to bring to mankind. We should make a mistake were we to assume that either this ideal or the means whereby it was to be realized was clearly and consistently presented to the mind of the time. It was a vague but deeply cherished aspiration.

CHAPTER IV

THE GOSPELS, CANONICAL AND UNCANONICAL

THE EARLIEST WRITING

IT was in this atmosphere that the gospels took their rise and they should be read in the light of it. They take many things for granted in contemporary history and the mind of the age for which the Old Testament does not prepare us—the figure of the Messiah, the supernatural character of the Kingdom that was yet to be a restoration of that of David, a catastrophic end to the existing order followed by a resurrection and a general judgment. It would be a waste of time to survey here in detail the established results of scholarship with regard to the origin and composition of the gospels. These results are easily accessible to any reader. We may assume a knowledge of their more salient features as we proceed. It is now customary to speak of Mark as the oldest and to make it the basis of any attempt at a sketch of the history of the doings of Jesus, but this is an assumption which can only be accepted with qualifications. Mark may be the oldest as a literary unit but there is a stratum in Matthew and Luke and even in John of perhaps equal antiquity and certainly of equal value for any first-hand acquaintance with the mind of Jesus. The suggestion is worth hazarding that the oldest part of the New Testament writings is the notes of our Lord's discourses taken down from His lips by Matthew the publican on the spot where they were delivered. There are also a few extracanonical sayings of Jesus which may be quite genuine; it stands to reason that He must have said a great deal more than is fragmentarily recorded in the gospels and may have repeated Himself on occasion; there are signs in the gospels themselves that He sometimes made use of the same observations in different connections. The saying quoted in Acts xx. 35, for instance, was evidently well known in the apostolic Church—"it is more blessed to give than to receive"; and it bears a certain resemblance to some that are preserved by the evangelists—"freely ye have received, freely give"; "give and it shall be given unto you," etc.

Perhaps Matthew's notes constitute the Hebrew gospel mentioned by Eusebius on the authority of Papias,[1] but if so they could not have been identical with the present gospel which bears his name. By Hebrew the historian must have meant Aramaic, the Syrian dialect spoken in Palestine in Jesus' day and most likely by Jesus Himself. But Greek was the literary language; hence the gospels as we have

[1] *Hist.*, iii. 39.

them now were written in Greek, though on the whole rather rude Greek, the Greek of unlearned provincials. Did Jesus Himself ever speak in Greek? It is not impossible though the overwhelming probability is that His mother tongue was Aramaic. Still it is likely enough that He could speak Greek, seeing that Galilee was so extensively penetrated by Greek influences; the gospels themselves are evidence that Greek was the most widely used literary medium of communication in hither Asia at that period.[2] That the author of our canonical Matthew could have written in Hebrew had he so chosen is evident from his many quotations from the Old Testament which are apparently taken direct from the Hebrew original and not from the Greek of the Septuagint.[3]

THE GOSPEL OF MATTHEW

Matthew writes for Jewish readers,[4] as Luke for Gentile, and the matter in the first gospel is carefully selected from this point of view. His object is firstly to present Jesus as the Messiah of Jewish expectation and secondly as the universal Savior—

[2] And as we now learn from contemporary Greek letters in papyri unearthed in Egypt, the Greek of the gospels was the colloquial Greek of the period outside Palestine as well as in it.

[3] Or, as argued by some authorities, from a small collection of Testimonia or proof-texts to illustrate the view that the Messiahship of Jesus was the true fulfillment of Old Testament prophecy on the subject.

[4] But evidently was not familiar with Jerusalem, and though he knew Palestine well may have been resident outside it, perhaps in Alexandria. Evangelist and apostle can hardly have been the same person though the latter may quite well have been the recorder of the collection of the sayings of Jesus drawn upon by both the first and third gospels.

hence the large number of quotations which are made in this gospel from the Jewish scriptures, the writer's intention being to show that Jesus is the true fulfillment of Messianic prophecy. Some of these quotations are according to modern standards rather far-fetched in their relation to the subject in hand, and they are not always exact; in one instance at least there is nothing to show from what scripture the quotation is made—"He shall be called a Nazarene." The tone of this gospel is hostile to the Pharisees, which is readily understandable if the author be really Matthew the publican; he must have had to feel the bitter scorn of the Pharisees as no other of the evangelists would. But his Jewish outlook is evident in many ways all the same. He stresses Jesus' interest in the Jews as a people and in their Law, and he illustrates freely the Master's familiarity with Jewish custom. The matter of the gospel is assembled in five groups or clusters of subjects, thereby necessitating some divergence from Mark in the order of events; where this is so it is usually safest to follow Mark—in fact Matthew himself follows Mark except as suits the convenience of his method. But he shows no dependence upon Mark for more than the outline of events; for the sayings of our Lord he draws upon another source with which in a somewhat different form St. Luke also appears to have been acquainted. Was this source the notes the apostle had himself taken in Aramaic referred to above? It is at least a reasonable hypothesis. But it is also possible that the tradition upon which both evangelists drew was

mainly an oral one.[5] There are some important sayings peculiar to Matthew, such as the beautiful in-
vitation, "Come unto me," etc. Perhaps the author
of this gospel was a Jewish Christian who derived
his principal information from the apostle Matthew
and represents the tradition of the Jewish-Christian
church rather than the recollections of one mind
only. The gospel would appear to have been written at or near the fall of Jerusalem in A.D. 70 and
it contains some elements which point to the conclusion that the author and those for whom he wrote
expected the second coming of Christ to take place
soon after that great and tragical event. St. Luke
has another outlook altogether.

THE GOSPEL OF MARK

It was long before criticism was prepared to regard the second gospel as prior to the rest in date,
but it is now generally conceded that this gospel
as we have it to-day or with little alteration was
known to the writers of the other three and made
use of by them in preparing theirs—to some extent
corrected or modified by them in accordance with
their several standpoints. It is rudely written, and
without conscious art, which renders it the more
valuable as a document of first-rate importance for
an understanding of the subject of which it treats.

[5] There are strong objections to this theory, however. The further
suggestion (*Cf.* von Soden: *Early Christian Literature*, p. 140) that
Matthew and Luke used different translations of one original Aramaic collection of the *Sayings* does not solve the problem.

It is not quite complete in its present form, that part of the end being lost which describes the events between the resurrection and the day of Pentecost. The last twenty verses of our canonical Mark are a compilation from the others by a later hand. If we could find the original, as some day we may, it would possess great value for us as throwing light upon the apparent discrepancies of the others in relation to the order of events at the resurrection and immediately afterwards. It has been traditionally affirmed to be in substance Peter's gospel, that is Peter's special contribution to the apostolic tradition concerning our Lord's ministry. It is said to have been written at Rome by John Mark who was associated both with St. Peter and St. Paul. Perhaps the Galilean fisherman did not possess the art of writing but he certanly did possess an eye for picturesque and dramatic detail. The style of St. Mark is just what we might expect if a personality like that of the rugged and impulsive fisherman who was afterwards called the prince of the apostles supplied the major portion of its contents. It begins with Peter's association with the work of Jesus in Galilee, saying nothing about any previous meeting in Judea, and in the main the scene of the events it describes is the northern province wherein was Peter's home. The third and fourth gospels to some extent rectify this, the latter evidently of set purpose, and give us details of a Judean ministry as well. The second gospel never spares Peter himself whereas the others do, which is another indication of its Petrine origin. It is by far the most vivid and human of the four in the descriptions of the activities of Jesus and what befell Him. Papias (quoted in Eusebius' *Ecclesiastical History,* iii. 29) says that the matter is not given in chronological order but consists of reproductions of different discourses of Peter written down as the disciple remembered them. This is probably true in some degree; the gospels are not chronologies but brief first-hand statements of fact, memoirs of incidents and sayings which may not have occurred precisely in the order displayed, nor would the preservation of the exact sequence be a matter of first concern with the authors. But, however that be, we can do no other than rely upon Mark's presentation as being on the whole the nearest in point of time to what it records. When difficulties arise we may have recourse to the others where they seem deliberately to have deviated from his narrative, but this outline should form the basis of any attempt to reconstruct the life of Jesus from the few materials at our command.

Mark sees no necessity to tone down anything. He, or rather Peter, sets down in a rough Greek dialect his intimate recollections of Jesus as the disciples saw and heard Him day by day. He is much bolder than the others in showing us the Master's true humanity—His feelings of anger and pain, of surprise and sadness, of loneliness and dread. The evangelist does not shrink from telling us frankly some things that do not easily fit in with the dogmatic view of Jesus' person and self-knowledge. And yet no gospel of the four is more emphatic upon the superhuman quality of Jesus' nature; this is not insisted upon but rather spontaneously assumed throughout as the one thing that impressed the beholder most. It is not Mark (Peter) that is our best source for an acquaintance with the teaching of Jesus; it is what the Master did rather than what He said that chiefly interests the second evangelist. Nevertheless here again what he does record is of inestimable value; some of the sayings of Jesus as recorded in Mark are the indispensable key to similar sayings preserved by the others.[6] And with the exception of about thirty verses all the narrative portion of Mark appears in the same order in the first and third gospels, nearly always in fuller and more vivid detail in the original source.

In making use of Mark, Matthew and Luke frequently improve on his phrasing from a literary point of view. Most of his Aramaic expressions are smoothed away by them. Occasionally they agree with each other as against him in presentation of detail or turn of expression, and this has led to the question being raised whether they were acquainted with another Mark than ours. That is not likely to have been the case, however. The synoptic problem is very much minimized if we allow sufficiently for the fact that all the written gospels derive originally from an unwritten tradition, the oral witness of the apostles and their fel-

[6] But it is possible that later copies of Mark may have incorporated some sayings from the non-Marcan document mentioned above.

[7] This is not to say that they did not employ literary sources or that the later did not depend on the earlier.

low-workers.[7] This was authoritative and exact to
a degree that would be now unthinkable. With the
universal development of the art of writing we have
lost something of the powers of memory possessed
by our forefathers and by many orientals at the
present day. There is very little doubt that our
canonical Mark is substantially the same gospel as
that which was written by Peter's disciple for Roman Christians, Jew and Gentile, some little time
before the destruction of Jerusalem. Had it been
otherwise its Greek would have undergone revision
and its provincialisms been pruned away. That this
has not been done points to its authenticity and in-
tegrity. The Aramaic expressions which jut out
of the Greek narrative, like rocks in a greensward,
are just what we might expect of Peter the fisherman who thought in Aramaic and could not keep
it entirely out of his speech. Protestant archæolo-
gists are now prepared to admit the probability that
St. Peter really was in Rome and was martyred
there after ministering to the little Christian church
that met near the house of the senator Pudens in
what is now called the catacomb of St. Priscilla.
What more likely than that John Mark would remember Peter's vivid and characteristic way of giving from time to time the very Aramaic words
spoken by our Lord at important moments! Perhaps the translation which Mark usually adds
would be Peter's own, the apostle first giving to
his congregation in his mother tongue the very expression that the Master used, as he remembered
it on some given occasion, and then turning it into

the universal Greek as well as he could for the benefit of his Roman converts.

THE GOSPEL OF LUKE

The first and third gospels make elaborate use of Mark but apparently are not acquainted with each other.[8] Luke is much more cosmopolitan in outlook than Matthew, probably for the reason that he was not a Jew. Luke's sequence of events in the gospel history differs widely from that of Matthew, probably for the reason already mentioned that Matthew groups his under subjects whereas Luke attempts to keep to something like chronological order—not that he always succeeds in doing this or indeed is careful to maintain it. He follows Mark where he can but does not hesitate to fit in matter of his own as he chooses. For example, he inserts the charming narratives and sayings (chapter ix. 51 to xviii. 14), derived from a source peculiar to himself, right in the middle of Mark's story and then goes on with the story where this special contribution terminates. His omissions are significant as showing that he writes for Gentile, not for Jewish readers, and therefore wishes to emphasize the universalism of the Christian evangel.

[8] But Prof. Turner, in his university lecture on New Testament study already noted, speaks (p. 45) of "the *vera causa* which has of all been most steadily overlooked or underestimated, namely, the influence of readings introduced from the text of one gospel into the text of another." This consideration leads him to discuss further (p. 62) the possible reactions of Matthew and Luke on later versions of Mark.

This is a complicated and technical phase of the general subject of gospel criticism which goes beyond our present limits.

For instance he says nothing about our Lord's apparent repulse of the Syro-Phœnician woman, nor about Jesus' journey through heathen territory (Mark vii. 31 to viii. 10), nor does he dwell as Matthew does, writing for Jewish readers, upon the inferiority of the Old Testament revelation and standard of conduct; sometimes also he gives to a saying of Jesus a different association from that of Matthew, thereby altering a little its bearing. This may be accounted for by the fact that he records a saying in a connection that agrees best with his general outlook—that is on the hypothesis (which is probable enough) that our Lord gave utterance to the same saying on different occasions. Matthew's context for some sayings is altogether different from Luke's. The most important example of this is the prophecies relating to the second advent. Matthew combines these with the definite forecast of the destruction of Jerusalem, thereby suggesting that in the mind of Christ and the apostles the former was to synchronize with the latter. Luke rightly separates the two consummations. Why? Was it because the destruction of Jerusalem had taken place when he wrote and the second coming had not, whereas when Matthew wrote both were still in the future? This would seem the most reasonable theory.

In his version of the Sermon on the Mount, or rather of the compendium of teaching which we are accustomed to group under that title, he has quite a number of very important sayings (vi. 24-26; vi. 27, 34, 35, 37, 38) which are not in Matthew at all, and he scatters many other portions of this famous sermon throughout his gospel and gives them a quite different association. The denunciations which Matthew records (iii. 7, xii. 34 and 38, and xvi. 1) as having been uttered against the scribes and Pharisees Luke definitely states as applying to the indifferent and wicked amongst Jesus' hearers generally.

Where did Luke get his facts and the point of view from which he presents them? It is a reasonable assumption that his gospel was colored by Pauline influences just as Mark's was by Petrine. But we must not make too much of this. St. Paul was not a first-hand authority for the life of Jesus as Peter was. But as a man of education Luke would find more to interest him in Paul's way of looking at things than Peter's. Paul was familiar with the Greek mentality and regarded himself as having a special mission to the Gentiles although no doubt he always began with the Jewish synagogue in every city he entered. Luke is a Paulinist in his general outlook, though whether he would have taken the same outlook if he had never come under Paul's influence is not quite so clear; it is at least conceivable that he might, judging from his antecedents and from the fact that Christianity was now being preached to the Gentiles as a universal religion. But he did not keep to one source; he appears to have taken the utmost care to collect evidence and verify his facts. For the nativity stories he must have had an informant in or connected with the holy family, and it is not unreason-

able to conclude with Sir William Ramsay that this
informant may have been no other than the mother
of Jesus herself.[9]   It is not necessary to conjecture
as Dr. Sanday does [10] that Joanna the wife of
Chuza, Herod's steward, and an associate of the
Virgin, may have been the person from whom Luke
derives what he so beautifully narrates concerning
the birth and childhood of Jesus. Luke could without difficulty have had access to Mary direct or to
James the Lord's brother who was head of the
church in Jerusalem. The Virgin is the more probable source because, as has been well remarked, the
restraint and delicacy of the nativity stories in the
third gospel in matters of such an intimate personal
character suggest that a woman is behind them, and
if a woman why not Mary? Had it been any other
member of the holy family we should have had
Joseph's point of view introduced also which is not
so. It is Matthew who gives Joseph's point of
view, although Luke did not know this at the
time of writing any more than Matthew was aware
of the facts which Mary alone was in a position to
reveal.

But Luke appears to have consulted many authorities in his search for materials for his gospel.
It would be interesting to know where he obtained
the exceedingly beautiful and precious collection of
sayings and parables (ix. 51 to xviii. 14) referred
to above which, though peculiar to this gospel, are
as characteristic of Jesus as any that find a place in

[9] *Was Christ Born at Bethlehem?*
[10] *Outlines of the Life of Christ,* pp. 172, 196.

the entire evangelic record. If anything as valuable
as this existed either orally or in written form within
the apostolic Church and as part of the subject matter of the primitive Christian tradition it is possible
that other portions of the teaching of Jesus equally
early and credible may yet come to light. Luke has
here laid hold of a collection of the Master's discourses with which the other evangelists did not possess a first hand acquaintance. Did he obtain this
also from Mary and her circle? Again it might
easily be so, for all a woman's tenderness breathes
through it. There are other fragments of fact
and teaching which find a place in the third gospel
alone and need accounting for. Possibly Luke
picked these up in touring the localities where they
were originally delivered and the memory of them
cherished among the little company of believers that
continued to worship Jesus there. There must have
been a number of such local traditions even after the
fall of Jerusalem as long as Palestine continued
populous. There is no evidence that Luke ever went
to Galilee to push his inquiries; if he had one would
think he would have known something of the Galilean appearances after the resurrection, none of
which he mentions. But this is not a conclusive
argument. Only a comparative few of the company of disciples in Galilee or elsewhere could have
known of these appearances at the time. And it is
plain that Luke's interest in the ministry of Jesus
was not confined to the south. In his description
of the Master's movements towards the end, to give

one outstanding example, he is on very sure ground. He shows, what is quite probable, that much of our Lord's most impressive teaching was delivered to His intimates during His last journey to Jerusalem; Matthew puts a considerable part of it in earlier connections.

Luke's sympathy with the poor and downtrodden comes out on every page although he himself belongs to a superior class. He stresses every saying of the Master which contains a denunciation of the heartless rich and illustrates His compassion for want and suffering. None of the other evangelists tell us of the important fact that Jesus was on several occasions a guest in the house of individual Pharisees, thereby indicating that there was not for some time a pronounced breach between Him and that body.

Another characteristic feature of St. Luke's gospel is that he always spares the reputation of the twelve apostles when he reasonably can, and one of his surprising omissions is the description of our Lord's agony in the garden so vividly given in St. Mark as well as in the others. The view that he shrank from including this lest it should tell against belief in the superhuman dignity of Jesus may have something in it, but on the other hand it is more likely to represent his own reverent attitude in the presence of a great mystery. Nothing was better known to the apostolic Church or formed a more prominent part of the story of the passion. Luke was familiar with it in the pages of St. Mark, to go no further, and he must have heard it again and again in the course of apostolic preaching or in Christian assemblies. He had no more reason for concealing it from his readers than for concealing the crucifixion itself.

Of St. Luke himself we know but little beyond the fact that he was a friend and companion of St. Paul in the latter's missionary journeys. As the name implies, and his gospel confirms, he was most probably of Greek origin, and there is some likelihood that he was a brother of Titus. His character is obvious from his writings; and tradition supports the view that he was gentle, modest, tender-hearted. His gospel is superior to the others in style and reveals the man of education as contrasted with the comparatively unlettered Jewish Christians who first preached Christ to the Roman world. There is an interesting tradition that he was also an artist and painted a picture of the Virgin—an indirect testimony that he knew the mother of Jesus personally, which would account for much in his narrative.

THE LATEST OF THE GOSPELS

It is evident even from the most cursory examination that the three earlier gospels are more or less similar in character and have their subject matter in common while the fourth is in a category by itself. The synoptic problem as stated above is the problem of reconciling or accounting for the different strata in the composition of Matthew, Mark, and Luke. The fourth stands altogether apart and constitutes an exceedingly complicated problem in itself to which there is no full and final solution with our present knowledge. Its traditional author is John the son of Zebedee, a view which the majority of scholars have for some time past united in rejecting, perhaps rather too hastily.[11] To the present writer it seems most probable that the apostle John is behind the gospel that bears his name just as Peter is behind Mark, and Paul to some extent behind Luke. Perhaps we may go further and say that he is as directly responsible for the bulk of the contents as Matthew for the first gospel.[11a] It has been held impossible that a Galilean fisherman should have written this profound spiritual treatise—for that is what it is—with its elaborate symbolism and philosophical background. But this is to assume too much. There are indications in the New Testament that the two sons of Zebedee were of fairly good social status. For instance it was through John that Peter obtained entrance to the house of the high priest on the night when Jesus was arrested, the former evidently having some influence in that quarter.[11b] He was the only one of the apostolic band who could with impunity remain near the cross at the time of the crucifixion; and the very request of James and John, made through their mother, that they might sit on the Master's

[11] *Vide* Principal Drummond's work: *The Character and Authorship of the Fourth Gospel,* in which a distinguished Unitarian scholar defends the traditional view.

[11a] Assuming that Matthew recorded the non-Marcan logia.

[11b] Assuming that the anonymous disciple of the fourth gospel was the apostle, and it is difficult to see what other conclusion is possible.

84

right hand and on His left in His kingdom suggests
that they considered themselves superior to the rest.
As for the philosophical conceptions exhibited in the
Prologue and the Alexandrian training which they
presuppose, criticism may be altogether on a wrong
track. As Dr. Rendel Harris suggests, the affinities of the Prologue may be rather with the Wisdom
literature of ancient Israel than with the Greek
Logos doctrine elaborated by Philo of Alexandria.[12]
Why not both? It is quite reasonable to suppose
that the parallelism which Philo himself saw between Wisdom personified and the Greek Logos
conception was perceived or communicated to all
thoughtful religious minds at the time this gospel
was written. This is not the most intractable problem connected with this gospel by any means. Internal evidence shows that the author was a Palestinian Jew, that he knew all about Jewish manners
and customs and the Messianic expectation, and
that he was thoroughly at home in his knowledge of
the districts to which he refers; he is always exact
in his descriptions and his local color. The only
difficulty in admitting this is his consistent reference to our Lord's most implacable opponents as
the "Jews," but here again criticism is inclined to
see stumbling blocks where none exist. Taken as
a whole the Jewish people, especially the inhabitants of Jerusalem, did reject Jesus; and by the
time this gospel came to be written the center of
gravity of the religion of Jesus was no longer in
Palestine but on Gentile soil; the church at Jerusa-

[12] *Origin of the Prologue to St. John's Gospel.*

lem ceased to be the headquarters of the movement after the destruction of the capital in A.D. $\overline{70}$.

Again, the author of this gospel knows all that he relates from the inside; he is personally acquainted with the various characters he depicts. He knows the principal forces at work in the Sanhedrin, and he is able to tell us with a degree of intimacy the others do not possess exactly what was going on and what dictated the policy of the rulers; he is *au fait* with it all right through. His very silence regarding his own name points to John the son of Zebedee as the source of the gospel, as otherwise it would be inexplicable why an apostle so prominent and a companion of St. Peter in the supreme crisis should go unmentioned. A common-sense reading suggests that St. John is meant every time the author is referred to. The beautiful self-designation "the disciple whom Jesus loved" has been found fault with as a claim to special favor on the part of our Lord and designed to show that John counted for more than Peter.[13] It is the exact opposite. It is used in the same spirit as St. Francis of Assisi habitually used the self-description, "Christ's poor little one, Francis." It is meant to suggest, taken in conjunction with his continued suppression of his own identity in his gospel, that John's only claim to worth or honor was the fact that he was loved by Jesus. It is he and he alone who emphatically records in detail the final com-

---

[13] Schmiedel: *Johannine Writings* argues that the cognomen is so presumptuous as to indicate that it could not be a self-designation by the apostle John, but might be used to describe him by a devoted admirer.

86

mission to St. Peter after the resurrection, which gave to that apostle an undisputed primacy in the primitive Church. There is an intimacy also in the description of the scene in the Upper Room at the Last Supper which can only represent the work of an eyewitness, and who could that eyewitness be but the apostle John? [14] The stamp of truth is on the whole narrative which supplies us with many valuable details lacking in the synoptics. Jesus must have been in Jerusalem a good deal oftener than the latter relate; it would be strange indeed if He were not. Why should He lament His failure to influence the people of Jerusalem if He had had no more acquaintance with them than the synoptics indicate? In this John supplements our knowledge in a very important degree. In fact it is fairly clear that the task which he proposed to himself was that of supplementing the synoptics rather than reproducing their matter; that he was well acquainted with their contents there is abundant internal evidence to show. [15] In some details he deviates from them though perhaps not so much as we might at first sight conclude. It is quite possible, for instance, that the discrepancies with regard to time and the sequence of events from our Lord's entry into Jerusalem until the resurrection could be reconciled if we had more data; the mutual

[14] Sanday: *Criticism of Fourth Gospel*, p. 179. "The gospel is the work of an eyewitness of the events, who is describing for us what he had himself actually seen."

For an exhaustive discussion of the identity of the beloved disciple, *vide* Prof. Stanton's *Gospels as Historical Documents*, Vol. III, pp. 132-146.

[15] Prof. Stanton, *ut sup.*, pp. 219-20, suggests that the fourth evangelist may have known Mark only.

relations of the Jewish and Roman calendars are very confusing.

It is not so easy to explain the difference in the style of teaching attributed to our Lord in the synoptics and the fourth gospel respectively. In the former He is terse, epigrammatic, parabolic; in the latter long, argumentative, dogmatic. In the synoptics the subject-matter of His discourse is generally some aspect of the Kingdom of God; in John it is mainly Himself and His claims. This difference may be partly due to the fact that He was dealing with quite another class of hearer in Jerusalem from that to which He had been accustomed in Galilee—fiercer, more fanatical, less disposed to listen to simple teaching of the kind which succeeded in Galilee among the humble fisher-folk there. It should be remembered that Jesus did not begin with parables even in Galilee but adopted the parabolic method after a time and for good reasons. John does not record any parables, perhaps because his predecessors had already done so, but partly also because the few miracles which he includes are all given a parabolic application—made, and very suggestively made, the vehicles of spiritual truth.[16] It is this elaborate use of symbolism which is the distinguishing feature of this gospel. In everything it contains there is an inner as well as an outer meaning, a higher as well as a lower, a spiritual as well as a literal. That the author selects his material out of a rich abundance is confessed. He tells

[16] Latham: *Pastor Pastorum*, pp. 84, 91, suggests that some of the miracles recorded in the synoptics are also to be regarded as acted parables.

us that there are many other things that Jesus did which are not written in his book, but that his special contribution is written with the object of demonstrating that Jesus is the Christ the Son of God. Need we go further in looking for the reason why so large a part of the book is taken up with controversies with the Jews in which Jesus is represented as putting forward claims which they on their part are not prepared to admit? That Jesus used a different style of teaching at other times may be presumed, and the writer knew it from his acquaintance with the other gospels even had he not been a first-hand authority himself, but he reports what was needed for the development of his main point. A close examination of the text will show that Jesus did not commit Himself in regard to His Messiahship in the fourth gospel any more than in the others until near the end, nor in Jerusalem more than in Galilee.

Very striking are the omissions of St. John. He says nothing about the virgin birth, not because he disbelieved in it, but because his Logos doctrine supplies as it were the view of the person of Christ which is its *raison d'être*. He says nothing about the baptism of Jesus but much about his relations with the Baptist himself. The temptation in the wilderness, like the transfiguration, he passes by as having already been described and not needed for his purpose. The same is obviously the explanation of his reason for not including the solemn institution of the Lord's Supper whereas he does dwell upon the fact that Christ is the bread of life. Like Luke he omits the agony in the garden, the cry of dereliction on Calvary, and the fact of the ascension, but in every case parallels to these experiences are supplied in the course of the narrative, and no other of the evangelists gives so much of our Lord's teaching on the subject of the Holy Spirit.

EXTRACANONICAL WRITINGS

Of the apocryphal gospels—that is, gospels which the Church has not thought fit to include in the New Testament Canon—some further mention ought to be made here.[17] They contain but little of value which is not to be found in the canonical gospels but are of considerable interest nevertheless as throwing light upon the mentality out of which the canonical gospels arose and which is taken for granted throughout the New Testament. They fall into different categories according to their character. Some are plainly meant to be historical, and in that respect bear a certain resemblance in style to our three earlier gospels. There may indeed be, as already remarked, some amount of genuine first-hand apostolic matter to be found within them. Of this order are the Gospel according to the Hebrews, the Gospel according to the Egyptians, and the Gospel of Peter. Perhaps we ought also to add the Fayum fragment discovered in Egypt in 1882 and the Oxyrhyncus group of sayings unearthed by Messrs. Grenfell and Hunt

[17] It is said that fragments of at least fifty of such pseudo-gospels are traceable in early Christian writings. Few are known in entirety.

in 1897 and 1903.[18] Some again are doctrinal in tendency and bear evidence of having been written mainly to support some particular heretical view of the person and work of our Lord. Such are the Gospel of the Twelve Apostles, the Gospel of Thomas, the Gospel of Philip, and the Gospel of Marcion. Then there are the gospels of the childhood. These profess to supply information about our Lord's immediate ancestry and the long period of His childhood and youth concerning which the canonical gospels are silent. Amongst these the Protevangelium of James occupies the first place as claiming to be an actual history written by James the Lord's brother concerning the birth and parentage of the Virgin. It is a composite production and clearly could not have been written by a person of Jewish origin. Two others derive from it, namely, the Gospel of pseudo-Matthew and the Gospel of the Nativity of Mary. Both of these, however, are quite late in point of date—not earlier than the sixth century A.D. In the same category with the Protevangelium of James must be included the Childhood Gospel of Thomas and a late Arabic gospel which covers much of the same ground, together with the history of Joseph the Carpenter, somewhat earlier than the foregoing, and a book which has greatly influenced Catholic tradition, the Assumption of Mary, which may have been written in the late fifth century. There are some writings whose theme is chiefly the incidents appertaining to

[18] For a careful and scholarly examination of these, *vide* H. G. E. White: *Sayings of Jesus from Oxyrhyncus* (Cambridge Press).

the passion of our Lord and His appearances after death. Of these the Acts of Pilate and the Descent of Christ into Hades are the chief and were combined in the Middle Ages into a single book called the Gospel of Nicodemus. The legend of Abgar belongs to the same group and is fairly early though without historical value. It is the story of the message sent by Abgar, king of Edessa, to Jesus asking the latter to come and cure him and live in Edessa. It gives also our Lord's reply, that He would send one of His apostles after His resurrection. This supposed letter of Jesus has been greatly esteemed for ages in popular use.

The Gospel according to the Hebrews is evidently not much later in date than Matthew, Mark, and Luke, and the same may be true of the Gospel according to the Egyptians also. Both are ascetic in tendency and the former is distinctly Jewish-Christian in standpoint. Another ascetic gospel is the above-mentioned Gospel of the Twelve Apostles which regards Jesus as a man and nothing more.[19] All of them, except possibly the first-named, depend chiefly upon the synoptics for their material which they work over in accordance with their particular point of view. The Gospel of Thomas is Gnostic in origin but the childhood stories are orthodox. No doubt there were many gospels written to commend Gnostic opinions.[20] We only know most of

[19] *I.e.* of Ebionite origin, but with the Gnostic accretion that the heavenly or supernatural Christ took possession of and used the man Jesus.

[20] Harnack's *History of Dogma*, Vol. I, gives perhaps the best survey of the subject. *Cf.* Dorner *ut sup.* and G. R. S. Mead: *Fragments of a Faith Forgotten.*

these from the frequent references to them in Christian legend; but they have exercised an enormous influence upon sacred art. To the foregoing should be added the Diatessaron of Tatian which professes to be a harmony of the existing gospel narratives woven into one.

The Gospel according to the Hebrews was in use among the Jewish-Christians of Alexandria as distinguished from the native Christians of the same district who used the writing known as the Gospel according to the Egyptians. It may be assumed that the former was written in Aramaic and the latter in Greek. Only fragments of either have come down to us. Their names were given to them in common use, not as written by Hebrews or Egyptians respectively, but as designating the circles in which they were read. The former especially would possess great value for us if we could recover it in its original completeness. It is said to have been written in the dialect of our Lord and the apostles themselves, a fact which alone would invest it with peculiar interest. It must have contained a good deal that the synoptics record but with notable variations, as, for instance, that it was in obedience to the suggestion of His mother and brothers that Jesus went to be baptized by John in the Jordan but that before doing so He disclaimed any consciousness of sin. There is no mention of the Holy Spirit descending in the form of a dove at the baptism but the description of what is said to have taken place has a beauty of its own: "It came to pass, when the Lord was come up out of

the water, that the whole fountain of the Holy
Spirit came down and rested on Him and said unto
Him, My Son, in all the prophets I awaited thy
coming, that I might rest on thee. For thou art
My rest; thou art My first-born Son, who reignest
for ever." In the story of the healing of the man
with the withered hand this gospel tells us that the
sufferer appealed to the Master to help him on the
ground that being a mason he needed his hands in
order to earn his bread. The rich young ruler is
represented as being displeased with Jesus' require-
ment that he should sell all he possessed and give
to the poor, and that Jesus then sharply remonstrated with him for his presumptuous claim to
have kept the precepts of the Law. "How sayest
thou, I have obeyed the Law and the prophets?
Since it is written in the Law, Thou shalt love thy
neighbor as thyself, and behold, many of thy brethren, the sons of Abraham, are covered with filth and
are dying with hunger, while thy house is full of
many good things, and nothing at all goes out of it
to them." This version of the episode throws some
light on the account of the same contained in our
canonical gospels.

The view formerly held by some scholars that the
Gospel to the Hebrews might be identical with the
original Matthew has now been generally discarded,
but a good deal is to be said for the opinion that it
represents an oral tradition partially if not completely independent of the synoptics and of equal
antiquity. But this does not apply to the whole

of the gospel; some portions of it are late, representing—in the resurrection narratives for instance —another stratum of tradition than that of the New Testament. The Gospel of Peter is docetic [21] in tendency and tells us explicitly that our Lord felt no pain upon the cross. Origen cites this gospel along with the Protevangelium of James as authority for the view of those who maintained that Jesus' brothers were Joseph's children by a former marriage.[22]

[21] *I.e.* that body of Jesus was an appearance merely and not real, and, therefore, not exposed to suffering. On this heresy *vide* Harnack and Dorner *ut sup*. Prof. Rendel Harris and Prof. Swete have both produced works on the Gospel of Peter.

[22] The literature concerning the apocryphal gospels is very large and constantly receiving fresh additions. Westcott's *Introduction to the Study of the Gospels* gives an excellent survey, but recent translations of the more notable portions of apocryphal gospel matter are available.

CHAPTER V

THE NATIVITY AND CHILDHOOD

The Virgin Birth

We cannot pass over the problem of Jesus' birth. The Church is committed to the view that He was born of a virgin, but it has to be frankly admitted that this article of the faith constitutes a great difficulty to the modern mind and hence many among both clergy and laity have avowedly given it up. It is not mentioned in the earliest gospel or in the still earlier writings of St. Paul; the writer of the fourth gospel who is well acquainted with the other three deliberately omits all reference to it, thereby indicating, in the opinion of some competent authorities, that it possessed no value for him.[1] Moreover, the several accounts of the Nativity as given by Matthew and Luke do not coincide; the genealogies especially are utterly different. These are weighty arguments and are not countered by the assertion that our Lord's divine dignity required a miraculous birth or that His sinlessness necessitated a breach with ordinary human generation.

[1] But *Vide* p. 88.

He would not be either more or less divine through being born of a human father, and if a sinful taint were transmissible by heredity it would be as much so through Mary as through Joseph. The Roman Church gets over this difficulty by making a dogma of the immaculate conception of Mary herself but only by removing the problem a stage farther back. If it were possible to break the entail of sinfulness in this way for one person by a direct act of God it could be done for the whole human race without calling in any other redemptive agency. We may as well say at once that if there be no other argument for the virgin birth than that our Lord's divine origin and spiritual perfection necessitated this mode of His entry into the conditions of earthly humanity it rests on no solid foundations.

On the other hand we must not be too positive in saying what is or is not possible to God in His dealings with man. There is a charm and sweetness as well as a dignified restraint about the Nativity stories which have given them a powerful appeal to the devout imagination in all ages and we have no right to fling them aside merely on the ground that they are not consonant with normal human experience. The question resolves itself mainly into this, Did the coming of Jesus into the world represent the intrusion of a higher principle of life than what had hitherto been known as human into our concerns? Was the new start thus made as great a departure in its way as that which separates man from the brute creation? If so, what more likely than that it should be signalized by something that would in a measure anticipate the sexless humanity which is to be? for this is what the virgin birth does. Keeping therefore closely to the standpoint with which we began this work, we ought to refuse to consider the case against the virgin birth as closed by any *à priori* considerations concerning what is inherently probable or improbable. The whole life of Jesus is one long miracle; He Himself, as we have seen, is the supreme miracle; why hastily conclude that in the manner of His birth there could be nothing supernormal, nothing differentiating Him from mankind at large?

Nor when we come to examine the evidence available are the difficulties as great as commonly represented. That Mark does not mention the birth and childhood is not surprising. He was giving Peter's memories of the public ministry and did not profess to do more. Assuredly if he does not affirm the virgin birth neither does he deny it. No more does St. Paul. His words are that Jesus was "born of a woman," but he nowhere says born of a man. If St. John omits any direct statement of the virgin birth he at least does not contradict it, and in the present writer's opinion he does the opposite of what the authorities referred to above attribute to him, namely, evince disapproval of the Matthæan and Lukan view by falling back on the doctrine of the eternal Word made flesh. That he does the latter rather strengthens than weakens the traditional view. He means to show that such a person as Jesus had never appeared among men before and never would again. Was it likely that such a being would be born as ordinary human beings are born? He goes on further to insist upon a spiritual birth which all believers undergo—"not of blood, nor of the will of the flesh, nor of the will of man, but of God"—a birth whereby we are to enter upon the kind of life which was already Christ's before He was born into this world in the likeness of man. *Not of the will of the flesh nor of the will of man*— what can this signify but that He Himself came to earth by the act of heaven and not by ordinary human generation?

That St. Luke, who was always careful of his facts, knew the family of Jesus is evident enough from xxi. 18 if nothing more. His intimacy with the personages of whom he and the synoptics speak in common as having been of the company of Jesus is equally marked. Dr. Sanday says that in Luke's visit to Jerusalem in 57 and 58 he had opportunity for meeting and knowing Mary the Virgin of which he would be sure to avail himself for the purpose of his gospel.[1a] But surely the matter would be well known in any case to the church at Jerusalem of which James the Lord's brother was head; there would be no great difficulty in getting at the facts. It should also be remembered and taken into account that a virgin birth would not be as incredible to the ordinary mind of that time as it would be to the ordinary mind of our time. There was a widespread belief, as the rabbinical literature shows, that a world-redeemer would shortly be born who would remain hidden until the time for His appear-

[1a] *Outlines of the Life of Christ*, p. 194.

ance was ripe. Everything connected with this mysterious person was supernormal.

THE GENEALOGIES

The problem of the genealogies has been much exaggerated. To begin with, there is no cogent reason for concluding that the author of St. Matthew's gospel is not also the compiler of the genealogy which is prefixed to it; and therefore it is obvious that to him there was no discrepancy between his statement of the descent of Jesus and his emphatic assertion that the latter was born of a virgin. The reading in the Syriac version of this gospel, "Joseph, to whom was betrothed Mary the Virgin, begat Jesus, who was called the Christ," does nothing to invalidate this view.[2] The only question is why the canonical Matthew takes the trouble to give us a genealogy of Jesus which is not that of Mary but of Joseph, and the answer is that the genealogy is symbolical only and was not intended to give the actual physical ancestry of Jesus but rather the moral and religious. That both Mary and Joseph belonged to the house of David is quite probable judging by the consistent witness of the New Testament to the fact of our Lord's Davidic descent. But Matthew's gospel is characteristically Jewish and rabbinic in the use it makes of illustrative Old Testament names and quotations for the sake of edification. The genealogy is a plain indication of this. Its contents are presented in

[2] Because it might merely indicate legal paternity.

three groups of fourteen names each as the author is careful to remind us—fourteen being a double of the sacred number seven—but such a lengthy period would require a far longer list if we were to take it literally. And when we scrutinize the names themselves we come upon some strange introductions—Tamar the adulteress, Rahab the harlot, Ruth the Moabitess (of a race which according to the Law was never to mingle with Israel or share in the Messianic promise), Bathsheba the paramour of David. What can this mean but to show that all Israelitish history is in a manner summed up and fulfilled in the Messiahship of Jesus and that even the sinner and the foreigner are from this point of view to be brought within the scope of divine grace? The artificiality of the structure of this illustrative summary is therefore seen to have a very definite purpose: Jesus is the flower of the Jewish race, that in which its age-long hope is fulfilled, but in such a way as not to exclude the Gentile from participation in its benefits or the sinner from its efficacy. The word "begat" is used in the legal sense only, to indicate succession. Thus one man is said to have begotten another after many generations' interval. This is the sole explanation of Matthew's version of the genealogy of Jesus which has much weight and it is the simplest and most reasonable. It does not follow, of course, that it is necessarily inconsistent with Luke's because the list of names is different. We could write two exhaustive genealogies of any one which would have little in common. Of the present King of England, for instance, it would be easy to prepare a genealogical table which could leave out some of the most notable names in English history and yet be full and accurate and that without skipping a single generation.

St. Luke follows something of this method in tracing the descent of Joseph through the line of Nathan the son of David and rejecting others. His omissions are even more numerous than Matthew's but there is no indication that he wrote with the same object; on the contrary Luke's well established character for care in the verification of his facts would suggest that he took some trouble to make sure of his ground. Why then does he also give Joseph's pedigree instead of Mary's while affirming the virgin birth of Jesus with as much emphasis as the first evangelist? It is impossible to say with confidence, but a fair supposition is that Joseph and Mary had a common ancestry upon one side of the house and that Luke deliberately chose to trace the descent of Jesus through this line, using for that purpose the record which existed at the time wherein Joseph would appear as the putative father of Jesus. It has to be admitted that this is mere conjecture but it solves a problem. Here we have descent from Joseph described in what has rightly been looked upon as the gospel in which the Nativity is presented from Mary's side. Why give the genealogies at all? Perhaps in part as explaining Joseph's journey to Bethlehem for the purpose of being enrolled at the command of Augustus Cæsar.

THE NATIVITY AND CHILDHOOD

THE CENSUS

Until recently one of the most perplexing problems in connection with the gospel accounts of the life of Jesus has been this enrollment or census but Sir William Ramsay has done a great deal towards clearing it up.[3] Apparently its purpose was not primarily for purposes of taxation though ultimately it may have been so. Luke is careful to say that it was the first one of the kind, thus showing that he was perfectly aware of another and better known one at a different period. There is nothing to show that either Joseph or anyone else was obliged to make the journey to his native place in order that the census should be properly taken. What is more probable is that he had his own reasons for going such as the possession of family property in or near Bethlehem. It is now beyond dispute that these provincial censuses were taken periodically throughout the empire, in some cases annually. We know also that the Jews hotly resented the national census which was taken in A.D. 6 and which appears to have been conducted in the Roman fashion (Acts v. 36). A revolt headed by Judas of Galilee broke out on account of this, no doubt because of the taxation attaching to it, and this revolt led to the foundation of the party of the Zealots to which, as we have seen, one of the apostles originally belonged.[4] There is no record of the earlier census nor any explanation of the acquies-

[3] *Was Christ Born at Bethlehem?* Part II.
[4] It has been argued that we have an anachronism here; but the point is not a vital one.

cence of the Jews in the one and their resistance to the other beyond the implication that the former was conducted by households and without the direct interference of the Roman authorities and the latter was not. Luke says indeed that the census associated with the birth of Christ was an enrollment only. That it was universal and extended to the whole Roman world would mean that it took a considerable time and was meant to establish a basis for later fiscal, military and commercial statistics. It is a fair inference that the emperor was dissatisfied with Herod's method of carrying out his instructions in the first instance and that it was because of this that the supplementary and stricter census was ordered which provoked the rising mentioned in Acts. We may be sure that Luke would not venture upon the definite statement that a decree of world enrollment was actually issued by Augustus unless he knew that the fact was beyond challenge. Leaving aside his reputation for accuracy we have still to allow for the existence at the time the gospel was written of many thousands of people who were contemporary with what is thus recorded, to the extent of knowing all about the matter at first hand.

If we had only Matthew's account to guide us we should conclude that Bethlehem and not Nazareth was the home of Joseph and Mary at least until after the return from Egypt, but Luke as definitely says that the annunciation to Mary took place in the Galilean city. The hypothesis is a reasonable one that Nazareth was only the temporary abode of Mary and her espoused husband for some time prior to the Nativity and would never have been more but for the hostility of Herod after that event. This makes plain too why Mary made the journey south in her then delicate condition; she wanted to get home, not merely to be enrolled in her native place but that her child should be born there; it would not be likely that she should mistake the significance of the angelic announcement that her Son should inherit the throne of His father David.

THE ANNUNCIATION

Concerning the form of the announcement itself, nothing need be yielded to prosaic modern rationalism. Once grant that the coming of Jesus into the world was a unique fact as already depicted, the irruption of a new principle into earthly conditions, and it becomes certain that that advent was prepared for on both sides of the veil. The beautiful stories in Matthew and Luke concerning this mystery have been styled the poetry of the Nativity, and the description is true enough, for poetry is truer than prose. More took place around the cradle of Bethlehem than could be expressed in terms of ordinary human experience. And granted that the birth of Mary's child was the stupendous event that Christians have always believed it to be and that history has justified them in affirming, Mary must have had some idea of it beforehand; it would be incredible that she should be left without some intimation of the august privilege that was to be hers. Hence the Lukan account of the appearance of a celestial messenger represents not more but less than the truth of what happened. The same applies with even greater force to the winsome narratives of the angelic appearance to the shepherds on the hillsides near Bethlehem, to the journey of the Magi, and all the other supernormal incidents which center in that marvelous birth in David's city. It could not have taken place without supernatural accompaniments, for little though earth know about it heaven knew all. So far from the supernatural being a difficulty here its absence from the narrative would create a greater difficulty. There is no difficulty save in the mental attitude of our age.

> The angels keep their ancient places:—
> Turn but a stone, and start a wing!
> 'Tis ye; 'tis your estrangèd faces,
> That miss the many-splendored thing.

What Happened at Bethlehem

Sentiment has played a great part in the description of the conditions under which our Savior was brought into the world. Thus Joseph and Mary have often been described as vainly seeking shelter from the hard and heedless company in which they found themselves, they being too poor to be able to command the accommodation which wealth could have secured. Much eloquence has been expended on the supposed fact that the humble pair could find no other chamber than the rude stable hard by a crowded inn. Tradition has embellished the story by adding that animals occupied it at the same time. There is no word about any woman being present except Mary herself, and it is she who is said to have wrapped her baby in rude coverings and laid Him in the manger where animals usually fed. The scene is suggestive of indigence to the verge of want and of utter callousness on the part of the multitudes outside who cared nothing about the poor travailing young mother in her extremity.

But we must beware of too positive conclusions here. There is no evidence to bear out this view and probabilities are against it. Mary and Joseph would travel together to Bethlehem in the company of a caravan. They would have some friends therein and it is unlikely that Mary was the only woman. The journey was, as always, slow and not exacting. Mary perhaps was not expecting to be delivered immediately or at any rate had no clear certainty on the subject. Doubtless the pair had relatives in or near Bethlehem if they came from that neighborhood themselves, but there would be no immediate reason for seeking them out unless Mary were in urgent need of seclusion, and this appears to have been what happened. On their arrival the open yard of the caravanserai would provide a sufficient resting place for them and their belongings, including the beasts of burden whereon the journey was made. But when it became evident that Mary must withdraw from such a public place they would first try to obtain admission to the inn itself and then finding that full would look elsewhere. The most obvious covered place that suggested itself would be one of the rock caves hard by and of which some are still to be found in that locality, used for the housing of animals when necessary. There they would go, and for aught we know,—indeed it is more than supposition,—Joseph would seek out a friend or friends of Mary's own sex to be near her at such a time. That they did not lack friends is evident from the many hints that are given later. Perhaps Mary's own sister Salome, the mother of James and John the sons of Zebedee, may have been of the company—if this Salome were indeed Mary's sister and if there be any foundation for Sir William Ramsay's theory that it was she who was the source of St. Luke's Nativity stories.[5]

Whence, again, came the Magnificat? It was an early Christian hymn and always attributed to Mary. Is there anything strained in the suggestion that she was indeed the composer during her journey south to visit Elizabeth when her soul was exalted with the divine revelation that had been made to her? There are signs that, as we now have it, it derives from an Aramaic original, and there is nothing far-fetched in the assumption that the humble Jewish maiden deliberately based her song on that of Hannah because of the similarity in the experiences of the two women. This hypothesis fits the facts just as the song itself fits the situation as it then existed but would have failed to do so later on. She sang of the future as one with her Jewish training would see it, and took for granted no more than any one with her antecedents would.

The story of the revelation to the shepherds and that of the coming of the Magi cannot reasonably

[5] *Ut sup. Was Christ Born at Bethlehem?*

be set aside as without historic foundation either. The shepherds on the hills outside Bethlehem were engaged in the work of rearing the paschal lambs for the Feast of the Passover which, judging from the fact that they were in the fields all night, must have been near at hand. Such men, with such an occupation, would be of devout character, just as the men of the medieval masonic guilds gave a religious flavor to their organizations because their work was to erect sacred edifices. Why did the shepherds receive any intimation of what had taken place in Bethlehem that night? There is an explanation which has at least some serious title to credence. It is that they were from the very nature of their vigil passing the time in devotional exercises and conversation concerning God's promise to His people. If in the solemnity of that prayer meeting under the stars they rose to heights of religious feeling, like thousands of the servants of God before and since, and if their one concerted earnest desire was that God should show some speedy sign of coming to the deliverance of Israel and in blessing to mankind, what wonder if they were suddenly made aware that their petition was in process of being answered? Something of the stir being made on the higher side of the very thin veil that stretches between earth and heaven broke through to their astonished senses and they saw and heard for a moment what is ordinarily hidden from our grosser perceptions but none the less real. Something happened; of that we may be sure; it would be strange if it had not, considering how stupendous was the event that was taking place and how deep the interest in it on the superphysical plane. Heaven knew what earth could not know, knew and rejoiced therein, and for a fleeting moment the senses of humble men at prayer in the midnight hour were enlarged to receive a glimpse of that celestial knowledge.

Be it remembered that such supernatural occurrences would not be received with the same incredulity at that time and place as to-day and amongst ourselves. If people speedily forgot the wonder thus revealed they would at least be susceptible to what they were told of it for the occasion. Bethlehem would be greatly excited by the news as it spread from lip to lip. We are assured that it was so, and we might infer it even if the record were silent on the point. A corroborative item is supplied in the implication that Joseph and Mary did not stay long in their lowly lodging. The evangelists do not comment upon the fact, but we next meet the little family in a house. Where would this be? Not a word is spoken about the host or hostess: Is it possible that it belonged to members of Joseph and Mary's own family? Was it in Bethlehem itself or some little distance away? Why did they not go there at first instead of putting up at the caravanserai mentioned by Luke? We do not know unless it were that there were some difficulty in obtaining access to it at short notice: hence it may have been their own, the property which they had come up to attest, and needed preparing before it could be made a home. Further, it is suggested that they went there quietly because of the publicity given to their affairs by the shepherds; this may be inferred from the fact that a little later no one knew where to find them except after exhaustive inquiry.

A good deal appears to have happened in the interval. The humble pair had been up to Jerusalem and presented the infant in the Temple with the customary usages, and He had been circumcised on the eighth day like all male Jewish children. Hints are afforded us again of supernormal revelations to holy and pious persons concerning this little one who had come so strangely into the world, but nothing is told concerning these experiences which would now be considered fanciful in the light of what we know of the operation of exceptional gifts allied to carefully disciplined religious character. What was vouchsafed to Simeon and Anna was not one whit more wonderful than may be paralleled repeatedly from the lore of saintship and even of psychic sensitives at the present day. What is specially interesting in the case of these holy people is that they were representative of a class. We are expressly told that they belonged to communities of persons who were banded together in Judea and especially in Jerusalem for the express purpose of praying and watching "for the consolation of Israel." It is in accordance with God's ways of working that they should not pray in vain. Anna the prophetess soon spread the glad tidings far and near throughout these quiet retired circles.

It is not likely that this kind of thing could go on for long without attracting some amount of attention. The jealous Herod would get to hear of it though at first he might not pay much heed. Perhaps the news traveled farther afield than Palestine itself and roused some interest here and there in persons not of Jewish race. Be that as it may, the next stage in the unfolding story is marked by the coming of what must have been a fairly large company forming the train of three travelers who had journeyed to Jerusalem with the express object of discovering the whereabouts of a child who, they had reason to believe, was destined to play a sovereign part in the history of the race, a child of destiny in fact.

There is much that is mysterious in this episode but well worth examination. Who were these three men and where did they come from? Were they persons of consideration or the reverse? What led them to undertake their journey and how did they regard the object of their quest? Tradition has it that they were petty chieftains or sheiks; the New Testament tells us no more than that they were sages, that is, persons who made a study of prophecy and occult lore; the indications are that astrology came within their purview. We know that at that period there was a widespread belief amongst surrounding nations that a prince would be born of Jewish race who would change the face of the world.[6] These pilgrims appear to have been familiar with that prophecy and may possibly have

(handwritten marginal note:) (1) Some have stated astronomy not astrology.

---

[6] Edersheim: *Life and Times of Jesus the Messiah*, i, 293.

heard of its fulfillment in the remarkable story of
the birth at Bethlehem. Where they came from
there is nothing to show. Justin Martyr (Dial. 77,
88) says they came from Arabia but does not indicate the source of his information. Matthew's account is not necessarily a contradiction of this statement, for the phrase "the star in the east," probably only means in astrological terms "in the as-
cendant" or "in the rising." In their observation
of the heavens they had noted a sidereal phenomenon which, coupled with some tidings which may
have reached their ears concerning the happenings
at Bethlehem, led them to conclude that the hero-
king of prophecy had appeared: hence the journey which they undertook in order to pay their
homage to Him. Jesus by this time may have been
as much as a year old or more, and a journey from
the borders of Persia would take many months,
from Arabia not so long.

They made no secret of their quest. Knowing
no more than the bare fact that the child of destiny
was somewhere in Palestine they made straight for
the capital and interrogated the authorities concerning the whereabouts of the little one. A caravan of such size would have attracted attention in
any case, but before long the news of their coming
was brought to Herod who was greatly perturbed
thereat. We are told that the whole city shared his
interest though we may rightly infer, with very
different feelings. Everyone knew that Bethlehem
was in traditional belief the place of the national
deliverer's nativity, and in response to Herod's

question on the point the Temple authorities and doctors of the Law told him so. But how to find this child of prophecy was not so easy. As we have seen, Joseph by this time had apparently withdrawn mother and babe into seclusion, well knowing what would befall if he allowed them to become a center of public curiosity and perhaps of something more. At the first hint of danger he would remove his charges elsewhere. Hence Herod set a trap for the Magi, speaking them fair and asking them to discover the habitation of the infant prince and afterwards disclose it to him that he might have the opportunity of tendering a similar tribute. They succeeded, how we are not informed, but it requires no great exercise of imagination to understand that they would have misgivings on the subject of Herod's purpose. Herod's subjects would supply sufficient testimony to make them hesitate about returning to Jerusalem. We can imagine the conversations about this which they would have with Joseph and the consequent uneasiness of the latter; hence it is not at all remarkable that the subject should recur to all of them in visions of the night. The visitors took the precaution of journeying home by a route which avoided Jerusalem, and Joseph in his anxiety shortly afterwards fled the scene also, taking Mary and her child to Egypt for safety.

THE SETTLEMENT IN GALILEE

How long the holy family sojourned in Egypt is not stated in the New Testament though the extracanonical literature of the infancy has much to say about it, perhaps with some foundation of truth. The stay could hardly have been prolonged if only because the date of Herod's death occurs so soon after the events above narrated, though of course it does not follow that the exiles left Egypt immediately on hearing the news. From Matthew's account it would appear that they were on their way back to Bethlehem—another sidelight showing that their interests were really there—but hearing that the tyrant Archelaus had succeeded his father as ruler of Judea they turned their footsteps northward and settled in Nazareth. Presumably they had associations with that part but may have had no fixed habitation there until after the return from Egypt. The third evangelist calls it "their own city Nazareth."

The apocryphal gospels, as is but natural, try to fill for us the gap in the record between the infancy and the commencement of the public ministry of our Lord. Curiosity on this subject would be sure to exist in apostolic times as now; but it cannot be said that the extracanonical books add anything valuable to our knowledge. For the most part they supply a mass of thaumaturgical detail in marked contrast to the dignity and wholesomeness of the New Testament memoirs. Jesus is represented as performing ill-natured miracles on His playmates occasionally when they angered Him, and indeed as moving through a succession of marvels of the most incredible and meaningless nature. We are better off with the brief and reverent

evangelic statement that He "increased in wisdom
and stature, and in favor with God and man." We
are meant to understand from this testimony, no
doubt, that He lived a natural, gracious, unfolding
human life in Joseph the carpenter's house in the
little Galilean city which is forever to be associated
with His name. The Nazareth of to-day is a
poorer and meaner place than it was in the prosperous times of the Cæsars. As Galilee was a flour-
ishing province, permeated by Græco-Roman life
and manners it is a fair inference that Nazareth
partook of the general conditions which followed
order and good government as unlike as possible
to the misrule which had prevailed in the same region for centuries past. In the synagogue which was
at once a place of worship, a court of local law, and
perhaps a school, Jesus would receive His first instruction in the history and faith of the race to
which He belonged. How strange to picture Him
sitting in company with children of His own age
listening to what the rabbis had to say in that plain
unadorned meeting place so like the Nonconformist
chapel of our own time! The centralization
of worship in the Temple at Jerusalem had
given a great local importance to the synagogue
as providing for the immediate religious and social
wants of the people. There and at home Jesus
would be thoroughly grounded in the ancient Law
of Israel and the writings of the prophets. It is
plain to be seen from His later public teaching that
He knew the Old Testament intimately from beginning to end and no doubt also knew what the

chief rabbinical schools had to say of the books of
the Jewish Canon. His training at home must
have been still more valuable, and we can infer the
depth and richness of the type of piety maintained
therein from the quality of the epistle of James the
Lord's brother. Jesus stands in a category by
Himself, and it is possible that He might owe little
to the instruction of a pious mother and upright
foster father, though such lives as theirs would supply Him with a fitting spiritual environment; but
in the case of James and the other inmates of the
home we are on sure ground in saying that the debt
to Joseph, if not also to Mary, was great. James
shows by his allusions the kind of character that
was produced by a thorough training in the Old
Testament tradition; he is the pious Jew at his best,
sober, prayerful, reverent, sincere. His animad-
versions on the rich perhaps indicate that Joseph's
family had come down in the world and had had to
put up with a good deal at the hands of wealthy
neighbors who had acquired their patrimony. That
James again became head of the church in Jerusalem points to the fact that their principal connection was with the south. A pure Galilean would
not be so suitable in that position. Sir William
Ramsay has shown that the education Jesus received was a very good one according to the standards of the time, for indeed in all the essentials of
a worthy life the Jewish youth of that period might
be accounted the best educated in the world.[7]

[7] *Education of Christ,* p. 67.

THE LIFE OF CHRIST

The Boy Jesus in Jerusalem

Only once during these formative years is the silence broken. Luke tells of the pilgrimage to Jerusalem at the Feast of the Passover when Jesus was twelve years old. In accordance with custom He had to be presented in the national sanctuary on reaching adolescence, a ceremony akin to our confirmation at about the same age. The present writer remembers seeing a number of children gathered round a bishop in St. Peter's at Rome in 1903, receiving instruction and answering questions, with other clergy of that great head center of Roman Catholic Christendom standing by, listening and looking on, and the picture instantly suggested to him the kind of scene that probably took place at Jesus' catechism in the Temple. There was nothing unusual about it. He was there with others that He might show the doctors of the Law how He had been taught and in His turn put questions to them. They found Him so exceptionally intelligent and well informed that the venerable rabbis gathered round Him with interest. Joseph and Mary left Him there while they went about their own concerns. Most children would not have stayed longer than was absolutely necessary and then would have rejoined the caravan in whose company they had come up to the capital. But Jesus took His instructions literally and remained in the Temple precincts full of the joy of being in the courts of His Father's house and hearing of the things that meant more to Him than anything else in life. Hence His reply to Mary's gentle reproach, "Thy father and I have sought thee sorrowing." The word "sorrowing" reveals something of the nature of the relationships in that lowly home; the ties of affection were close. The boy's defence was fully reasonable. Why should they seek Him? He had not been lost. They might have known that He would be where they had placed Him and engaged in the exercise for which they had brought Him to the Temple itself. It is to be noticed that Mary calls Joseph His father, but that in Jesus' reply it is a heavenly Father who is meant. "Wist ye not that I must be about my Father's business?"—or, "in the things of my Father" or "my Father's house." Where did the divine boy learn to call God His Father? He utters the name as if He expected to be understood and as though it had been often on His lips. Perhaps Mary herself was the teacher, a thought full of beautiful suggestiveness when we ponder how much it implies. James in his epistle uses the same word with the same reverent familiarity, and perhaps he did not learn it first from the lips of the brother whom he had now come to recognize as his Lord. Perhaps both learned it from the same source.

No mention of Joseph appears in the inspired record from this time forward, but that he lived until Jesus was entering upon manhood may be inferred from several facts. One is the remark expressing the surprise of His former neighbors: "Is not this Jesus, the son of Joseph, whose father and mother we know?" Or on the occasion of His first

address at Nazareth: "Is not this Joseph's son?"
They would hardly have spoken thus if Joseph had
been very long dead, and yet there is no indication
that Joseph was alive after the public ministry began. It is the mother and the brethren who are referred to on occasion but never the supposed father.
In one instance at least the onlookers enumerate
the inmates of the household: "James and Moses
and Simon and Judas," together with some sisters.
On this occasion also Jesus is described as the son
of Mary, the name of Joseph being omitted, and
He Himself is called the carpenter, not merely the
son of a carpenter. He must have been old enough
to learn His trade before Joseph died for the indications are that He followed Joseph's calling and
therefore we may take for granted that Joseph was
His instructor.

Jesus' Kindred

What was Jesus' exact relationship to the other
members of this household? It is evident that He
was generally regarded as the son of Joseph. But
were these brothers and sisters of His the children
of Joseph and Mary? The best tradition is against
this view and maintains that they were the children
of Joseph by an earlier marriage, he being much
older than Mary.[8] This would explain a good deal,
as for instance the slowness of Jesus' brothers to

[8] Two of the apocryphal writings already mentioned, Protevangelium of James, and Gospel of Nativity of Mary, both state that
Joseph was greatly Mary's senior. Origen and Clement of Alexandria amongst the Fathers of the Church affirm that the brothers
of Jesus were older than He and sons of Joseph but not of Mary.

recognize the significance of His personality, though when it is said that they did not believe in Him we need not read more into the statement than that they had not yet associated themselves with His fortunes or come to understand what He was seeking to do; it does not follow that they were actually hostile or scornful of His claims and teaching; it is much more in keeping with the situation as thus portrayed to conclude that they had left their father's home and set up homes of their own before Jesus was of an age to impress them greatly, otherwise it would be inexplicable that they could have been members of the same household with Him day by day and year by year and failed to realize the transcendent quality of His nature. That they realized it after the resurrection is evident from the epistles of James and Jude.[9] Both of these brothers describe themselves as "servants of Jesus Christ." James calls Him the Lord of Glory. The earnest piety and character of both men are revealed in their writings, and it is highly improbable that they were ever to be found among Jesus' active opponents. It is noteworthy that they never refer to Him as their brother but only as their Lord; their attitude towards Him is exactly that of the rest of the primitive Church, wherein indeed they did not exercise the same authority as the apostles. James the just, as he was reverently styled, was made head of the Church at Jerusalem, partly perhaps because of his relationship to Jesus, but more likely because

[9] The authenticity of Jude is more open to question than that of James.

of his own gifts of wisdom and goodness. One extracanonical tradition of a beautiful character concerning him may well be authentic, namely, that he was already a follower of Jesus before the crucifixion and was so convinced of His Lord's triumph over death that he vowed neither to eat nor drink till he heard of His resurrection, and that Jesus knowing this appeared to him privately on the first Easter Day and breaking bread gave it to him saying, "Eat, my brother, for the Son of Man is risen from the dead." [10]

The fact is worth noting in the same connection that Jesus would not have been likely to commit His mother to the charge of the beloved disciple if she had had sons of her own still living in the same home with her. Clearly that was not so. Joseph's children were not her sons and perhaps had long had families of their own to support. Jesus in all likelihood not only inherited His foster father's trade but continued to support His mother and perhaps His unmarried stepsisters also in the same house after Joseph's death. This may be the reason for the slight differentiation between brothers and sisters in the comments of the inhabitants of Nazareth, "Are not His sisters here with us?" The brothers apparently were not at that time living in the old home or perhaps in Nazareth itself.

Of Jesus' other relatives not much can be affirmed with confidence. That Mary had a sister or sisters is expressly stated, and there is strong traditional support for the view already mentioned

[10] *Gospel According to the Hebrews.*

that one of these sisters—perhaps there was only one—was the mother of the apostles James and John. If there is no confirmation of this in the New Testament itself at least there is nothing to contradict it. James and John would be thus more nearly related to Jesus by blood than the sons of Joseph and would naturally be much associated with Him in childhood and youth—another reason for committing the virgin mother to John's care.

That John the Baptist was, though more distantly, Jesus' kinsman we are informed on the authority of St. Luke who says that John's mother Elizabeth was Mary's cousin. And seeing that Mary was sufficiently intimate with Elizabeth for the latter to be the first person she wished to see after the Annunciation, and seeing too that they were both selected for the high privilege of bearing sons who should be epoch-makers in the world's history, the one as forerunner and the other as fulfiller, it is but natural to conclude that they met at intervals while the children were growing up and that the two boys were well acquainted. This again explains much. Elizabeth, being already advanced in age when her son was born, had in order of nature, passed away before the latter's prophetic ministry began, but while she lived some measure of intercourse between the home at Nazareth and hers must have continued. After Elizabeth's death this intercourse may have been less frequent. John could not have come forth as a flaming prophet without long preparation and that would involve a period of solitary brooding and self-mortification.

All the evangelists agree that he was a denizen of the wilderness and something of an anchorite. Whether he had even been associated with the community of the Essenes there is nothing to show. He was not an Essene; he approximated much more nearly to the type of the ancient prophets and especially Elijah who was a man of like habits and temperament.

Very fine and devout reproduction. N. E.

CHAPTER VI

ON THE THRESHOLD OF THE MINISTRY

RELATIONS WITH JOHN THE BAPTIST

WHAT did the Baptist think about himself? His own testimony as preserved in the evangelic record shows that he disclaimed either being the Messiah or the prophet who was popularly supposed to return to earth as the herald of the Messiah. He said he was neither Christ nor Elijah nor Jeremiah. He seems to have regarded himself merely as a herald of the Messianic advent which he had become convinced was near at hand. His words would imply that he possibly thought of himself not so much as the herald of the Messiah as the herald of the herald. "There standeth one among you whom ye know not," etc., might refer rather to the prophet who was expected to appear than to the Messiah Himself. His preaching shows that he believed the Messiah would come in judgment. His message to Israel was that it was not only the Gentiles but the seed of Abraham who needed to repent, and his words were stern and uncompromising, especially in dealing with the Pharisees and Sadducees. He

introduced baptism as a ceremony indicative of repentance—not that it was new; it was already in
use as symbolic of the passing from one kind of
life to another. In John's use of it there was no
suggestion of a new life begun by the regenerating
operation of the Spirit of God; the rite was merely
what he declared it to be, a solemn way of indicating that the person undergoing it was putting
away old and evil modes of living and entering
upon a new course of action more in accordance
with the will of God and a fitting preparation for
the impending judgment and the coming of the
Kingdom. Christian baptism of course signified
something more, but it is questionable whether baptism into a fellowship of Jesus signified more during His earthly ministry. Jesus' disciples, when
He made disciples, seem to have been baptized by
the apostles in much the same sense as John's;
Jesus did not do any baptizing Himself. But it is
nowhere stated that this baptism which preceded the
passion was ever repeated afterwards or needed to
be.

John's relations with Jesus constitute a problem
which is yet far from being solved. Why Jesus
chose to undergo baptism at all has been a puzzle
to many from the very first. He made no confession of personal sin and yet submitted Himself to
an ordinance which was stated to be a baptism of
repentance. The perplexity thus occasioned would
of itself be enough to prove that the incident is
historic and was well remembered as marking the
end of Jesus' long period of silent preparation for

His mission and the commencement of His public
work. The cousins may not have met for some time
previously. Jesus journeyed south with the rest
of the family to listen to John's preaching and to
witness the phenomenal impression it was making
through Judea. Perhaps He there and then took
the decision of thus publicly and solemnly turning
His back upon His old quiet life and entering upon
the path which was to lead Him to the cross. He
could not be other than deeply moved by what He
saw and heard, and He realized that the hour had
come for Him to begin what He must long have
felt to be His mission to the world. We may be sure
that such a soul as His could not have arrived suddenly at the conviction that He had something to do
in the world such as none other ever had. He had a
hidden life with God into which we cannot pene-
trate, but everything He afterwards said or did in
public as preserved for us in the New Testament
goes to show that He was fully master of Himself
from the hour His ministry began, and spiritually
mature. This baptism was no conversion; He was
already as completely at home in the mysteries of
the Spirit as He was ever likely to be; He was only
waiting, and now He knew that the great moment
had arrived. Stepping down into the water of Jordan therefore meant something different to Him
from what it did to those about Him. It meant the
closing of one door and the opening of another, the
end of the thirty years of silence and the beginning
of the brief public activity which has had a greater
cumulative effect upon the destinies of mankind

than the combined witness of all other prophets and religious masters who have ever spoken and wrought.

John appears to have recognized Him at once as perhaps is not to be wondered at; and his protest, "I have need to be baptized of thee and comest thou to me?" may have meant no more than that he already knew full well the pure unearthly spiritual quality of Mary's son. But there is also the suggestion that in a sudden flash of insight he beheld in Jesus the greater than himself—not necessarily the Messiah—whom he had announced as coming after him. It does not seem to have occurred to John that he himself was filling the rôle traditionally ascribed to Elijah, that of being the forerunner of the Messiah. Who then did he perceive Jesus to be? But for the details given in the fourth gospel we might conclude that he thought of Jesus as merely the true herald of the Kingdom; but this can hardly have been the fact in view of the explicit declaration attributed to Him by the fourth evangelist, "Behold the Lamb of God which taketh away the sins of the world." Could such a declaration be historic; and why the metaphor of a sacrificial lamb? The most reasonable view on an examination of the facts is that John, from previous knowledge of Jesus as well as from swift intuition at the moment, discerned in Him a being of wondrous potency, greater far than himself, and therefore shrank from baptizing Him. Both experienced in the actual performance of the rite the mysterious spiritual visitation which has been variously recorded as the descent of the Spirit upon Jesus. But it was not

until after the latter's return from the wilderness
and after further conference between the two that
Jesus revealed Himself to the Baptist as the Messiah. John may have been quite prepared for the
revelation, but the indications are that it was made
after the temptation and not before. Such indeed
is suggested by the form of John's announcement;
for it was not until Jesus had gone through the
ordeal in the wilderness that the nature of His Messiahship was fully settled in His own mind. He
definitely put aside all idea of political leadership
and based His conception of Messiahship upon the
idea of the Suffering Servant of God as portrayed
in the second Isaiah, the chosen one who suffers
for the sins of his people and whose sufferings have
a redemptive efficacy.[1] In His forty days' lonely
vigil He definitely chose a suffering Messiahship
as His lot and the Father's will—at least until its
earthly consummation in the sacrifice of Himself
as the paschal lamb slain for the sins of the world.
If this be not admitted the character of Jesus' ministry is inexplicable, and we are not taking too much
for granted. The word Messiah was a rather vague
term, connoting many different things to those who
were accustomed to use it. Jesus could have dis-
pensed with it. He adopted it because He found it
at work as the symbol of God's appointed representative through whom the regeneration of the
world was to take place. What was really important was the latter expectation, not yet fulfilled in

[1] For the "Servant" passages in Isaiah consult G. A. Smith in Expositor's Bible.

its entirety, the establishment of God's Kingdom among men. Jesus submitted to convention in regarding Himself as the anointed one through whom this change was to come about, and He did not err; His advent has meant far more to mankind than that of the Messiah of Jewish expectation would ever have done. What was original to Him in so doing was His association of the idea of Messiahship with that of the Suffering Servant. This was striking, impressive, un-Jewish, and went straight in the teeth of popular conceptions of the Messianic office.

Did He succeed in making John understand it? It would appear so if the fourth gospel is to be credited; otherwise we are unable to account for the expression "Lamb of God" which is quite in place if Jesus had explained to His cousin the forerunner the result of His battle with the tempter and the reasons for His choice. John may have found difficulty in assimilating it, for it must have gone counter to his own prepossessions as illustrated in his discourses. For him, no more than for his contemporaries, could the Messiah be a sufferer. There is just the possibility that the word Messiah was not used between them; nowhere is the statement made that it was; and the Baptist's description of Jesus as the Lamb of God may have been no more than a metaphorical allusion to the character of His coming ministry. This is unlikely, however. The phrase is too august to admit of any lower interpretation and implies too much. On the other hand it did not necessarily convey to anyone else the belief that Jesus was the Messiah. Messiahship and sacrifice were too distinct for that in the minds of John's hearers.

The view that the fourth gospel account of this episode is unhistoric, and that it was because of the success of Jesus' ministry that John afterwards sent to ask Him, "Art thou He that should come or look we for another?" is untenable on several grounds. Tradition is wholly against it as is psychological probability. But the question might conceivably mean, Was Jesus Himself the forerunner or not? This is perhaps how it was understood by John's disciples who brought the message, for it was only there and then that Jesus pronounced the Baptist to have fulfilled the part of Elijah towards the new dispensation. One fact which emerges clearly from a careful study of the gospel narrative is that neither John nor Jesus ever made specific public claims for themselves in relation to Messianic prophecy.

The attitude of John's followers to those of Jesus remains a problem of which as yet there is no full and complete solution. A hint is given us indeed that at an early stage in the ministry of the latter John's disciples were jealous of His influence and also condemned His greater laxity on the subject of fasting. But after John's very specific declaration of the transcendent significance of Jesus it is puzzling to find that John's following seems to have remained separate from that of the Master. After the intrepid Baptist's death they came to Jesus with the information but do not appear to have associated themselves with Him forthwith as one would expect. They appear to have held together then and afterwards, for as a fellowship they continued for a time even after the crucifixion and the organization of the Christian Church. Then, too, there is the saying of Jesus to be accounted for, that he that was least in the Kingdom of Heaven was greater than John, albeit no greater than John had ever arisen. We can only conclude that to Jesus the new law and the new life, imparted by Him to those willing and able to receive them, were held to be an immeasurably higher blessing than had ever otherwise been experienced; and in this view Christian history will sustain Him. Humanity made a new start from Jesus, not from John or from any other than John.

THE SPIRITUAL CRISIS FOLLOWING THE BAPTISM

In the light of the foregoing the episode of the Temptation is not so mysterious as it has often been made to appear, nor is there any justification for the theory that it was a transference into Christian story of the mythical ordeals said to have been endured by other great personages, notably Buddha. What could be humanly more natural than that after the illumination received at the Jordan Jesus should wish to go away by Himself to think out what was now before Him and the course on which His career must be shaped? Nor would the experience be entirely subjective.[2] If there be forces of

[2] Gore: *Dissertations on Subjects Connected with the Incarnation*, p. 23 *ff*.

evil in the spiritual universe as well as good—and who would deny it?—it is certain that they would assail the soul of one so transcendently great as Jesus upon whose will at this time such momentous decisions hung; all future history waited upon this fateful hour, for if Jesus had chosen differently nothing is more certain than that the whole direction of modern civilization would have been other than it is. The change wrought by the impact of Christianity upon the world may be exaggerated in the mind of Christians—*pace* Gibbon—but that there has been a change, and an enormous change too, resulting from the combined influence of the Gospel and the Church few would deny. Did Jesus know this beforehand? Whether He did or not scarcely matters. Heaven knew it; perhaps hell knew it; the tremendous nature of the spiritual crisis involved could not have been hidden from the plane or planes whereon are the springs of most of the spiritual forces that affect humanity for good or ill. The will of Jesus at the beginning of His ministry was the storm center of a conflict of forces just as it was at the end, and as perhaps in some degree every human life is also. Limited as we are limited in knowledge and power, though not to the same extent, He found Himself tempted to compromise with His own highest vision for specious reasons. The order of the temptations is differently given in Matthew and Luke, but the discrepancy is not important. The whole story is plainly symbolical and must have been told by Jesus Himself to those in His intimate confidence. After a long fast—which does not necessarily mean entire abstinence from food but only the taking of sufficient to sustain life—in His weakened physical condition the thought came to Him that He never need undergo privation; He need not share in the disabilities of ordinary humanity in anything; He had somehow become aware—when or how is immaterial—that He possessed a certain power over nature; why should He not use it for the satisfaction of His own creature wants? There was the further suggestion thus conveyed that throughout His earthy ministry He might exercise this sovereignty in the interest of His mission; He need never suffer; His outward man need know nothing of what the sons of men are habitually called upon to endure of the struggle to live. His answer might also be ours, the answer of the spirit to the flesh at all times. "Man shall not live by bread alone, but by every word that proceedeth out of the mouth of God." Not first that which is of earth but that which is of heaven should be the object of our quest—the body for the soul, not the soul for the body.

The metaphorical significance of the other two temptations is apparent on the face of them. Jesus was not literally transported either to a pinnacle of the Temple or to a mountain of such a height that a view could be obtained therefrom of the entire inhabited earth. But the question was thrust upon Him whether it would ever be right to put God to the test, as it were, by venturing that which might bring others to destruction.[3] Was God necessarily bound to save Him from ruin and disaster if with no higher motive He presumed upon His unique consciousness of vocation and sonship? Again the answer was that He could be guilty of no such presumption. No more morally than physically would He put forth claims that could not be honored in the case of ordinary men; He asked for no immunity from such trial and sorrow as was the portion of the race.

Lastly there came to Him the temptation to which so many lesser masters have succumbed, the temptation to win secular power, to accommodate Himself to men's baser motives that He might rule them for their own good. And easily He might have done it, as easily as Mahomet did afterwards or the Maccabees had done before Him. There was that in Jesus which could have swayed men imperially had He so chosen; He could have aroused all the fanatical heart of Israel and been the founder of a mighty empire driving that of Rome from the Orient had He made His Messiahship of that order. It was the kind of Messiahship the Jews wanted, passionately longed and prayed for, and He could have fulfilled all their hopes and more. This is not mere speculation but sober sense. Jesus could have swept the Roman eagles from Palestine and been the founder of a secular empire which might have challenged that of the Cæsars. The

---

[3] Edersheim: *Life and Times of Jesus the Messiah* gives another and striking though more literal view. But from any standpoint the meaning of Jesus' choice in this instance is that He would not gain spiritual ends by unspiritual means.

material was all ready to His hand; the conditions
were favorable; the people only waited for a leader;
and He was not as other men. He knew it, but
He would not. His Kingdom was not of this
world.

THE GOOD NEWS OF THE KINGDOM

What then was His Kingdom? Here we are
on very debatable ground. There are authorities
who maintain that His ideas on the subject were
not widely different from those of His contemporaries of His own race but that He waited for supernatural intervention, believing that a crash was
imminent in human affairs, that all His hopes were
centered on the future and the sudden and catastrophic intervention of heaven to bring the established order to an end. It must be admitted that
there are passages in His recorded teaching which
go some way to support this view, but it is equally
clear that these do not serve to demonstrate it.
Briefly put it may be said that in the thought of
Jesus the Kingdom of God and eternal life implied
each other. By the former He meant the supernatural order, that state in which God and His
angels dwell, the realm of all-perfection; and by
the latter He meant the life proper to that state,
life as it is lived in heaven, timeless life. He spoke
indifferently of the Kingdom of God or the Kingdom of Heaven because to Him either phrase meant
that state wherein the will of God was the only
rule and to which complete obedience was rendered;

in a word He meant the *summum bonum* of which
all great dreamers have dreamed, the eternally real
which is also the ideally perfect, the good to which
nothing can be added, that which is as contrasted
with all that merely seems. If we start from this
point of view regarding the mind of Jesus on the
central theme of His discourses the rest clears itself
as we go along. To Him the Kingdom was always
present in its fullness in heaven but also in some
degree on earth. It was present wherever any human heart was willingly yielded to God or in any
human deed which glorified God. But in an unideal world such as ours it could only be fragmentarily present at the best, therefore He bade
His followers look to the future for its complete
realization "in earth as it is in heaven." [4] The ordinary Jewish dream of a restored kingdom of Israel
was not this. It was mainly political. An oppressed race, they looked back to a dim glorious
past, to the great days of David and Solomon when
Israel reached its greatest height of material splendor and bade fair to be a political power of much
magnitude like some of its neighbors which had
risen from beginnings as small. For ages these
people had had to serve foreign masters but had
never given up their cherished hope. They not
only believed that they would have their own kingdom again with its capital on Mount Zion but that
it would be to the rest of the earth what Rome was
just then. They believed that a great king born

[4] Wendt: *Teaching of Jesus*, Vol. II, chap. vii,—Conditions of
Membership of the Kingdom of God.

of David's line would arise and play the part of a greater Cæsar. He would rule over a world-wide federation of peoples, and the Jews were to be a privileged imperial race.[5] This reconstituted kingdom of Israel was to be a veritable Kingdom of God, a kingdom of justice and righteousness, a kingdom of happiness and universal peace under the rule of God's vicegerent, the heaven-sent deliverer, the Messiah-King of prophecy.

It would be impossible to say by what proportion of the nation this belief was firmly held at the time Jesus began His ministry. Dr. Glover [6] thinks it was not very large, but if he be right it is remarkable that the expectation as shown in the New Testament should have been so generally known and so intense. It is only what we might expect in a high-spirited people with an ancient religio-political tradition. They could not acquiesce in the Roman dominion, and it was but natural that they should be looking eagerly for the appearance of some great national leader to throw off the hated yoke and restore their independence if no more.

THE KINGDOM AND THE MESSIAH

But that the Messianic expectation should be as clear-cut as their belief in coming deliverance from Roman overlordship is unlikely, and hence the personality of the deliverer afforded a fruitful theme for religious fancy and speculation. At certain periods the Kingdom occupies the foreground of

[5] Schaff: *History of the Church*, Vol. I, p. 155.
[6] *Jesus of History*.

popular thought and little is said of the Messiah; at other times expectation centers on the figure of the Messiah and only on the Kingdom as His Kingdom. Originally the king, any king of Israel, was a Messiah—that is, an anointed one—in virtue of his kingly office; hence restored kingship would of itself imply Messiahship. As time went on, and the hope of an heir to David's throne declined, the national desire for restored autonomy took the form of thinking of God Himself as the deliverer-king of His people, and any instrument He chose for that deliverance could rightly be regarded as a Messiah for the specific purpose. Thus Cyrus the Persian is described as God's Messiah for the deliverance of the Jews from Babylon, though he himself did not know it.[7] The Israel of that period was in the conception of the second Isaiah the Suffering Servant whose function it should be to witness God to the nations. But for some time before Jesus came Apocalyptic had been reviving and developing the idea of a personal Messiah who was to be God's instrument for the deliverance of His people from the oppressor by a mighty hand. Hence we have a most confusing series of oracular declarations of the function and character of this being; these are anything but mutually consistent, but the fact that there were so many of them is sufficient to show that there was a large public which dwelt fondly and piously upon this rekindled hope of a new and better world-order to be inaugurated by one who should be divinely raised up for that work. Jesus

[7] Isaiah xlv. 1-5.

must have been familiar with this literature or with a considerable part of it. His use of terms would suggest this, and the whole coloring of His picture of the future is a similar indication.

But it should not be forgotten that the Messiah as portrayed in such popular writings as the book of Enoch was after all but an idea, not an actuality, and never a very self-consistent idea. It is well to bear this in mind when the question is raised whether Jesus was the Messiah; the problem is, Which Messiah?—the Messiah of the Psalms of Solomon or that of Enoch, or neither? That He was not and never intended to be the Jewish Messiah in the sense of a leader of insurrection against Roman rule is abundantly evident both from His acts and utterances. That question, as we have seen, was settled at the Temptation. But that His view of Messiahship had affinities with Apocalyptic is equally evident to those familiar with what remains of the latter.

JESUS AND MESSIAHSHIP

The question why Jesus chose to identify Himself with the vague figure of the Messiah of Jewish national expectation is not an easy one to answer. It was the Messiah of Apocalyptic upon whom He seems to have centered His thought, not that of the native-born prince of the nationalistic hopes; and there is a considerable difference between the two. The latter was simply to be a man specially raised up for the work of freeing Israel from her oppres-

sors, a greater Judas Maccabeus but gaining his
end by much the same means; the former might be
anything, so many things were imagined and declared about him. The apocalyptic writers assigned
tremendous functions to Him. His glorious advent
was to mark the end of the age and the beginning of
an entirely new dispensation involving a drastic
all-round renewal wherein the whole creation was
to share. This was to be preceded by a general
judgment in which those who had wrought harm
to Israel were to be called to account; then the various world-powers were to be overthrown at a
stroke and the Messiah was to reign in their stead.
He was affirmed to be a preëxistent being who
would appear in the fullness of the time (*vide* Apoc.
of Baruch iv. 3 and lix. 4; and Assumption of
Moses i. 14-17). He was referred to under different names—the Restorer, the Son of Man, the Son
of God, the Son of David, etc. Criticism is not
yet fully agreed about the exact sense in which
Jesus adopted the title Son of Man as descriptive
of Himself. It could not have been universally understood in a Messianic sense, for nothing is more
apparent in the synoptic record than that He did
not at first intend His claim to Messiahship to be
generally known. Son of Man was a Messianic
title from the time of the Maccabees onward though
with a somewhat indeterminate connotation as designating either a person or a people, the latter principally. But in the book of Enoch it is used to signify a personal Messiah, a Man from heaven. Had
Jesus read Enoch? The conclusion that He had is

almost irresistible, but there is no evidence that the people who formed His audiences were equally familiar with it. The point has been stressed that in the Aramaic dialect the words "man" and "son of man" are the same.[8] But why then is the term never translated into the Greek of the gospels as "man" only? The evangelists agree, so far as we can judge, that Jesus gave it a personal and Messianic signification and used it consistently to indicate Himself. The Messianic implications of this self-designation would not be apparent to others until He chose to make them so which was not until near the end of His ministry.

The simplest conclusion to which we can come from an examination of the evidence in our possession is that from the first Jesus thought of Himself as the Messiah, but in a larger and higher sense than had hitherto been understood. He purposely refrained at first from declaring Himself the Messiah lest He should mislead His hearers into thinking of Him as what He was not, and thus vitiate His spiritual work at the very outset. But the chief reason on the other hand why He did think it worth while to regard His mission in this light was that He saw that all the spiritual hope of Israel had come to be centered upon the advent of a Deliverer, a representative of the Most High, for whom the name Messiah was the only and accepted name though it was made to cover so many different things. Above all it stood for a supernatural per-

---

[8] Notably by Lietzmann (1896) in an essay which first forced the question upon scholars generally.

son in the language of Apocalyptic, for one who should be at once both sovereign and judge acting in the name of God. The Messiah is so presented in Enoch and in the Sibylline Oracles (iii. 625). Hence His use of the title Son of Man could only have meant that He knew Himself to fulfill all these anticipations; He was the Man from heaven who had yet to be revealed. In the meantime He had to work and suffer.

The expression Son of God had not necessarily the same Messianic significance, though it is so used in Enoch and fourth Ezra. Evidently Jesus' use of it as applied to Himself exasperated the Pharisees and the Temple authorities, but not because of its Messianic implications; they probably recognized that in so describing Himself He claimed a special relationship with divine being.

Son of David is easier to understand. Jesus' descent from David does not appear to have been seriously challenged at the beginnings of Christianity. Perhaps the favorite Pharisaic title for the Messiah was Son of David because this sect ardently desired that a prince of David's line should come to sit on David's throne. The Pharisaic Psalms of Solomon contain the plainest expression of this hope. But it was in Judea only that the descent of the Messiah-king from David was principally cherished; the aspiration did not exist elsewhere to anything like the same extent. The Psalms of Solomon lay stress upon the fact that He was to be world-ruler and judge. Concerning the manner of His manifestation the Apocalyptic

writers have much to say (*vide* Apoc. of Baruch
xxix. 3 and II Esdras vii. 28). Some said that
He was already in the world but in concealment
owing to the iniquity of the people. It was universally believed that His advent would be specially
heralded. He was to regather the scattered remnant of Israel to Jerusalem and restore the Temple
(Psalms of Solomon xvii. 33). He was to destroy
the Roman empire and establish the Kingdom of
God upon its ruins (II Esdras xii. 31-33; Apoc. of
Baruch xxix. 9; Psalms of Solomon xvii. 22-25).

How far Jesus ever thought of Himself as fulfilling these various and diverse functions it would
be impossible to say. All that stands out definitely
from His words and still more from His course of
action is that He knew Himself to be the Chosen
and Anointed One, coming from above, who was
destined to be God's instrument for the purpose of
bringing salvation to mankind in all its aspects.
He was conscious of being sent into this world for
a specific object while belonging essentially to a
higher.

MYSTERY OF JESUS' SELF-KNOWLEDGE

The consciousness of Jesus constitutes a problem
which we can only reverently approach without pro-
fessing to be able completely to solve it. That He
was conscious of standing in a unique relationship
to God is evident from the testimony of all the
gospels. His superhuman quality is as strongly
presumed in the synoptical gospels as in the fourth

though less is directly said about it; there is no warrant for saying that the synoptics present us with a purely human Christ and the fourth with a divine. The first intimation of a unique quality in Jesus' self-consciousness is given in His reply to His mother in Luke ii. 49 though it is possible to explain it as the result of Mary's own teachng about Israel's God. Also whatever happened at the baptism there is no doubt but that His divine sonship was present to His knowledge from that moment though it does not follow that He was not thoroughly aware of it before. The Gnostic glosses upon this saying have no historic justification nor is there any ground for the argument that it was in the waters of Jordan that Jesus received the special illumination and endowment which made Him the receptacle of divine life and power above all other men;[9] indeed one of the most remarkable things about the record of His life is that from first to last it contains no trace of what we should call spiritual development; He is mature from the day He first appears in public, sure of Himself and His heavenly Father, strong, calm, authoritative in His declaration of the divine word. Throughout He adopts an attitude towards God which no other has ever dared to do and yet He does it with sane dignity and perfect collectedness, not as a self-deluded visionary might who in his madness had come to imagine himself divine.[10] He speaks of the Son as revealing the Father (Matt. xi. 27) in a classical

[9] As in apocryphal *Gospel of the Twelve Apostles.*
[10] Liddon: *Bampton Lectures on Our Lord's Divinity,* Lect. IV.

passage as pronounced in its Christology as anything to be found in John, and evidently He means Himself though the third person is used. It is the same in the parable of the wicked husbandmen where this unique sonship is affirmed as at once fulfilling and exceeding all the witness of the prophets. In John v. 18 He makes Himself equal with God, if this be what we are to understand by the force of the passage; the same is plain enough in John x. 30, "I and my Father are one," and even more impressively in His reply to Philip in the upper room. Again and again He declares that He comes from and will return to God (John vi. 38, 46, 62; vii. 28, 33, 36; viii. 14, 18, 26, 42). With astonishing consistency He always distinguishes in His references to God between His own sonship and that of others. Instead of saying our Father it is constantly, "My Father and your Father" or "When we pray say our Father." He claims that only He had seen the Father (John vi. 46); others must see the Father through Him (Luke x. 22, etc.). He was conscious of His own preëxistence (John iii. 13 and xvii. 5), and is equally explicit about His own future coming in glory to judge the world (Matt. xxv. 31 ff., Mark viii. 38). There is nothing more notable in all history than this astounding combination of self-assertion with utmost humility. He claims a personal homage outstripping anything that the mightiest master of men has ever dared to demand and does it as of right; He is not irritated when it is withheld, being so sure of Himself; but He identifies the supreme good for every individual with a submission to Himself which is without parallel except as given to God. He states that He is greater than David, Abraham, Solomon, the Temple, the Sabbath, and the Law; men's greatest self-offering is that which is made to Him and for His sake; and yet He Himself is the servant of all (Matt. v. 11, 22, 28, 34; vii. 21, 22, 28, 29; viii. 4, 10, 22; x. 15, 22, 32, 37-39, etc., etc.). He never doubted, hesitated, or wondered if He might be mistaken in regard to the truth of what He taught; He knew with an immediate assurance that had nothing in it of speculation or inference. He never exhibits the slightest consciousness of wrongdoing, and there is only one passage which is even susceptible of being interpreted as a confession of imperfection.[11] Remorse and fear form no part of His experience; He asserts an unbounded moral authority which is fully justified by the impression made by His character on those who knew Him best and enjoyed His intimacy. The test of daily companionship which with others would have revealed weaknesses only deepened the awe and reverence which His friends felt for Him. That He was subject to ordinary limitations in other ways, notwithstanding His possession of extraordinary powers He Himself plainly averred.[12] He did not know the day and hour of His own advent, He confessed astonishment at men's unresponsiveness to His message, He shrank from the last dread ordeal of shame, ignominy and maltreatment. We may well

[11] Mark x. 18, reproduced in Matthew and Luke.
[12] Gore: *Dissertations on Subjects Connected with the Incarnation*—"The Consciousness of Our Lord," pp. 96, 97.

say that all other miracles recorded in the New Testament pale beside the supreme miracle of the self-consciousness of Jesus Himself. There is no parallel to it in all that is known of human life on this planet.

In the main He seems to have confined His ministry to people of His own race and country. He avoided foreign cities in Palestine itself with the possible exception of Cæsarea Philippi and there is no statement that He ever wrought or taught in a Gentile community as such. The incident of the Syro-Phœnician woman and the Roman Centurion are remarkable exceptions to His general rule. There are some indications that in the earlier stages of His ministry He thought He could win the allegiance of Israel; He does not appear to have known with certainty that He would be rejected by His own countrymen. What would have happened if they had accepted Him? It is hardly any use inquiring. Such a life as that of Jesus would be certain in any event to come to a Calvary of some kind; He would have had to meet His passion at the hands of men. More we do not know; the mystery is deeper than concerns mankind only; there are superhuman forces of ill to be reckoned with as well as of good. In descanting upon the limitations of Jesus it has often been remarked that He believed disease to be of Satan's making whereas we now know better. Do we? It may be gravely doubted. Here is a complex problem of which no complete solution is forthcoming by any means at our present command, but there is at least some

(1) Jesus economised time. Men ought today. many a
public teacher spends his time of irrelevant things. We
have gained But little out of the composite authorship
controversy —

THRESHOLD OF THE MINISTRY

ground for suspecting that our insight into the
causes of human suffering is after all not so superior
to that of the Light of the World as we have been
too ready to assume. But He mistook epilepsy
for demon possession! Did He? Have our wise
men mistaken demon possession for epilepsy? If
there be one thing almost beyond question to those
who know the evidence in these days it is that
demon possession is not only a fact but a fact of
our time as well as of New Testament times.

Concerning our Lord's accommodations to the
ideas of His contemporaries in other ways little
need be said. If He spoke as though Moses wrote
the books of the Law and David the Psalter, He
was only speaking in terms of the knowledge of the
time, perhaps even of His own, and the intellectual error touches no vital principle. ✓ (1)

More important questions are whether He need
have perished if He had not allowed Himself at
His trial to be accused of claiming Messiahship;
why He chose to labor in the world in such a humble capacity; what immediate significance He attached to His earthly life and ministry; and why
in His own mind, and consequently in that of the
apostles, His passion apparently had so much
greater significance than His teaching. We cannot answer these questions without taking full and
serious account of the development of Christian
doctrine as a whole.

If ever Jesus underwent the kind of agonizing
spiritual crisis which with great men often precedes
vocation to a life-work, it must have been before

His emergence at the baptism; there is not a hint
of such a thing afterwards, for neither the Temptation nor the agony in the garden were of this
nature. On the other hand His public ministry
was perhaps too short to have contained much
room for the gradual development which would
take place in an ordinary public life spread over
many years. It is noteworthy that while He declared Himself able to forgive sins in God's name
there is no suggestion that He ever asked or felt it
necessary to ask forgiveness for Himself. To His
death He attributed a mysterious efficacy in relation to the sins of the world; but He had no sins
of His own that required atonement. Until the
dark hours on Calvary He lived ever in the light
of the Father's presence and knew many more
things concerning the Kingdom of heaven than He
was able to declare to those about Him. He never
attempted to define His relationship to God; perhaps it never has been defined; mystery it was,
mystery it is.

He valued human friendship and longed for sympathy in trial and affliction as ordinary human beings do. He was not self-contained and self-
sufficient in the same sense as some hard masculine
natures frequently show themselves to be in this
world. He loved little children and they evidently
came to Him freely. He mixed with ordinary
human life and shared in the simple homely joys
of His neighbors; His sheer naturalness stands in
sharp contrast with the poses of many other pre-
ceptors and leaders of men. He was full of com-

passion for the weak and sorrowful, but could be stirred to deep indignation by meanness, cruelty, or hypocrisy. He was never other than self-controlled and there was a majesty and force about Him which impressed even His enemies in spite of themselves; no one seems to have found it easy to take a liberty with Jesus. His courage was only equalled by His patience and forebearance. He had none of what is ordinarily termed worldly wisdom but an unfailing supply of the wisdom of goodness; He saw straight to the heart of good and evil in those about Him without making a mistake. Morally and spiritually He is without a compeer in the annals of the race.

Such then was Jesus at the beginning of His public ministry and such He remained to the end. We have now to ask what that ministry was and how it shaped itself towards the goal He had in view. The most obvious reason for His having undertaken a public ministry was that He might create a new Israel, the Church, and introduce to the world a new vision of God and a new and higher kind of life than any that had gone before.

very suggestive on the line of Christ's Self Consciousness —

N E.

CHAPTER VII

THE COMMENCEMENT OF JESUS' PUBLIC LIFE

The First Disciples

A PROBLEM of some magnitude in connection with the proper sequence to be observed in attempting to trace the doings of Jesus from this point onward now presents itself. If we had only the first three gospels before us we might conclude that after the Temptation, Jesus went straight back to His home at Nazareth and remained there until He heard that the Baptist had been imprisoned, and that then He came forth in Galilee as a public teacher. But if we are to accept the fourth gospel as an historical authority—and the trend of recent evidence is more and more in favor of so doing, for it removes not a few difficulties from our path although it creates others—we become aware, as the evangelist manifestly intends us to do, that some activities of considerable importance took place in the period intervening between these two capital events. The intercourse between Jesus and the Baptist appears to have been resumed immediately after the Temptation, and they would seem to have remained in association for some time, though how close that association was there is nothing to show. On four successive days, according to the account given in St. John, significant events took place. On the first of these the Baptist was questioned by a deputation of priests and Levites from Jerusalem upon the significance of his mission, and he took the opportunity of saying in the course of his reply that he now knew that the greater than himself, for whom it had been his work to prepare the way, was already come. This confession goes far to suggest that he had been holding private conversations with Jesus and had been confirmed thereby in the impression he had received at the baptism concerning Jesus' destiny. The day following, as he saw Jesus coming towards him, he uttered the solemn proclamation referred to above, though how many persons heard it is not stated. But on the day succeeding this he said almost the same thing to two of his own disciples. One of these was Andrew, brother of Simon Peter, who afterwards so specially associated with the person and work of Jesus. The evangelist does not state who the other person was, but the inference is that it was himself. If so, and if the chief source of the information contained in the fourth gospel is the apostle John, then we have here a record of the first meeting between the beloved disciple and his Master at the beginning of Jesus' ministry. John's presence in the south at this time is explained by his eager earnestness in listening to the preaching of the Baptist, to whom he appears definitely to have joined himself as a learner. That Andrew was with him and was his friend shows that they were already acquainted. No doubt the little group of Gallileans came down to the Jordan together and remained in company, for we gather that Simon was there also, though not present when Jesus was pointed out by the Baptist to John and Andrew. These two instantly followed Jesus, who turned and asked them what they sought. Their reply was in substance a request to be permitted to hold conversation with Him at their leisure. They asked Him where His lodging was, and in return He invited them to come and abide with Him as it was late, only two hours before dark. Whether Jesus was still staying with the Baptist is not indicated, but there is nothing in the account to forbid such a supposition which is consonant with all the rest that is recorded of this momentous time. The herald of Jesus was now deliberately handing over certain of his disciples to the new teacher, and nothing is more likely than that the important first interview between them and Him should have been held in the privacy secured by the Baptist.

One would like to know what was said that night by the light of a flickering oil lamp as Jesus sat face to face with these two men, one of them a mere youth. That they were deeply impressed is evident from what they did. Apparently before he went to rest Andrew went and found his brother Simon and brought him also into the presence of Jesus, for it is stated that it was on the day following His meeting with the three that Jesus decided to return to Galilee. There is some difficulty about

Andrew's way of describing Jesus to Simon. He frankly calls Him the Messiah, which is strange in view of the fact that it was on this very point that Jesus Himself was so silent that Simon's own avowal to the same effect much later on should have drawn from the Master the exclamation: "Blessed art thou, Simon Bar-jona, for flesh and blood hath not revealed it unto thee, but my Father which is in heaven." How then does it come that at the outset of this same Simon's acquaintance with Jesus, the reason given for making that acquaintance at all is that in his brother Andrew's opinion Jesus is none other than the Messiah? The question is a difficult one, perhaps not to be fully and satisfactorily answered. But to the present writer it seems that the only way of accounting for the application of this title to Jesus thus early in His ministry is that it was not used with the nuance afterwards given to it by the apostolic preachers. It is not said that Jesus Himself endorsed the declaration. It was not for nothing that He took time tacitly to instruct His followers in the depth of significance to be attached to the word. Probably it was only very vaguely understood at first by any of these simple men; they may not have given much attention to the subject as a practical one till they heard the Baptist preach, and even then had no very clear idea of what Messiahship ought to mean except that it was bound up with the nationalistic hopes of Israel. Hence when after being in His company for many months Simon at last confessed spontaneously his conviction that Jesus was the Messiah, the Master knew that His object had been attained and that the idea had now become associated in the thought of His followers with a new conception of the nature and quality of Messiahship. Is this the reason why He joyfully replied to Peter's confession at Cæsarea Philippi, *"flesh and blood* hath not revealed it unto thee"—that is, not Andrew's nor anyone else's impulsive testimony this time—"but my Father which is in heaven?" Was the expression "flesh and blood" an allusion to the earlier announcement now confirmed on other and higher grounds? He had maintained silence on the subject and waited till this spontaneous confession became inevitable.

A friend of Andrew and Peter, their near neighbor in Bethsaida in Galilee, was added to the little company next day, Philip by name. Philip in turn introduced a fourth to the fellowship, Nathanael of Cana. The text of the narrative implies that Jesus was on His way home to Galilee when this happened, and that His three new adherents were traveling with Him or just about to start when they fell in with Philip and afterwards with Nathanael. There is some ground for identifying Nathanael with Bartholomew the apostle. Nathanael was meditating and praying under a fig tree on his homeward road to Galilee when Philip came to him with the announcement, "We have found Him of whom Moses in the law and the prophets did write, Jesus of Nazareth, the son of Joseph." The form of this description of the

156

Savior shows that something was known or had recently been learned by Andrew, Peter, and John of Jesus' habitation and family. But it was not an impressive revelation. The subject of Nathanael's thoughts and prayers at the moment was that of the deliverance of Israel and the coming of the Messianic king. Hence to be told that the Messiah was the son of a carpenter in the obscure village of Nazareth was to him like utter nonsense. It would be equivalent to telling an ordinary Englishman of the present day that the future sovereign of the British Empire was at that moment serving as a mechanic in a provincial town. "Can there any good thing come out of Nazareth?" was Nathanael's sarcastic reply. "Come and see," said Philip. Nathanael left his devotions and at once accompanied Philip to the Master's presence. No sooner did Jesus see Nathanael coming towards Him than He greeted him with the words, "Behold an Israelite indeed, in whom is no guile!" Nathanael was startled, for apparently the observation was upon the line of his own thoughts. He had been reflecting upon Israel, her sorrows and her sins, and here was some one who evidently knew this. "Whence knowest thou me?" he demanded. "Before that Philip called thee," was the answer, "when thou wast under the fig tree I saw thee." Astounded, Nathanael cried out, "Rabbi, thou art the Son of God; thou art the King of Israel." He could scarcely have been in that august presence without being impressed in any case, but to learn that Jesus had known all about him beforehand

clinched the matter. There could be no doubt but
that Andrew was right. Here stood the holy One
of Israel, God's chosen, the King who was to sit
on David's throne. And the memorable colloquy
closes with the intimation on the part of Jesus that
the grounds upon which Nathanael believed were
but small compared with what were to follow.
Clairvoyant vision was unimportant when viewed
beside spiritual revelation, and it was to the latter
privilege that Nathanael was now bidden in being
made one of Jesus' friends and intimates. "Henceforth thou shalt see heaven opened and the angels
of God ascending and descending upon the Son
of Man."

In Cana of Galilee

It may have been, as already suggested, that this
meeting took place before instead of after Jesus'
return from Judea to Galilee after His parting
with the Baptist. If so, the fact that the Master
was present at a wedding feast in Cana directly
afterwards suggests that Nathanael persuaded
Jesus to visit him for this occasion and to bring His
mother. It is stated also that Jesus' new disciples
were there. What more likely than that they were
there because of the fellowship established with Nathanael on the banks of the Jordan and that they
had all traveled home to Galilee together? Jesus
then went down to Nazareth to fetch His mother
to Nathanael's house as a guest. Philip and the
others rejoined Him shortly afterwards under Na-

thanael's roof where the wedding festivities **were** in progress.

Here He performed what we are informed was His first great miracle, the purpose of which appears to have been neither more nor less than the giving of happiness to a group of humble folk at a social gathering.

Of late years the mental atmosphere of our time has again become more favorable to belief in the credibility of the miracles attributed to Jesus in the New Testament. It is certainly not too much to say that for fifty years previously the chief difficulty in connection with the study of the life of lives has been just that of admitting the historical character of the marvels Jesus is said to have wrought. But it has been found impossible to disentangle the life from the works. As the late Professor A. B. Bruce says,[1] the evidence for the miracles of Christ stands on as good historical ground as the best accredited parts of the teaching; indeed, the teaching is so intertwined with the miracles that the one may be said to depend to a great extent upon the other. A miracle is only a phenomenon which we are as yet unable to refer to some governing principle to which we are accustomed. What we call natural laws are observable sequences of phenomena or of the conditions governing phenomena. A miracle is not a violation of natural law, but the supersession of one sequence by another. Thus, it is a law that water will run down hill; but water in solid form will not run at all; and again

[1] *Expositor's Greek Testament.* Vol. I, p. 23.

water in the form of vapor will actually rise instead of falling. And so all the way through; what we call miracles to-day are phenomena for which we cannot account in the present state of our knowledge. What would once have been called miracles are now commonplaces of experience, such as the action of radium, the X-rays, wireless telegraphy, and all the wonders of electricity. And what we are still obliged to call miracles, miracles in the New Testament sense, are taking place in our midst to-day, such as levitation, faith-healing, and the like. There is hardly one of our Lord's recorded miracles which cannot be paralleled in our own time in some degree, though doubtless in His case the phenomena are exceptionally wonderful because He Himself is exceptionally wonderful. And let us keep in mind the point of view with which we began this study: Given a transcendent person we may expect transcendent facts. Given a transcendental world of eternal perfection, from which a mighty being comes into ours, we should not be surprised if something of transcendental power and glory is manifested, too. As for this miracle in Cana of Galilee, it has been well remarked that the very same thing, namely the turning of water into wine, only with a longer time to do it in, can be seen going on all over the world to-day by the ordinary processes of nature wherever grapes are ripening in the sun.[2]

(1) The fourth evangelist tells us that at this wedding feast there was no wine. He does not say that

[2] So said early Christian apologists, as Irenaeus Adv. Hær. iii. 11.

(1) It suggests "The Wine having failed" all through the story.

they had any wine at all to begin with, though if
the feast were in Nathanael's house this is strange.
Literally the Greek rendering is "the wine having
failed," so perhaps the obvious conclusion to be
derived from it is that the feast had been going
on for some time and that the supply of wine had
given out. We know that these wedding merry-
makings were sometimes prolonged for days and
even weeks, and it would be no unlikely thing that
even a large quantity of the wine of the district
would be exhausted in such circumstances especially if free and generous hospitality were shown
to all and sundry. Learning of this, the mother
of Jesus said to Him, "They have no wine." This
was a not unnatural remark, but it must have been
made with a deeper import than the words convey, judging by the response it evoked and which
sounds harsh in its English form: "Woman, what
have I to do with thee? mine hour is not yet come."
Our ordinary New Testament translation of these
words ought not to have been allowed to stand.
"Woman" was a title of respect, not as in our
idiom an almost slighting mode of address. "What
have I to do with thee?" is also misleading. It
should be, "What is that to me and thee?" In colloquial English we might render it, "Mother, can
you and I interfere in this? The hour for me to
declare myself publicly has not yet arrived." It is
clear that Mary must have known that her divine
Son was possessed of miraculous powers. She must
also have known something of the crisis through
which He had recently passed and His intentions

regarding the immediate future. He would have
no reason for keeping these from her who up to then
had been His principal confidante and from whose
lips He had learned the story of His supernatural
advent. The presence of His disciples in the house
showed that a new departure was imminent. If
Nathanael were the host, then in all probability this
wedding feast was the end of the old life. Jesus and
His friends intended to begin their new work together directly it was over, and had perhaps post-
poned their joint action till then.

But it is pleasing to note that it was at His
mother's special request that Jesus anticipated His
public ministry in this way. He demurs at first,
and then does what she suggests, as she seems to
have known He would. "Whatsoever He saith
unto you, do it," she observes quietly to the servants. What did she suppose He could do? The
only conclusion from the testimony is that she must
have been aware from previous experience that He
had power to make good in some way the want of
wine; and yet we have no evidence that He had
ever worked a miracle before, the apocryphal infancy stories notwithstanding. What can we conclude but that Mary was in her son's confidence at
this time about everything, including the nature
and meaning of the Temptation in the wilderness?
It was from this source that she knew of His latent
mastery over the forces of nature, His endowment
of supernatural power; hence her request and expectation of its fulfillment. Jesus bade the ser-

vants fill the water pots with water—great jars, like the amphoræ which were such a feature of Roman civilization long ago, earthenware vessels for holding considerable quantities of either water or wine. They obeyed, and at His further command drew of the contents and carried them to the table. The water had become wine, and that of the best quality; for the governor of the feast, whoever he may have been, complimented the bridegroom on its excellence, speaking evidently in the name of all who partook of it. "Every man at the beginning doth set forth good wine; and when men have well drunk, then that which is worse: but thou hast kept the good wine until now."

This, the first recorded miracle of Jesus, is told only in the latest of the gospels, the one traditionally attributed to St. John. In consonance with the ingenious symbolism of the book we may take it that the author of the gospel, in preserving for us the story of the miracle at Cana, means us to think of it as a figure of our Lord's relation to the ancient religion of Israel.[3] This had once contained a true divine revelation, the wine of spiritual life, in the united witness of prophet, saint, and seer. But the life had given out; the prophetic fire had died away; there was no longer any fervor or inspiration in the official faith and worship of the time. The religious forms were utterly colorless, devoid of meaning and power. The wine was gone; there was only water left. Then comes the world's Redeemer and recharges the revelation of old with

[3] Schmiedel: *Johannine Writings.*

a new spiritual content, with new moral energy. The best wine had come last.

THE FIRST CLEANSING OF THE TEMPLE

What happened after the wedding feast at Cana? Here the three earlier gospels tell us less than the fourth. If we had nothing but the accounts of the former before us we might suppose that the Master began His public ministry at once—indeed, directly after the Temptation and before this social occasion at Cana. But John shows us otherwise. He says that after the wedding feast Jesus, His mother, and His brethren went down to Capernaum and stayed there "not many days." Near to the beginning of the ministry, and from that time onward, Jesus fixed His dwelling in the town thus named. The first gospel explicitly says so. "Now when Jesus had heard that John was cast into prison, he departed into Galilee; and, leaving Nazareth, he came and dwelt in Capernaum, which is upon the seacoast in the borders of Zabulon and Nephthalim." The mission of the Palestine Exploration Fund identifies Capernaum with the modern village of Tell-Hum.[4] If this is correct it would be about a short day's journey from Nazareth.

But a good deal had evidently taken place in the meantime. If Jesus came into Galilee *after* hearing of John's imprisonment, where was He before? Was the Baptist imprisoned previous to the wed-

[4] But consult G. A. Smith: *Historical Geography of the Holy Land*, p. 456, and Sanday: *Sacred Sites*, p. 36 *ff*, for discussion of this question.

ding feast at Cana of Galilee? If so, it was from this moment that the Galilean ministry began. But John the evangelist's special contribution to the subject leads us to infer that Jesus made a short visit to Capernaum and then immediately went south again for the feast of the Passover. The synoptics are silent about this journey, the mention of which, indeed, in this particular connection, creates some knotty problems. Possibly Mary and her family had been thinking of moving to Capernaum, and now took the preliminary steps to that end; or it may be that they went there as the guests of Jesus' new disciples, who evidently had a good deal to do with Capernaum, and that later on when He was expelled from Nazareth the Master fixed His permanent headquarters there.

The most remarkable thing about His movements as thus described is that, so the fourth gospel states, during this visit to Jerusalem after the short stay at Cana and Capernaum He went publicly into the Temple and drove out all the persons who were buying and selling within its precincts, whereas the earlier gospels describe a similar act as having taken place at the close of His ministry. Is there a contradiction here? The synoptics do not mention this Passover visit at all, and in their very vivid and dramatic accounts of the cleansing of the Temple immediately antecedent to our Lord's betrayal and arrest, they say nothing about His ever having done the same thing before. Yet here we have it in St. John under much the same conditions. This gospel says that Jesus made a scourge of small cords and drove all the sheep and oxen out of the Temple, together with the money-changers, saying as He did so, "Take these things hence; make not my Father's house an house of merchandise."

There is one marked difference between the two narratives, however. The synoptics have it that His words on the occasion were: "My house shall be called a house of prayer; but ye have made it a den of thieves." Both expressions are impressive and memorable, and as the author of the latest of the gospels was so evidently acquainted with the others, he would not have deliberately contradicted them in such a detail as this. There may easily have been two such expulsions, one at the beginning and one at the end of Jesus' brief career as a public teacher.[5] The scandal was admittedly great, the Temple authorities deriving considerable financial profit from their practice in relation thereto. It was the custom for vendors of victims for the Temple sacrifices to pay for the privilege of taking their stand within the walls for the purpose of plying their trade, and as pilgrims of Jewish nationality came up to the feast from all over the world a brisk business was carried on in money-changing likewise. Everybody knew it was unseemly, and the occasion only required that some one of strong personality and with something of prophetic force about him should become the embodied conscience of the worshipers at large in re-

[5] This is admitted by many authorities. *Cf.* Liddon: *Sermons on Some Words of Christ,* xix.

gard to the matter. The whip of small cords referred to in this particular instance—not in the other—was only a handful of fibers picked up from the ground whereon the cattle stood, and was not used upon human beings but to drive forth the animals.

Naturally on this occasion, as on the later one, the officials in charge came to Jesus when the disturbance was over to ask for His credentials. If He were entitled to speak as a prophet, so they argued, He should be ready to give them some sign that He was one. This is not quite so strong a demand as that recorded of the later cleansing: "By what authority doest thou these things? and who gave thee this authority?" In fact, much more impressive notice seems to have been taken of the second cleansing than the first, and with good reason; by the time the second cleansing took place our Lord had become a generally known public figure in sharp antagonism to the religious ideals of His time, especially as embodied in the priesthood and the Pharisaic order, which on the former occasion He was not. And His reply to the challenge is different also. In the first instance when asked for a sign, He responded with the enigmatic saying: "Destroy this Temple, and in three days I will raise it up." In the later episode as recorded by the synoptics, the reply is a counter question concerning the baptism of John demanding to know whether they considered it to be of heaven or of men.

The more closely the several narratives are

scrutinized the more evident it becomes that Jesus cleansed the Temple twice, the second time more overwhelmingly and impressively than the first. His comparative mild remonstrance on the earlier occasion, "Make not my Father's house an house of merchandise," is replaced on the second by the stern indictment, "Ye have made it a den of thieves." The greater strength of language can be fully accounted for by all that had happened in the interval, by the growing antagonism between Himself and the religious leaders of the nation. In asking for a sign to justify His exceptional action at the beginning, the Temple authorities show that as yet they did not know with whom they had to deal and were uneasily conscious of the widespread discontent caused by their shameless cupidity; they felt that in expelling the money-changers He was only doing what many people wanted done and the like of which prophets had been known to do before; the best way of challenging His conduct was to request that He should comply with the ordinary popular expectation that a prophet should be able to produce some indication that he was heaven-sent. But at the end of the ministry they had no such scruples; they were prepared to resist Jesus to the death. He gave them their sign when they first asked for it—"Destroy this Temple," etc.—a most striking utterance in view of all that had to follow, and they could have had little idea of what it meant. Not so with His ironical demand concerning the baptism of John when His own earthly ministry was drawing so near its tragic close. At the moment of the first cleansing John was still living; by the time the second took place he had been dead long enough to become, as it were, canonized in the estimation of the people and Jesus had taken His place as a public personage. He speaks of John's ministry in the past tense. Well did the secular-minded, crafty priests understand the purport of Jesus' reference to the noble Baptist. He had placed them in a dilemma. They dared not make light of the credentials of the martyr whose name was now held in reverence by the multitude, and yet neither could they admit that He had spoken by the authority of heaven, seeing that they themselves had not paid respect to his word. They, therefore, took refuge in evasion. "We cannot tell," they said. Jesus' scornful comment on this feeble trick was no evasion, however. "Neither tell I you by what authority I do these things." He had not the slightest objection to telling them by what authority He acted; it was the same authority as John's, namely, that of innate moral force, the "needs must" of all prophetic souls, and they knew it. They were reduced to silence and desperation. Henceforth it became imperative for their own security that this bold and formidable successor of the Baptist, and a far mightier and more impressive personality than he, should be got rid of in some way. By fair means or foul He must be put to death.

We have anticipated considerably in thus comparing the separate accounts of the two cleansings, but it is worth while bringing out the important disparities between them. The circumstances are as different as the terms employed by the respective participants are said to have been.

But to return to our examination of the original sequence of events, it should be noted that the fourth evangelist adds a comment on Jesus' reply to the request for a sign. He says: "But He spake of the temple of His body. When, therefore, He was risen from the dead, His disciples remembered that He had said this unto them." Here the writer is once more true to his method of the systematic employment of metaphor, of meaning within meaning. John the divine, an old man looking back upon these memorable days when as a youth he walked by the side of Jesus, could not fail to see in the saying above quoted a double reference—one to the sacred body that was laid in the tomb, and the other to the mystical body of Christ, His holy Church. The old religion of Israel was indeed being destroyed by such blatant materialism and hypocrisy as the presence of the money-changers in the Temple denoted. The religious leaders of Israel were destroying all that the Temple was supposed to embody and express, but it was the mission of Jesus to raise upon its ruins a world-wide spiritual fabric which should never be destroyed. And just as St. John supplies the record of the episode which produced this impressive forecast, because the synoptics omit it, so he in his turn sees no necessity for recording the second cleansing which the synoptics relate at length.

If we are thus to adhere to St. John's sequence

of events, we must recognize this first cleansing of
the Temple as the definite beginning of our Lord's
public ministry. Not in Galilee but in Jerusalem, as
was most fitting, were His first words spoken to listening assemblies. And when we come to reflect
upon the subject it is clear that this is what we
ought to anticipate. If Jesus meant to address
Himself to Israel there was every reason why He
should begin His work in the capital and at the
feast of the Passover, the greatest religious gathering of the year. The contrary assumption, based
upon the record of the earlier gospels, that Jesus
first began to teach in the neighborhood of His own
Galilean home, has nothing to support it beyond
the fact that the earlier evangelists naturally em-
phasized this part of the ministry because the companions of Jesus on whom they chiefly depended
for their information were Galileans, and also because our Lord Himself lived in Galilee. John
deliberately supplies omissions, knowing quite well
what he is doing. He may have been with his new-
found Master in Jerusalem on this preliminary occasion, whereas it is less probable that Peter was.[6]
In his reminiscences he emphasizes this fact, whoever may have made literature of them—at least it

[6] There are indications that the sons of Zebedee were more prosperous than Peter. They had "hired servants" and a fleet of fishing
boats—"ships." They would, therefore, then as now, obtain some
amount of social importance and freedom of movement denied to
the man who had to toil for a livelihood. If, as is reasonable and
probably intended, we are to identify the apostle John with the beloved disciple, then we must also conclude that he possessed influence
with the circle of the high priest. He was able to gain admission
to the judgment hall for Peter as well as himself, and he was present with impunity at Calvary, which no other member of the apostolic circle dared to be.

is legitimate to infer as much. If in after years, recalling for the benefit of his Ephesian church what he could remember of his relations with his Lord, he commented specially upon some things not included in the synoptic reports, can we be surprised? Is it not just what any one would do in his place? He had the other gospels there before him; they were read in the little Christian communities whenever these met for worship; he knew all they had to say. Would not those about him request more, and so the Johannine tradition grow up as supplementary to the Petrine and Matthæan? He here tells us that many present in Jerusalem at this particular feast of the Passover believed on Jesus through seeing what He had done—that is, they were awed by His moral greatness and transcendent force of character. "But," significantly adds the evangelist, "Jesus did not commit Himself unto them, because he knew all men." He never obtained much of a hearing in Jerusalem; it was from the humbler fisher-folk of Galilee that He won the greatest response to His word, despite the scornful Pharisaic comment of a later period: "Search and see, for out of Galilee ariseth no prophet." The hard, fanatical, fierce-minded Jewish crowd found little in Jesus to understand or revere.

THE INTERVIEW WITH NICODEMUS

One incident stands out conspicuously, however, in contrast to the general barrenness of spiritual re-

sult in Jerusalem at this beginning of Jesus' manifestation to Israel. A certain member of the
Sanhedrin, named Nicodemus, was greatly impressed by what he had heard and seen of the new
teacher during the few days of the feast. The Talmud mentions a person of this name of great wealth
and influence whose family was afterwards reduced
to poverty through its Christian sympathies. This
may have been the Nicodemus in question; in fact,
indications point that way. It is clear from other
references to him in this gospel that he must later
on have become one of the friends of Jesus, though
not openly identified with His cause. At the beginning of their acquaintance he is shown coming
to the Master by night and seeking speech with
Him. Evidently he did not at this stage wish to
incur the hostility of his colleagues in the Sanhedrin, and yet confesses himself deeply moved by
what he had heard and seen of Jesus. The Temple
cleansing was no doubt part of this, and Nicodemus
himself may have been a member of the deputation
sent to ask Jesus for a sign of His prophetical gifts.
He now begins the private conversation by addressing the young Galilean carpenter as rabbi,
a title of respect and courtesy which would not be
bestowed lightly. "We know that thou art a
teacher come from God," he continues, "for no man
can do these signs that thou doest, except God be
with him." Who are the "we" thus referred to?
Was this Nicodemus' way of stating that other
members of the deputation, or of the Sanhedrin,
had been convinced in the same way as he of Jesus'

173

right to speak in the name of God? He puts no question in so many words, but that on which he sought enlightenment is clear enough from the Master's response. Like all earnest spirits of the time Nicodemus wanted to know about the advent of the heavenly Kingdom and what the conditions of its manifestation might be. The answer was surprising: "Except a man be born again, he cannot see the Kingdom of God." The expression puzzled Nicodemus, so Jesus went on to explain: "That which is born of the flesh is flesh, and that which is born of the Spirit is spirit." And this time also He added, "except a man be born of water and of the Spirit, he cannot enter into the Kingdom of God."

The authenticity of these words has been questioned on the ground that they reflect the later practice of the Church rather than our Lord's own teaching at the very outset of His ministry. This may be true, but there is a prior explanation. We are here dealing, not with the ordinary Galilean public which listened to His words on the hillsides and by the lake shores, but with a fully instructed doctor of the Law. "Art thou a master of Israel, and knowest not these things?" continues the passage attributed to Jesus. Obviously He expected Nicodemus to understand. The moral significance of baptism by water was familiar enough to Pharisees at this period as we have already had occasion to observe. The Baptist had prescribed it as a definite act denoting the passage from the ordinary life of the world to that of obedience to the com-mandments of God and preparation for the Messianic advent. Jesus Himself had undergone baptism at John's hands; so had some of the Pharisees, including perhaps Nicodemus. What should this have conveyed to the mind of the suppliant who stood in the presence of the new teacher? It should have taught him that the Kingdom of God for which he so earnestly longed was not merely to be an external institution but a condition of mind and heart; only those whose souls were right with God could attain to membership therein. The formal act of the will, the state of repentance or consecration to God, denoted by submission to baptism, and accepted of God as witnessed by the gift of the Holy Ghost, is the essential condition of the new and higher mode of life which the very phrase the Kingdom of God assumes. The Kingdom must be inward and spiritual in order to become outward and material. Nicodemus ought to have known this, and in a sense perhaps did, but his conventional world had still a great hold upon him and he was unwilling to break with it. Once after this we hear of him from his seat in the Sanhedrin putting in a plea for moderation in the attitude the majority were taking towards Jesus; and again he appears after the tragedy of Calvary, to assist with Joseph of Arimathæa at the burial of the Lord.

We may reasonably take for granted that this public appearance of Jesus in the south had still some connection with the preaching of the Baptist. But the Baptist was arrested by Herod Antipas directly afterwards for his boldness in rebuking the tyrant's adulterous union with his brother's wife. Consequently Jesus decides to return for the time being to His own province. The evangelist tells us that immediately previous to his arrest the Baptist had been exercising his ministry at a place called Aenon near to Salim, probably a few miles distant from Jerusalem; and that Jesus and His disciples also went out into the country round about the capital and there carried on a ministry similar to that of John, the disciples baptizing their Master's converts. Some of John's disciples brought word to their master about this: "Rabbi, He that was with thee beyond Jordan, to whom thou barest witness, behold, the same baptizeth, and all men come to Him." John's noble answer is a testimony to his moral greatness. "A man can receive nothing, except it be given him from heaven"—or rather, "can take nothing upon himself." "This my joy therefore is fulfilled. He must increase, but I must decrease."

It should be pointed out that here, as in the conversation with Nicodemus and elsewhere throughout the book, it is difficult on occasion to say where the words reported leave off and the comment of the evangelist himself begins. "He that cometh from above is above all," etc.[7]

The first intimation of Pharasaic hostility to Jesus is now forthcoming and has given us the immediate reason for His departure to Galilee. He

[7] "A blending of fact and interpretation," Sanday: *Criticism of the Fourth Gospel*, "The Nature of the Discourses," p. 169.

was told by the disciples that it was seen and heard
that He baptized more disciples than John, though
it was the disciples and not Himself that did the
baptizing. He had no desire to come into collision
with the authorities as yet, so He thought it best
to withdraw from the neighborhood. With John
in prison and his movement suppressed, there could
be small protection for an imitator or one who was
thought to be such. Nor would the Temple officials
be likely to forget or overlook the slight to themselves implied in His action in turning out the
money-changers shortly before. So He took His
way north, going by the short road which lay
through Samaria. The author of the gospel is
careful to note the fact that this was His second
visit to the region where He had been brought up,
since the Baptist's public announcement of Him as
the chosen of God, for the narrative runs, "He left
Judea and departed *again* into Galilee."

The Woman of Samaria

On this journey He paused at a place named
Sychar—perhaps the modern Askar—A-sychar—
near to what is still called Jacob's well. Feeling
tired He sat down on the parapet of the well while
His traveling companions went into the city to
purchase food. A woman belonging to the place
came to the well to draw water, and the Master
asked for a drink. Without directly refusing, the
woman expressed extreme surprise at the request,
for, as she said, the speaker was evidently a Jew,
and Jews were not accustomed to ask favors of

Samaritans. It should be observed that she was not accusing Jesus of presumption in entreating a kindness which she had no mind to grant, but was simply expressing her astonishment that a person of Jewish race should condescend to have anything whatever to do with a Samaritan. She may have given Him the drink; it is not stated that she refrained from doing so.

In reply to the woman's expression of surprise at a Jew asking to drink from a Samaritan waterpot, seeing that the Jews regarded every Samaritan as vile and unclean, Jesus told her that if she only knew who it was that asked this favor, she in turn would have asked of Him the gift of living water. "Whosoever drinketh of this water shall thirst again: but whosoever drinketh of the water that I shall give him shall never thirst; but the water that I shall give him shall be in him a well of water springing up into everlasting life." Her prosaic mind does not understand. "Sir, give me this water, that I thirst not, neither come hither to draw." The request may have been ironical; if so, the mood did not long continue. The Master speedily made her aware that He knew all about her private history, concluding with an impressive declaration both of His own Messiahship and of the universality of the new dispensation. "The hour cometh when ye shall neither in this mountain, nor yet at Jerusalem, worship the Father. . . . God is Spirit; and they that worship Him must worship in spirit and in truth." The immediate sequel of this remarkable conversation was, we are told, that many Samaritans believed on Him as "indeed the Christ, the Savior of the world."

Here again we encounter the difficulty already discussed, that Jesus is represented as explicitly stating that He is the Messiah, numbers of people openly acknowledging the fact, whereas elsewhere He is shown preserving the strictest reticence on the subject, a reticence not publicly broken until He was actually on His trial before the high priest and afterwards before Pilate. We are more than once informed also that people in general differed among themselves on the question who and what He was. It is doubtful whether these discrepancies of statement can be completely reconciled by means of the knowledge at present at our command. Here before the Galilean ministry commences at all, Jesus without hesitation declares His identity, and yet afterwards consistently and of set purpose refrains from doing so. We can but conclude that His self-disclosure in this connection did not carry with it to His Samaritan hearers the full implications that might be supposed. This, as already suggested, is the only theory that will fit the facts—if any theory will fully fit the facts. Messiahship cannot have received the definite content in all minds that we are accustomed to ascribe to it, and Jesus was such a Messiah as no one anticipated. What pleased Him most in Peter's avowal later on was that, after knowing Him as He really was, the simple-hearted fisherman should still be willing to think of Him as the desire of Israel; it meant that a certain shedding of preconceptions of the nature of Messiahship had been going on in the apostle's mind. That the word Messiah was a more loosely used term than we should otherwise infer is demonstrated by the evidence of the earlier ministry. There was no distinctively Samaritan ministry: hence our Lord's frankness on the occasion here described may be accounted for on the hypothesis that no harm could be done by the passing disclosure, the significance of which was not likely to be fully grasped or to cause strife. He planted His spiritual seed, and, leaving it to germinate, went His way.

The problem is much more difficult when we come to examine the Jerusalem discourses attributed to Jesus in the fourth gospel. From the very first, according to these, He spoke of Himself in terms which implied, if they did not expressly assert, His Messiahship. To put it at the lowest He claimed a position in relation to God greater than that of any prophet. He is said to have antagonized the Jews by this. They objected to His referring to God as His Father, thus "making himself equal with God." He then falls back on the third person, but claims for the "Son" a lordship and a power to execute judgment which could hardly be predicated of any other than the Messiah. He declares that the scriptures wrote of Him and that He is come down from heaven to give life to the world. The Jews objected to this statement also on the ground that they knew His earthly parentage; and His life was no longer safe amongst them. On the other hand, it is equally clear that they were not agreed upon the question whether He actually meant to lay claim to Messiahship. They regarded His words as enigmatic and disputed about their significance. There is no explicit utterance of a public character in St. John's gospel any more than the others which shows that Jesus made such a claim before the very end. That He drew special attention to His own person and to His authority to speak in the name of God is beyond doubt, but that He ever said in so many words that He was the Jewish Messiah is not affirmed. He uses freely the title Son of Man, and on occasion Son of God, but the meaning of this self-designation is no less a problem of the synoptics than of the fourth gospel. One thing stands out plainly in the latter as in the former, and that is that His accusers could produce no evidence at His trial that He had ever said He was the Messiah. If He had not avowed it Himself there and then they would have been at a loss. The Roman governor did not trouble to inquire what His idea of Messiahship was, but had Him put to death as a would-be king of the Jews and, therefore, a possible center of insurrection against the Roman overlordship of Palestine.

This digression anticipates somewhat a subject whose treatment more fitly belongs to a later stage but is presumed from the first.

THE EARLY GALILEAN MINISTRY

It is now that the Galilean ministry begins with which the earlier gospels are principally concerned,

According to St. John Jesus obtained His hearing in the first place in the neighborhood of His own home because of what had been reported there concerning His doings in Jerusalem at the feast of the Passover.[8] A short period of retirement may have intervened, but it could not have been long before that wonderful period of teaching and healing activity commenced which made Jesus generally known in the province and even beyond. It is noteworthy that in St. John's version again we have the statement that He returned to Cana of Galilee on this occasion, and while staying there paid a special visit to Capernaum and performed another miracle—this time the healing of a certain nobleman's son who was at the point of death.[9] There is so close a resemblance between the account of this miracle and that of the healing of the centurion's servant as given in St. Matthew[10] and St. Luke[11] that many persons have been inclined to identify them. But the identity cannot be regarded as certain; if there are remarkable coincidences in the narrative of these two events there are no less notable differences.

How did the Galilean ministry open? And was there anything therein to distinguish it from the brief Judean activities recorded in St. John? The evangelists testify that Jesus began to teach in the synagogues, which custom permitted competent persons to do; and we are led to infer that He made a practice of this for a time, beginning, not at

[8] John iv. 45. [10] Matt. viii. 5 ff.
[9] Ibid. iv. 46-54. [11] Luke vii. 1 ff.

182

Nazareth, but at Capernaum. Capernaum may thus have been chosen from the consideration already advanced, that the first disciples had associations with that place. But He did not confine His activities to one center only, and His fame soon spread everywhere round about. It is stated by St. Luke that He did at Nazareth what He had already been doing in other centers, stood up in the synagogue on the Sabbath to read and expound the scripture. His old neighbors were very desirous to hear Him because of the stories which had reached them concerning His doings elsewhere.[12] He read and applied to Himself the words of Isaiah lxi. 1: "The spirit of the Lord God is upon me," etc. "This day is the scripture fulfilled in your ears," He declared. The claim irritated His hearers, they regarded it as gross presumption; and they promptly showed their displeasure by expelling Him from their community and in their fanatical rage attempting to fling Him over the cliff on which their little town stood. Something in His demeanor, however, excited sufficient awe within their breasts to restrain them from proceeding to extremities, and "He passing through the midst of them went His way." Henceforth He dwelt in Capernaum, but there may have been another occasion when He visited Nazareth, according to Matthew and Mark. This time the assembly in the synagogue was sufficiently impressed not to exhibit any violence towards Him, but was still

[12] Luke iv. 23.

jealously antipathetic.[13] "He did not many mighty works there because of their unbelief." "A prophet is not without honor, save in His own country and in his own house," was the Master's comment upon His failure to reach their hearts.

His reception in Capernaum was very different. For some time He taught there in the synagogue on the Sabbath days, a high testimony to the impression He produced upon His new neighbors. If there had not been a considerable desire to listen to Him He would certainly not have been allowed by the synagogue authorities to assume the position of a teacher there week after week. From now His public work begins to take on a character distinct from that of the Baptist. The call and selection of the twelve apostles, and afterwards of a larger band of seventy disciples,[14] we may regard as the forming of the nucleus of the Christian Church. If we possessed only the synoptic record of events we might suppose that the two pairs of brothers, Simon and Andrew, James and John, were summoned from their occupations without any previous preparation or acquaintance with the Master. This would be unlikely in any case, but from John's account, as we have seen, we are made aware that there was a previous association of a very definite character. It is evident that these men had been much in the company of Jesus from the time when He and they were first brought into touch by the Baptist at the Jordan. No doubt they

[13] Matt. xiii. 54 ff; Mark vi. 1-6.
[14] Luke x. 1 ff.

had returned to their customary avocations in Galilee, but with the mutual understanding that when Jesus was ready for their coöperation He would come for them. This is what now happened, and according to promise they immediately left everything and followed Him. The third evangelist places the call some time after the commencement of the synagogue ministry in Capernaum, accompanied as it was by miraculous cures of disease. The Master healed Simon's wife's mother of a fever; He also made use of Simon's boat as a pulpit wherefrom to address the crowds on the shore of the Sea of Galilee, and at the close of the discourse made the fisherman thrust out into the deep and let down his nets. Then ensued the miraculous draught of fishes, which so impressed Simon that he fell upon his knees crying, "Depart from me; for I am a sinful man, O Lord." It was in this connection that Jesus uttered the words, "Fear not; from henceforth thou shalt catch men." [15] The first two gospels have it, "Follow me and I will make you fishers of men." [16] St. Luke's version is interesting as showing the events which immediately preceded the call. It is John who tells us how the name Peter, used in the synoptics from the first, came to be bestowed. Their message was the same in every case. They were to announce the near advent of the Kingdom of God. There is no indication that they were authorized or qualified to teach; their function simply was to declare that the hope

[15] Luke v. 1-11.
[16] Matt. iv. 18-22; Mark i. 16-20.

of generations was about to be fulfilled; they did not enter into any particulars as to how it was to be fulfilled.

It is this proclamation of the Kingdom, and the association of it with the person of Jesus that is the new feature in His preaching as distinct from that of the Baptist. Otherwise He began with the very same words as those which characterized John's ministry: "Repent, for the Kingdom of heaven is at hand."

WORKS OF HEALING

A subject of outstanding importance from this point onward is that of the miracles attributed to Jesus.[17] The miracle of Cana was not publicly performed, and the guests themselves who were present at the wedding feast do not appear to have realized that anything out of the common had taken place. But a constant accompaniment of the public activity of Jesus was His beneficent exercise of supernatural power. He is said to have performed miraculous cures from the very beginning of His public appearances in Galilee. In the synagogue at

[17] We cannot expect to find ancient evidence that will come up to modern standards. Consequently we can neither accept nor deny, in any dogmatic way, such psychical stories as those in Herodotus, or the miracle narratives of the world's sacred writings. But in so far as the happenings described in the old narratives conform to types which are recognizable in the phenomena of to-day, they may at least provisionally be considered likely enough. For example, all the miracles of the New Testament are credible to any one who has done much psychical investigation, for he comes across more or less similar things; things, at any rate, sufficiently similar to warrant the belief that where the modern phenomena fall short of the ancient, the reason is that in the case of these latter a higher and more powerful Personality was concerned.—J. Arthur Hill: *Psychical Investigations*, p. 247.

Capernaum, henceforth regarded as His own city,
and on the Sabbath day, He healed a man with an
unclean spirit.[18] This event caused the greatest excitement in the region round about, and from that
time forward He was expected to heal sickness and
disease wherever He went. That the news of His
wonder-working powers spread rapidly throughout
Galilee is illustrated by what St. Luke tells us of
His reception in Nazareth. "Whatsoever we have
heard done in Capernaum, do also here in thy country." Immense throngs now followed Him everywhere, and He found it difficult to secure privacy.
"All men seek for thee" [19] was the salutation of the
apostles when they discovered Him in one place of
retreat. He worked no wonders for the sake of
impressing people; His healing ministry was from
first to last simply one of mercy, and He repeatedly
desired that too much attention should not be directed to it. A great wave of popularity carried
Him very high in public estimation for a time, but
He was never deceived thereby; He knew that there
was little spirituality in the attitude of His contemporaries towards Him. The Pharisees themselves are represented as at first associating with
Him and being ready to use Him as an instrument
for the furtherance of their own peculiar aims; but
soon this feeling on their part changed. He refused to honor their punctiliousness in matters of
ritual observance and the like. Ere long, as we
shall see, He made the breach complete by deliberately going to the outcast classes which were de-

[18] Mark i. 23-28. [19] *Ibid* i. 37.

barred attendance at the synagogue. The orthodox became openly hostile to Him and He to them.
They were scandalized by the fact that not only
did He eat and drink with publicans and sinners,
but that He and His followers were not in their
judgment sufficiently rigid about fasting and keeping the Sabbath. Worst of all He dared to forgive sins, which to them seemed blasphemous. In
time this opposition drew to a head, and the Pharisees of Galilee made common cause with the priestly
party at Jerusalem, and also with the Herodians,
in the effort to destroy Him. How far popular
favor waned it is hard to judge. There is nothing
to show that the poor people of Galilee among
whom His best work was done ever wholly turned
against Him. With the bigoted, intractable mob
at Jerusalem—the Jews as St. John calls them—it
was different.

How did the people think of Him? Plainly they
regarded Him as a mystery. They saw that He
spoke with a personal authority which ordinary religious teachers did not employ. They could not
but note also that in some way His personality was
connected with the Messianic hope. But beyond
that they knew nothing. They did not expect the
Messiah to come as a peripatetic preacher, nor did
they think of Him as likely to be born and brought
up in Galilee. Hence when they spoke of Jesus
it was usually as a prophet. "A great prophet is
arisen among us; and God hath visited His
people." [20]

[20] Luke vii. 16.

It is St. Matthew who presents us with the clearest picture of Jesus' method of working. He tells us that immediately after the first phase of the synagogue ministry people pressed upon Him from everywhere. "There followed him great multitudes of people from Galilee, and from Decapolis, and from Jerusalem, and from Judea, and from beyond Jordan." [21] This is the most distinct information we possess that the whole of Palestine was aroused by the news of the sayings and doings of Jesus, and that many made the journey from other parts to see Him and hear Him in Galilee. So far as Jerusalem was concerned the memory of the incidents attending His appearance in the Temple at the feast of the Passover following the Temptation would be enough to make dwellers there desire to know more of Him, and what they heard from Galilee would increase that desire. Samaria alone was apparently so cut off from sympathy with Jewish movements as to remain comparatively untouched, the brief visit to Sychar already mentioned being an exception. Nor is it likely that Samaritans would have been welcomed by those composing the Master's ordinary congregations.

PUBLIC TEACHING

Matthew states that early in the Galilean ministry "seeing the multiudes, he went up into a mountain; and when he was set,"—that is, had fixed His temporary abode there—"his disciples

[21] Matt. iv. 25.

came unto him." [22] Then follows the immortal compendium of teaching commonly called the Sermon on the Mount. But it was not a sermon in the sense of being a connected discourse. The late Professor A. B. Bruce remarked that it could more fitly be described as the Teaching on the Hill.[23] That there was such a special session there can be no doubt, though the allusions to it are so slight and the content of the teaching given on the occasion is so difficult to determine. It was a kind of summer school of religion held in the open air on the summit of a Galilean hill, and may have lasted for weeks instead of only for one day or part of a day. The account of it given by the first evangelist gives ground for supposing that it did not consist of a promiscuous assemblage of people, but rather of professed disciples who had come together in a comparatively secluded spot in order to be instructed in the mysteries of the Kingdom of God. The entire setting and subject matter of the so-called sermon attest this. To begin with, we have a withdrawal from public activity indicated in the terms wherewith the body of teaching is introduced— "multitudes" contrasted with "disciples." The latter are said to have come to Jesus, apparently by special arrangement, after He had established Himself in the mountain aforesaid. What can this mean but that the locality was chosen in order to be comparatively free from the bustle and disturbance of ordinary life, especially of the life of ac-

[22] *Ibid* v. 1.
[23] *Expositor's Greek Testament,* "Synoptical Gospels," p. 94.

tivity upon which Jesus had now entered? He wanted to get away from this for a time in order to come into closer relations with those who were henceforth to be accounted of His more immediate following and to form the foundation of the society that was to witness Him in the world. We can hardly be taking too much for granted in concluding that this was the Master's purpose. It is difficult to see what other purpose He could have had in mind, and that we are not mistaken in presuming so far upon the facts at our command is confirmed by several considerations. For one thing, the larger part of the collected sayings is manifestly addressed, not to Israel as a whole, much less to the world at large, but to selected persons, and who can these be but the nucleus of the new or spiritual Israel, the Church that was presently to be formed? [24] This view also explains some of the more difficult sayings; they were not for society in general, but for individuals gathered out of it and living in relation to a higher law. To this hour the meaning of the beatitudes is not beyond dispute, nor even their form. No one can avoid seeing that St. Luke's version of these does not say the same thing as St. Matthew's, but something widely different, and yet the resemblances between them are such as to demonstrate their common origin. Some authorities deny the ethical significance of the beatitudes altogether—a short-sighted judgment, indeed, but not without some literal justification. We have to look beneath the striking and imperish-

[24] *Vide* Hamilton: *People of God*, Vol. II, pp. 27-32 and 59-66.

able paradoxes, at the spirit rather than the letter of them, and to view them in conjunction with all the rest of Jesus' recorded utterances and His general ideal of life and conduct, in order to arrive at a true understanding of their eternal significance. Is not this a sign that they were originally spoken to an eclectic circle and one specially and carefully prepared to receive them?

This theory or more than theory is supported by what has been established concerning the composition of the non-Marcan document already referred to as the main source of our knowledge of the teaching of Jesus. Scholars call this by the technical name of Q because its origin is an unsolved problem. The most plausible as well as the most attractive view of its origin up to the present is that it is Matthew the publican's own first-hand report of what his Master said, especially at this memorable session in the hill country of Galilee. Expert critics of the gospels do not gainsay this possibility; Harnack in particular admits that there is a strong presumption in its favor, though no more can be affirmed positively.[25] The authority for it is Papias, quoted above, whose personal knowledge and recollection go back almost to apostolic times. According to Eusebius, Papias credited Matthew the apostle with having written a collection of the sayings of Jesus in Hebrew— that is, no doubt, in the Aramaic dialect in which they were uttered. If this collection has not been entirely lost it may lie behind the bulk of what our

[25] *Sayings of Jesus,* p. 249.

canonical Matthew gives us of the sermon on the Mount and some other portions of the teaching of Jesus as preserved in this gospel. One would be glad to think so, for if this be the truth of the matter we are taken right to the fountainhead of the Christian Gospel.[26] And why should it not be true? Matthew's avocation required that he should be able to write in the vernacular, which is what Papias says he did in this instance. It is impressive to think of the publican-apostle taking down from the very lips of Jesus the words of eternal life substantially as we have them to-day; and if this memorable note-taking took place at the summer school in the heart of the Galilean hills the result would almost coincide with the content of Q. Let any student of the gospels read through the sayings comprised in Q as reconstructed by, say, Harnack, and he cannot fail to note the moral loftiness and spiritual purity of the content and its astonishing freedom from local and racial prejudices and limitations; in fact, its universality is its most outstanding feature and would serve to stamp it unique apart from all other claims to consideration. Harnack very justly says that it is without bias of any kind which criticism can detect.[27] Here

[26] Prof. A. B. Bruce says (*Expositor's Greek Test.*, p. 17) : "Jesus associated Matthew with Himself that He might use him as an instrument for initiating a mission to the class to which he had belonged. But if the Master might call a fit man to discipleship for one form of immediate service, He might call him for more than one. Another service the ex-publican might be able to render was that of secretary. In his old occupation he would be accustomed to writing, and it might be Christ's desire to utilize that talent for noting down things worthy of record. The gift would be most in demand in connection with the teaching of the Master."

[27] *Sayings of Jesus*, p. 168.

we have the key to the mind of Jesus, to all that He thought and said and to His view of the significance of His person and work. We are safe in interpreting everything else in the gospels from the standpoint of this body of teaching, Mark's history not excluded, for it should not be forgotten that in this collection of sayings we have an earlier record than Mark's—in all probability the very earliest stratum in the New Testament and the source which takes us nearest to Jesus Himself as seen and known by His contemporaries. Moreover, as we have seen reason to believe, this precious possession was preserved for us by Jesus' own deliberate act in gathering round Him on a Galilean hillside a company of persons who were later to form the Christian society at its beginnings and to whom He could at His leisure present the charter of the new order that society was to witness for and attempt to realize in the world.

The critical theory that the differences between Matthew's and Luke's versions of the greater sayings included in Q may be explained by assuming diverse translations from an Aramaic original will not carry us far in an attempt to find an elucidation of the problem. A much more satisfactory hypothesis, and not a far-fetched one, is that Matthew was not the only note-taker at the great hill session where most if not all of the teaching contained in Q was originally given, though portions of it might be repeated at intervals later and in modified form. If, for instance, we accept the reasonable supposition that each beatitude represented the subject of the lesson for one day we can readily discern a sequence of thought polarized by the two evangelists respectively. Take the first beatitude as presented by Matthew, to illustrate this method of exposition. It has been suggested that the addition of the two words "in spirit" to Luke's bolder and more abrupt, "Blessed are ye poor" is due to later ecclesiastical influence, the toning down of a hard saying to suit changing circumstances. But, taking for granted that at least one whole discourse was devoted to this particular phase of a spiritual ideal, and that there was more than one recorder of the aphorism or aphorisms in which the lesson was conveyed, there is no great difficulty in inferring what could conceivably have happened on the occasion. The bulk of Jesus' audience consisted of poor people one and all of whom were looking for the Kingdom of God but not quite sure what it would mean for them. If it meant no more than a sort of glorified restoration of the ancient kingdom of Israel, it would involve little change in social arrangements; those in authority would remain in authority; the poor would remain the poor, though better off and free from anxiety for daily bread; those in possession of riches would retain the extra importance riches had hitherto conferred. In a word, the revival of Israel's ancient autonomy, with a new splendor and prosperity added by special favor of the Most High, would not effect any very great change in the relative social status of the various individuals and classes that made up the Jewish nation.

Jesus had now to show these hearers of His that the Kingdom or rule or reign of God was before all else a spiritual state, not a secular dominion, Jewish or otherwise. He did not contradict the prevailing assumption because it had a germ of truth in it, namely, that a regencrated human society would be the social expression of the spiritual idea thus presented. But He must have startled the assemblage of humble people when He began His instruction by saying, "Blessed are ye poor for the Kingdom is yours"—that is, more easily accessible to you than to others whom you account more fortunate. Then would naturally follow the explanation, so true in that hard age as in most ages since, that the poor are by the very conditions of their lot less likely to be deceived about themselves and the realities of life than the rich and highly placed. They have fewer temptations to artificiality, pride, vanity, arrogance, and pretense. They are not so likely to overvalue themselves or to regard themselves as of special importance in the world. Simplicity, humility, sincerity are qualities which flourish better in the cottage than the palace. There is a spirit natural to the poor man which is not so commonly found among those who are not poor, or we do not expect so to find it in our experience of ordinary humankind. Yet occasionally we do so find it among the mighty ones of earth, the great, the powerful, the wealthy—rarely, it must be admitted, but a lowly heart does sometimes beat in the breast of one who gives law to nations, and the man of great possessions may also be a man of simple character and unpretentious mode of life. This remark applies to treasures of intellect as well as of gold and silver; it is hard for a man to estimate his own worth aright if he is marked off from his fellows in either way. Jesus knew this, and the beatitude we are considering is one statement of the truth just as the startling saying, that it is easier for a camel to go through the eye of a needle than for a rich man to enter the Kingdom of God, is another. If then He began with Luke's version of the beatitudes He would conclude His lesson with Matthew's: Blessed is that man who, whether he be poor or rich, can keep the spirit which is most natural to a poor man— "Blessed are the poor in spirit for theirs is the Kingdom of heaven."

To examine the teaching of Jesus in detail is impossible in a work like the present, and it has already been elaborately and exhaustively done by eminent exegetes. We can but draw attention to special portions of it as the gospel story passes in review. There is hardly anything in the words of Jesus as preserved by the evangelists which is entirely new. Much of it was anticipated or paralleled in such writings as the Testaments of the Twelve Patriarchs. His distinction consists rather, in grouping and condensing the best that Old Testament religion had bequeathed than in adducing an element indisputably original. It was He Himself that was original; He was the embodiment of what He taught. He had the difficult, one might think the impossible task, of addressing promiscuous gatherings of Palestinian Jews in terms which would suffice for all ages to come, and He succeeded. The teaching of Jesus never grows old, never loses aught of its power and charm. And when we remember that we only possess it at second-hand, that is, as mediated through the recollection of a few of those who originally heard it, the marvel becomes all the greater. Compare it with the letters of that man of genius, the apostle Paul, who wrote his epistles before the bulk of what now constitutes the New Testament had come into existence. Both Luke and John Mark were men younger than St. Paul and in a sense his subordinates. Yet there is a freshness, an elevation, and a wonderful directness in the sayings attributed to Jesus as recorded by these two men which do not characterize those of the apostle of the Gentiles. One of the mysteries connected with the production of the New Testament is this contrast in form between the involved though powerful theologizing of St. Paul, with its rabbinical background, and the terse, pellucid, altogether beautiful style of Jesus which laid such a hold upon the minds of His hearers that, long as it was before His words were made into literature, their innate power remains. What must it have been to hear Him!

He took hold of the commonest everyday incidents and turned them into sweet illustrations of spiritual truth—the shepherd walking along the hills in advance of his flock, the fisherman casting his net into the sea, the sower going forth to sow. He had an eye for natural beauty, which St. Paul

never had. It has been remarked that the apostle
on his missionary journeys passed through some of
the most glorious scenery in the world and never
gives a hint of it in his discourses. How different
with Jesus! The birds of the air, the lilies of the
field, the splendor of sunset and sunrise are all present to His observation and interest. He has time
to think of the sparrow falling to the ground, of
the ravens that God feeds, and of the ox or sheep
that falls into a pit and needs to be helped out on
the Sabbath day as on any other day. No wonder
the common people heard Him gladly. Not that
they always understood what He said. He did His
best to teach them by parable, but sometimes the
parable itself needed fuller explanation to the few
whom He was endeavoring to train for the work of
witnessing Him in the world later on. We need
not be afraid of admitting that some of the parables are susceptible of more than one interpretation, a tribute to their spiritual depth and range.
No doubt it was the intention of their author that
meaning should be discovered within meaning as
souls progressed in the spiritual life. This is specially the case with those in St. John's gospel,
where, indeed, as has already been pointed out, all
the miracles are used as parables. There is scarcely
a sentence in the whole book that is not capable of
being construed on different levels; there is always
an inner and an outer, a lower and a higher significance to be attached thereto.

The atmosphere of the teaching is something
wholly new. The spirit of Jesus moves easily and

naturally in the transcendental throughout, yet
without once losing touch with the workaday world;
He speaks familiarly and with first-hand knowledge of the things of God, yet without withdrawing
for an instant His sympathy from the needs and
sorrows of poor humanity. He made heaven and
the life eternal seem real to those He addressed as
no one else has ever done, and yet there was no
ascetic other-worldism either in His discourses or
His mode of life. Such lightness of touch, united
to such richness of spiritual content, has never been
seen in any religious utterances as in these. If His
object in part were to provoke people to think,
pray, and inquire into the great mysteries of our
life and death, He certainly succeeded by the very
method He employed as well as by His skill in employing it. In one saying He is represented as declaring that He adopted the parabolic form in
teaching so that people should not understand what
He meant.[28] Needless to say, that was not literally
so, but it was undoubtedly true that only those who
were spiritually ready to grasp the full implications
of His word would get out of the parables all that
was in them. To the rest they would be more or
less obscure. But everybody would get something.
It is so to-day.

It is sometimes remarked that if the precepts of
the Sermon on the Mount could be carried out in
their entirety human society would dissolve, and
that may be true.[29] If what has already been said

[28] Mark iv. 11, 12; Luke viii. 10. *Cf.* Matt. xiii. 10 *ff* and John
xii. 40.
[29] Gore: *Sermon on the Mount,* p. 110.

concerning this so-called sermon be correct—that is, that it consists of brief notes of a considerable body of teaching delivered to avowed disciples and spread over a somewhat lengthy period—it is clear that it was not meant for immediate and universal adoption; it is a statement of the ideal of conduct which would be followed in a Christian community; it is the law of the Church as it proceeded from the lips of its founder.[30]   There are large gaps in it, of necessity so.   It does not legislate for modern economic problems or for any of the complexities arising out of the relations of the modern State.

[30] Seeley's chapter in *Ecce Homo* on the "Nature of Christ's Society" is still a fresh and penetrating analysis of the factors that led to the expression of the mind of Jesus through an organized fellowship: the two cannot be considered apart.

covers vast amount of ground but does it well. Both instructive & suggestive.

N. E.

CHAPTER VIII

THE EARLY MINISTRY

THE SEQUENCE OF EVENTS

FOLLOWING St. Mark's order, which is at once the simplest and most primitive, and upon which with modifications the first and third gospels depend, we can obtain something like a coherent story of this period of our Lord's public activity. It is far from being a complete story or one wholly free from difficulties, but these are not so numerous as in the later period. Provided we do not adhere too strictly to any one theory of the manner in which the ministry developed or of the scenes in which it was exercised, a fairly distinct thread of connection is observable throughout. If the view taken above be accepted, that the writer of the fourth gospel did not conceive himself to be correcting the information given by the others but only to be supplementing it from the special Johannine traditions; and if, as is now generally admitted, the authors of the first and third gospels, writing independently of each other, both made use of Mark in giving their outline of the doings of Jesus while drawing upon another source for the teaching, we can at least make a reasonable attempt at an understanding of the Master's procedure and how it was gradually affected by influences from without. That a particular saying should appear more than once or in different connections in one gospel as compared with another is surely a matter of indifference. There is every likelihood that Jesus repeated portions of His teaching from time to time, and some of the most striking and original of His aphorisms may have been associated, now with this episode, and now with that.

These are comparatively unimportant questions; what matters much more is to determine, if we can, the general bearing of words and works and their true significance. It should be noted that most which we possess of the former belongs to the out-of-doors ministry. What Jesus may have said in the synagogues we are not told, with the one exception of the scene in the synagogue at Nazareth; nearly all the sayings preserved in the gospels were spoken to promiscuous assemblies. It is otherwise with the miracles; some of the most notable of these are said to have been wrought in the synagogues, and that it was partly in consequence of this that the synagogue ministry had to give way to the larger one towards which the Pharisees and scribes took up an attitude of increasing hostility. But this was not for some time, for the statement is definitely made that He first preached in the synagogues throughout all Galilee and cast out devils. There is no evidence that the syna-

gogues were wholly closed to Him at any time—
certainly not before the antagonism between Himself and the Pharisees became acute. It is much
more probable that the synagogues soon became
too small to accommodate the crowds which flocked
to hear Him. In the closing verse of St. Mark's
opening chapter, for example, it is stated that in
spite of our Lord's charge to the first leper whom
He cleansed, not to make the miracle known, the
man blazed the matter abroad to such an extent that
for a time Jesus could no more enter into the city
(Capernaum), but had to remain without in desert
places, and that people came to Him there from
every quarter. This alone would be sufficient to
account for His speedy substitution of a wider ministry for that of the synagogues, not to mention His
desire to come into contact with the non-synagogue-
going classes. Both types of ministry may have
run concurrently for a certain period. When He
went to a new locality He would begin by speaking
in the synagogue and afterwards betake Himself
to the open air. In the end His discourses were
delivered in the open air alone, though there is an
occasional suggestion of His speaking in private
houses, or, more probably, in the courtyards attaching thereto.

ADDITIONAL WONDER-WORKING

Besides the miracles already mentioned as belonging to this first period of our Lord's public
ministry, we have to note the curious episode of the

Gadarene swine (which may more fitly be considered later), the cure of the paralytic whose sins He also forgave, the raising of the ruler's daughter, the healing of the woman with an issue of blood, the opening of the eyes of two blind men, the deliverance of a dumb man possessed with a devil, the healing of the man with the withered hand. This last is stated to have been the overt cause of the enmity of the Pharisees towards Jesus thenceforth. Mark says that unclean spirits saluted Him as Son of God, but that He forbade them to make Him known. To this period also we may refer the stilling of the tempest on the lake of Galilee. The significant statement appears in Luke that Pharisees and doctors of the Law were sitting by on a certain day, which were come out of every town of Galilee, and Judea, and Jerusalem.[1] Apparently it was on this occasion that Jesus healed the paralytic on the Sabbath day. That Pharisees and doctors of the Law should have come down from the capital to watch His movements is evidence, not only of the general interest that had been aroused thereby throughout Judea as well as Galilee, but also perhaps of the fact that His earlier appearance in the Temple at Jerusalem had not been forgotten nor the questioning it occasioned been allowed to subside. It would seem also that the Master must have visited Jerusalem once more during this period, judging from what is recorded in St. John v. The events described in this chapter follow immediately upon the healing of the

[1] Luke v. 17.

nobleman's son at Capernaum, but there is room in between for all alluded to above to have taken place. It would not be easy to assign them to a later period, for the sixth chapter of St. John opens with a further reference to Galilee and a description of the feeding of the five thousand, which, in the synoptical account, follows more obviously upon the above series of events. John says that Jesus went up to Jerusalem on this occasion to be present at a feast of the Jews, but does not tell us what the feast was. It was not a Passover, but in the absence of express information it is of little use attempting to say which out of the number of lesser feasts was the one here indicated. Its mention in this connection is noteworthy because of the healing of the impotent man at the pool of Bethesda, to which we must refer again later.

In St. Mark's vivid way—a characteristic difficult to reproduce in English—and which the other evangelists do not possess in like degree, he tells us of the intense impression produced by these wonder-workings. "All the city was gathered together at the door," [2] he says—that is, the whole population was assembled at the city gate excitedly discussing what had come to pass in their midst. The city gate was the usual place of meeting for ordinary purposes. The evangelist tells us something of what was said. "What is this?" they questioned of one another. "A new teaching? With authority he commands even the unclean spirits, and they obey him." [3] It is Mark again who makes

---

[2] Mark 1. 33.   [3] *Ibid.* 27.

us aware of the rapidity with which the news traveled far and near, and not only within the province wherein the works were wrought. "And immediately His fame spread abroad through all the region round about Galilee." [4]

On Jesus' return to Capernaum after the short retirement which had been forced upon Him as indicated above, His advent was signalized by an instant rush of clamorous crowds to see and hear Him. Mark, as usual, is the most dramatic in his description of the scene and what followed. He says it was noised that He was at home, and that "straightway many were gathered together, insomuch that there was no room to receive them, no, not so much as about the door: and he preached the word unto them." [5] We need not assume that the excitement thus caused was more than parochial, so to speak, or that the throngs would be very great as compared with the vast popular demonstrations to which we are accustomed in European or American cities in our own day. Presumably this was our Lord's own house which was thus besieged, or the house belonging to one of the disciples in which He had taken up His abode some time before. It would not be very large and could not accommodate an audience of more than a score or two at most; and the crowd outside to which the Master went forth as suggested in the narrative might consist of a few hundred people. *(1)*

We here encounter our first great difficulty in attempting to reconcile with each other the various

(1) This does not consider future happenings sufficient in the analysis. 4000 - 5000 ree. that is not parochial.

evangelical records of this portion of the ministry.
Mark, with considerable verisimilitude, says that it
was on this occasion that the healing of the paralytic took place which provoked the first expression
of hostility from the scribes, because Jesus added
to it the forgiveness of the sufferer's sins. Matthew and Luke place it in an entirely different connection. To harmonize them is impossible, and we
can say no more than has already been said on the
subject, namely, that the evangelists themselves
have only a secondary interest in questions of
chronological order. We can but adhere to Mark's
version on the whole as the best as well as the
earliest.

According to the picturesque description of the
incident given, by the second evangelist, in which
we may detect Peter's vivid way of recollecting
what took place, Jesus must have been addressing
the assemblage from some elevated spot overlooking
the courtyard of the house in which He was domi-
ciled, the people filling the courtyard in every part
and overflowing through the gateway into the
street. Luke's observation relating ostensibly to
what followed, that doctors of the Law from Jerusalem were present, would be more relevant to other
occasions; on this particular one, few, if any, could
have known where to find the Master till, as Mark
indicates, the news spread like wildfire through the
little city that He had returned and was in the house.
On the other hand it is possible that these important
visitors from the south had been waiting in Capernaum for some time in the hope of being present at

His next public appearance. While the gathering was in progress, and Jesus in the act of speaking, four men came up bearing on a light pallet a fifth who was paralyzed and unable to move of himself. Finding direct access to the Master impossible because of the density of the crowd that blocked the gate, they had recourse to stratagem. They ascended to the roof, and either untiled a portion of it, or, what is more likely, rolled back a corner of the veil that shielded the courtyard from the direct rays of the sun, and then attaching cords to the bed lowered it with its occupant right down into the immediate presence of Jesus. All three of the synoptics affirm that Jesus was touched by the faith thus betokened on the part of the bearers, and, we may assume, by their loyal devotion to their afflicted friend also. But His first word in reference thereto was not what any one expected. "Son"— or, rather, "child"—He said, "be of good cheer; thy sins be forgiven thee." [6]

Doubtless there was more in this utterance than fell on the ear. This man's sickness, like much similar suffering at the present day, may have been, probably was, his own fault. He had sown to the flesh and of the flesh reaped corruption. No one else in the wide world perhaps knew of the bitterness of his regret and his desire for amendment. His prayer to God for forgiveness and restoration, which like Nathanael's under the fig tree, he had imagined to be utterly secret, he now saw, to his amazement, was known to the teacher who stood

[6] Mark ii. 5.

gazing compassionately down upon him. There
was an instant flash of understanding between the
two. Both knew that the soul needed healing as
well as the body in this case as in most others, and
the Master's word of absolution was addressed
straight to the paralytic's unspoken thoughts and
was the one he most rejoiced to hear, though never
expecting to do so. But it startled those round
about, especially the scribes, though it would seem
that for the present they kept their objections to
themselves. They reasoned in their hearts, "Why
doth this man thus speak blasphemies? Who can
forgive sins but God only?" Then came the second
surprise. "And straightway Jesus, perceiving in
his spirit that they so reasoned within themselves"
—or, as Matthew has it, "knowing their thoughts"
—"saith unto them, Why reason ye these things in
your hearts?" And to show that the Son of Man
had authority on earth to forgive sins, He bade the
paralytic arise instantly and take up his bed and
walk.

Better to like it thus, than as you purpose in the ensuing remarks.

It can hardly have been intended that this last
statement should be taken too literally. As it
stands it would suggest that our Lord healed the
paralytic simply and solely to demonstrate that He
Himself had authority to forgive sins. But would
He not have healed the poor man of his infirmity in
any case? Undoubtedly; He only began with the
root evil, the malady of the soul, and then com-
pleted the cure. His address to the critical onlookers merely amounted to saying, Observe what
follows; if I have power to heal the body, does it

not argue that my word of liberation to the soul, previously spoken, was valid also?

But a perplexing question thrusts itself upon us here. This is the first occasion on which Jesus is said to have used the mysterious self-designation, Son of Man, which appears, in all, in the gospels no less than eighty-two times. In what sense can He have used it? It could not have been Messianic in this instance at any rate, nor in most others, so far as His hearers knew, for, as we have seen, Jesus' Messiahship was not yet explicit, was not even suspected by the public He addressed. On the other hand the theory that the expression had an impersonal signification, and was merely equivalent to "Man" renders it meaningless in such a connection as this. The question is not only what Jesus Himself meant by it, but what those who heard Him understood Him to mean. Schweitzer declares the problem solved, and that Jesus spoke of Himself in this way because He knew Himself to be the Son of Man who was later to be revealed —that is, the Son of Man or Man from heaven of current apocalyptic prophecy.[7] To call Himself Son of Man openly under present circumstances would not convey this fact of His own self-consciousness to His hearers, while at the same time it would be consistent with what they must afterwards discover or which would at least be claimed on His behalf. This is plausible, perhaps more than plausible. It is reasonable to conclude that our Lord used the name with a purpose and that

[7] *Quest of the Historical Jesus,* p. 281.

it must have had something of Messianic significance in it unrecognized by the world until the time
came for Him to be proclaimed as the Messiah,
when it would be remembered that He had thus
described Himself all along. But why did not the
public associate the phrase with Messianic claims
in His person? It can only have been that they
never dreamed of the Messianic Son of Man as
coming in the guise of a Galilean carpenter preaching as a wandering rabbi, whereas they were acquainted with it in some other connection. And
what could that other connection be if not the somewhat vague and indeterminate use of the expression illustrated especially in the case of the prophet
Ezekiel? Ezekiel represents himself as being thus
addressed from heaven. There is nothing to forbid
the supposition that Jesus may have adopted the
phrase from this source, giving it at the same time a
connotation in His own mind which He did not
betray to others. In Aramaic the term a "Man" or
"Son of Man" has a significance not dissimilar to
that of the German "Man" in the sense of "One,"
the impersonal pronoun. This may explain why no
one thought of it with surprise when hearing it from
the lips of Jesus. Instead of saying "I" He could
quite suitably say "One" or "Myself," and "Son of
Man" may not have been understood necessarily to
mean more. It did mean more to Himself. Matthew adds a suggestive comment: "When the multitudes saw it (the miracle) they marveled, and
glorified God, which had given such power unto

men." [8] Evidently this is an allusion to Jesus'
statement above quoted, that the Son of Man had
power on earth to forgive sins as well as to heal. It
must have been understood in the sense that "Man,"
at any rate a divinely chosen and gifted man, might
do these things.

All three of the synoptics state that the call of
Matthew the publican succeeded almost immediately to this striking prodigy. Mark says that after
the healing Jesus came out of the house and went
down to the lake shore, His congregation accompanying Him, and that He taught them there. The
implication is that finding His domestic quarters
too straightened, especially after what had just
taken place, He stepped out into the open air, bidding His hearers follow Him, and that the same
meeting went on uninterruptedly. Whether it was
on the way to the beach or on the way back from it
that Jesus spoke to Matthew is not quite certain;
but Matthew's own account of the incident would
suggest the former. Matthew was a taxgatherer
under the Roman authority, and it was part of his
duty to collect the dues from the fisher-folk and
others at stated intervals along one section of the
Tiberian coast. He was sitting in his stall engaged in this work when Jesus passed with all the
excited company streaming around Him which had
just witnessed the healing of the paralytic. The
paralytic himself had already run forth shouting
his story. Business would be slack just then; the
taxgatherer would have little to do; everyone had

[8] Matt. ix. 8.

gone to listen to the new prophet and see what was
going on. Matthew sat alone and waited. Jesus
marked him from afar, and when He came opposite the publican's booth paused just long enough
to utter two words, "Follow me." [9] Matthew (or
Levi, as Mark and Luke call him) rose instantly
and obeyed. He knew that this was a special summons. Hundreds of others were following at the
same moment, but the call had not come to them
as it had come to him. This was the beginning of
a new life for him, entrance upon a vocation, the
extent of which as yet he little knew. He abandoned everything for it, just as the first companions of Francis of Assisi did in similar fashion
nearly thirteen centuries later. Probably at the
moment he had not much to leave; as we have said,
business had been suspended for the time in the
unwonted interest that had been aroused by the return of the Master after a brief absence; but may
it not have been that all Matthew's arrangements
were already made and that he only awaited the
signal, as Peter and the sons of Zebedee had previously done, to forsake all and attach himself to
Jesus? Mark says he was the son of Alpheus.
This being so he had a brother James who was also
included in the apostolic band, and there is every
likelihood that these men had had opportunities of
meeting Jesus previously during His residence in
Capernaum. Like the first four apostles they were
ready to come with Him when He needed them, and
an understanding may have existed to that end.

[9] *Ibid.* ix. 9.

Jesus needed Matthew now. He wanted to reach all classes; all classes wanted to hear Him; but not all were welcome to the synagogue. There were those without, not as large a proportion of the community then as now, but still considerable in number, between whom and the rest little intercourse was possible. These were despised, avoided, socially outcast. The publicans were the most hated among them, and with reason; they farmed the revenues for the Roman invader and thus joined in the oppression of their own countrymen. Some of them became very wealthy through this greedy and unpatriotic practice, but with the result that they were universally condemned and held in dishonor; their associations were perforce with those who were outside the pale of what was accounted respectable and of good report. It was a man of this order that Jesus now approached, and the inference is that one of His motives in doing so was that He might be brought into more immediate touch with the people who were never seen in the synagogues and would not have been permitted to enter.

That this was the Master's object is shown by what is next recorded, and especially by Luke's version of it. "Levi," says the third evangelist, "made him a great feast in his own house: and there was a great company of publicans and of others that sat down with them." [10] It is not without significance that the word "feast" might here better be translated "reception." Levi's occupation had brought him wealth, and he now used some of this wealth

[10] Luke v. 29.

in the holding of a reception—literally such, as we should understand it to-day—to enable the poor and the socially disreputable to make nearer acquaintance with Jesus. Another fact worth noting is that it is Matthew's own gospel which refers to him by that name; did Jesus give it to him as that by which he was to be known henceforth? It means "given by God." The old name of Levi might not be utterly discarded any more than "Simon" was discarded when the first of the apostles was surnamed by his Master "Peter," a rock.

END OF THE DISTINCTIVELY SYNAGOGUE MINISTRY

We might almost say that from the call of Matthew dates a new departure in the Master's methods, and it also marks the first open expression of disapproval on the part of the Pharisaic party in Galilee. It was to them a scandal that He should thus mix Himself up with those who were under the ban of orthodoxy. "How is it that He eateth and drinketh with publicans and sinners?" [11] they asked of His disciples—the first clear indication we possess that He already had a recognized following of disciples. Matthew's report of Jesus' impressive reply is best and fullest of the three and suggests that as host and principal agent on the occasion he had a keener memory for what happened than the rest. Some of the disciples must have come to Jesus with the information of the Pharisees' protest, and, continues the narrative in the first gospel, "When Jesus heard that He said

[11] Mark ii. 16.

unto them, They that be whole need not a physician, but they that are sick. But go ye and learn what that meaneth, I will have mercy, and not sacrifice: for I am not come to call the righteous, but sinners to repentance." [12] There is nothing provocative in this beautiful and tender justification; the complete break between Jesus and the representatives of the established order had not yet come about, but it was on the way. After this scene in Matthew's house the synagogue ministry could not be continued on quite the same terms as before. The citation of the words from Hosea vi. 6 was remarkably applicable to the situation. There could not have been a greater contrast than the idea of Jesus as thus evinced, concerning the scope of the heavenly Kingdom, and that of the majority of His Jewish contemporaries. He called all men to prepare for the advent of the Kingdom, and the call was specially directed to those who needed repentance. The word repentance is not included here in the best Mss., but it might as well be, for Jesus and the Baptist both insisted from the first on the necessity, for the change of mind or heart denoted repentance as preliminary to the advent of the Kingdom, which both declared to be near at hand. In the instance before us Jesus does not say who are sinners and who are not; He but gently insists that all should be included within the range of God's mercy, and that His mission is to all accordingly.

Whether the appeal to His critics made any im-

[12] Matt. ix. 12, 13.

pression is not explicitly stated. On the whole it is improbable, but there is one indication to the contrary which should not be passed over and that is supplied by St. Luke. Luke has a special source already mentioned which does not follow any chronological order, but which contains a good deal of matter that might more fitly be ascribed to the earlier than the later ministry. What this special source was there is no evidence to show, but none of the other evangelists has it and it is inserted in the third gospel almost *en bloc*. It is the fifteenth chapter which seems to have special relevance in relation to the gathering arranged by Matthew and which Luke also reports in his own fifth chapter. The fifteenth opens with the words, almost a repetition of those previously recorded in connection with Matthew's feast: "Then drew near unto Him all the publicans and sinners for to hear Him. And the Pharisees and scribes murmured, saying, This man receiveth sinners, and eateth with them." Then follow the three parables—the lost sheep, the lost piece of silver, and the prodigal son. There the discourse on this occasion ends, for the next chapter begins with one addressed specially to disciples. Does this fifteenth chapter contain, as Dr. A. B. Bruce suggests,[13] the bulk of the address which Jesus delivered to the strangely heterogeneous assembly in Matthew's house at the memorable feast which followed the call of the publican-apostle? If so—and the form of introduction certainly implies it—we have here the nearest approach to a full

[13] *Expositor's Greek Testament*, Vol. I, p. 577.

report of a connected discourse of Jesus which exists. This is much more truly a sermon in the modern sense than the so-called Sermon on the Mount, for it deals with a single theme, and develops it with great beauty and impressiveness. Who took the notes from which it was reproduced? To Matthew's jottings, as we have seen, we are perhaps indebted for the Sermon on the Mount and something more, but Matthew possessed no such skill as this and no such mastery of the Greek medium as was necessary for retelling at length a story so winsome and withal so searching. Either, therefore, this chapter represents Luke's own first-hand report of the Master's words on this great occasion or he had direct access to some one of his own order who could furnish it. Luke was probably old enough at this time to have been present in the assembly in question and to have written out an almost verbatim record of the discourse for himself; it is most lovingly and tenderly done, and the fact that it appears in Luke's gospel and Luke's alone would almost point to this explanation of its origin. It is the work of a man to whom writing came easier than to the other evangelists. It is told in detail and in Luke's characteristic style; it bears the marks of an educated yet sympathetic mind. Whether St. Luke, who writes so well in the Greek language, could understand Aramaic is, of course, doubtful; there are no Aramaic terms in his gospel as in Matthew and Mark. Neither is it anywhere specifically stated that he had ever seen or heard Jesus.

But there is one point which strongly suggests either Luke's own original report or that of an eye-witness very like himself in feeling and outlook, perhaps some one closely connected. It is the reference to the elder brother in the third parable. A brief survey of the whole will make this clear.

It will be noted that the first two parables end with almost the same words, namely, that there is joy in the presence of the angels of God over one sinner that repenteth. Neither the sheep nor the piece of silver repented in the sense we are accustomed to ascribe to that term. Both remained lost, helpless, passive until sought for and recovered by the shepherd and the owner respectively. What can this mean? It can only mean that in our Lord's thought repentance is a God-created state of mind; He has more to do with it than the sinner; it is He, and not the sinner, whose volition produces in the heart of the latter feelings of contrition and desire for amendment; God seeks man ere man seeks God —man seeking God is in itself a sign that God has first been seeking man. On the other hand, man has a will as well as God; God does not treat His children as if they were only of the status of the lost sheep and piece of silver; we are more than automata, we are free, self-determining beings; there can be no real spiritual life where the exercise of the will is absent. So Jesus introduces the figure of the prodigal to show that there is an important human side to the fact of repentance. The wanderer is made to say, "I will arise and go to my father." All parables, being merely illustrations,

220

are inadequate in some degree for the conveyance of spiritual truth. Jesus uses three here because He needed them all to teach both aspects of His theme. The first two without the third would present repentance as an experience in which the human will had no part, but only the will of God; and the third separated from the other two shows the initiative as coming from man, not from God. The prodigal has to make the long journey home before he comes to his father's presence; the father cannot be represented as in the far country with his son, whereas God is always with His children even at the darkest and the worst. But, lest His hearers should make the mistake of thinking that the human part is the principal factor in the total experience, Jesus uses two parables to enforce the truth that the divine comes first, and only one to teach that man has something to do in the matter also. The figures of the lost sheep and the lost piece of silver illustrate the priority of the action of God, and that of the prodigal the sinner's response thereto.

Why is the elder brother introduced at all? To judge from the conventional way of treating the subject, and from the fact that the elder brother as represented in this parable has become in Christian usage almost a synonym for spiritual pride, one might suppose that our Lord's intention in placing this addendum to the beautiful story, a story complete without it, was to make an attack upon the Pharisees and to hold up their self-righteousness to reprobation. Surely this is an entire mistake and completely misses the point. If these three parables really formed the substance of the address delivered in Matthew's house in the circumstances above described, there was as yet no open breach with the Pharisees. Suspicion of Jesus had begun to be entertained by them, but it was not until this moment that they openly opposed Him. They could not understand why a reputable teacher should thus be seen fraternizing with publicans and sinners, and they protested. Jesus' defense when the disciples told Him of this protest while the meal was yet in progress we have already noted. Now comes a further reply on His part, an attempt to break down their prejudice if possible. When He had finished His story of the prodigal, so compassionately applicable to His auditors, who with Him shared Matthew's hospitality, He raised His eyes towards the assembled onlookers, mostly synagogue-goers, who, after the usual oriental fashion, were permitted to stand on the outskirts of the assembly. Their disapproval was no doubt manifest in their demeanor. Addressing Himself directly to them He went on to make, not a denunciation, but an appeal. There is not a word in this part of the parable to suggest that the elder brother was an unworthy person, quite the contrary. His anger at the reception of the prodigal is shown to be natural; it is not condemned. The father is represented as freely admitting the elder son's claim that he had never at any time transgressed the father's wishes. Moreover, in making this admission the father drops into a tender diminutive. Instead of using the word "son" ($\nu\iota\acute{o}s$) as in the elder brother's angry outburst, "When this thy son came" that is, the heir of thy substance—he says "child" ($T\acute{\epsilon}\chi\nu os$). Child of my heart, he pleads, what you say is true; things have been well between us; we have always been in closest sympathy hitherto—"thou art ever with me, and all that is mine is thine." Therefore is it all the more fitting that we together should rejoice and be glad; "for this thy brother was dead, and is alive again; and was lost, and is found."

Was ever an appeal to the best in human nature more gently and nobly put? There is not a harsh word in it from first to last. We are told that when the elder son first heard of the merrymaking "he was angry and would not go in." But it does not say so at the end. The parable closes on the note just quoted, for the plain and good reason that it remained to be seen whether the elder brother, looking on at Matthew's feast, would respond to the appeal it contained or not. All the factors described in the parable were there in operation—the wanderers from the far country, the offer of God's mercy, the banquet of reconciliation, the frowning elders. Would they understand?

Did one at least understand that day? Was it St. Luke himself? Is this the reason why this man of education and refinement became a professed follower of Jesus? Does it explain the chief characteristic of his gospel—a characteristic which the others do not share in equal measure—his sympathy with the outcast and the lost, the downtrodden and the poor? One would like to believe that an affirmative answer could be given to these questions, and on the whole it seems justifiable. No other explanation agrees so well with the facts as presented in this winsome gospel.

BEGINNINGS OF DEFINITE OPPOSITION

Following upon the Master's answer to the Pharisees at the feast in Matthew's house, Mark recounts three other episodes in which Pharisaic objection to Jesus' practice is shown as increasing. The first of these relates to fasting. It was represented that the disciples of John and of the Pharisees observed a rule of fasting at prescribed periods whereas those of Jesus did not. In St. Matthew's version it is said to have been the disciples of John who came asking for the reason of this difference: Mark says both. The point is not important. The Pharisees would be sure to object in any case, but it is interesting to observe that up to the present the disciples of the Baptist, notwithstanding his imprisonment, keep together and observe a definite rule; they have not yet become merged in the following of Jesus. Jesus' reply to the question was the counter question, "Can the children of the bride-chamber fast while the bridegroom is with them?" etc.[14] In the same connection appears the double metaphor, "No man also seweth a piece of new cloth on an old garment," and "putteth new wine into old bottles"—that is, "wine skins." The sug-

[14] Mark ii. 19.

gestion in all these is that there was no particular occasion for the self-discipline indicated or for complying with the established usage in regard thereto. Jesus had come to bring good news. The relation of His adherents to Himself was one of new beginnings, of preparation and instruction for greater experiences to follow. They understood but little yet, nor indeed did any one but the Master understand the greatness of what was in store. It would be foolish to anticipate and futile to imitate. The mould of the Jewish religious system was not adequate to the new and mighty spiritual force which had come into the world.

These sayings are full of significance. They contain the first recorded hint that our Lord already knew of His coming passion: what else could He mean by His reference to the fasting to which the disciples would submit when He was taken from them? There is a suggestion of mourning in the thought, but it is no more than a hint. He emphatically affirms that their proper demeanor now is one of rejoicing, that there is nothing to be sorrowful about, but that one day it will be different because of the circumstances under which they will be deprived of His presence. That He was fully conscious also of the break with the past involved in His advent is clear enough from His use of the figures of the new cloth and the new wine skins. The Gospel associated with His person cannot be regulated by the old forms of ritual and worship: it is too radical a departure for that to be possible. It will create its own system, require new modes of expression, rise higher and strike deeper than any one then suspected. A more accurate forecast could not have been made, though in the nature of things neither the followers of the Baptist nor the Pharisees themselves could be expected to grasp its implications. It is an interesting sidelight on the question of the Master's own consciousness of His mission and His purpose in carrying it out. St. Luke's version of the incident adds the sentence, "No man also having drunk old wine straightway desireth new, for he saith, The old is better"—or, "The old is good (enough)." [15] This was literally true of the situation at the moment as of religious conservation in any age. None of these critics of the Master really wanted anything new in belief or practice; nor did they realize that His message had any deeper significance than that to which they were accustomed. Hence the pettifogging quality of the issues raised by them. Fasting was a small matter compared with the greatness of the spiritual boon that had come in Jesus, not only to Israel, but to the whole world, little though they knew it. They were treating it as a new phase of an ancient and sharply limited order of things, assuming that it was but a fresh local development within the old Judaistic system, as that of the Baptist was supposed to be; and they were entirely wrong. They did not want this new thing, did not realize its wondrous divine quality. How like human nature the world over! There is no reason to suppose that John's disciples expressed their perplex-

[15] Luke v. 39.

ity in other than a friendly spirit, whatever may have been true of the Pharisees. It was only that their outlook was circumscribed by their prepossessions.

The next episode, recorded in the same connection, is that of the Pharisees' protest against the behavior of some of Jesus' disciples in plucking and eating ears of corn on the Sabbath day as He and they were walking together through the fields. Luke, with his usual precision, makes an attempt to indicate for us the season of the year when the event took place, though it is doubtful whether we understand him rightly. He says it was on the second Sabbath after the first, which may mean the second Sabbath after the first month—that is, of the month in which the Passover occurred. But apparently it was before the Passover, if it preceded the feeding of the five thousand as recorded, not only in the synoptical gospels, but in John vi. To harmonize the several accounts chronologically is out of the question. In Mark and Luke it appears directly after the feast in Matthew's house, but in Matthew's own gospel that is not so; there is a considerable interval suggested between the two events, including the call and ordination of the twelve apostles and a whole series of discourses. All we can be sure about as regards time is that the act complained of must have taken place somewhere between the ripening of the barley harvest and that of the wheat some weeks later. There is, of course, the explanation that the second Sabbath thus alluded to was a forgotten technical term of synagogue ritual observance. But it is unsafe to build any theory of dates upon a single obscure phrase such as this.

This is the first instance in which, according to Mark, the Pharisees raise the question of Sabbath observance in relation to Jesus. They complain that the behavior of the disciples is a breach of the sabbatic law. In this case it is the disciples who are the offenders; in the next it is our Lord Himself. Perhaps Jesus had already offended in Jerusalem by healing the impotent man at the pool of Bethesda on the Sabbath; if He had not already done so it must have been soon afterwards. As we have seen, emissaries from Jerusalem were now keeping watch on His doings in Galilee. The Master's defence of His followers is to turn the Pharisees' own argument against themselves. If they appeal to the Scriptures, there is the example of David and the high priest in an emergency; and in the Law itself there is the prescription relating to the priests when certain manual work has to be done in the service of the Temple on the Sabbath. Again we notice a pregnant comment: "In this place is one greater than the Temple" [16]—or, perhaps better, "a greater thing than the Temple"—a further reference to the fact that the Gospel He had come to proclaim was of vaster import than the system centering in the Temple at Jerusalem. "The Son of Man is Lord also of the Sabbath," He added —a saying preceded in Mark's version by the still more striking expression, "The Sabbath was made for man, and not man for the Sabbath." [17]

[16] Matt. xii. 6.   [17] Mark ii. 27.

The issue was accentuated quickly afterwards. Matthew says that He went into their synagogue, presumably the synagogue of the Pharisees who had made the complaint—perhaps Capernaum, for Mark says, "He entered again into the synagogue," as if it were the one in which He was accustomed to teach—and saw a man there with a withered hand. Evidently they were waiting to see what He would do in regard to this. From what had already taken place He must have known that this would be so even without the exercise of any supernormal faculty. Mark tells the story best. Jesus first bade the afflicted man come out into the middle of the assembly, and after the command had been obeyed, He put the direct question to the Pharisees present: "Is it lawful to do good on the Sabbath days, or to do evil? to save life, or to kill?" [18] As they were only on the watch to find something wherewith to bring an accusation against Him they made no answer. The pathetic sight of the man's infirmity did not move them to any compassion. Jesus' action in directing the sufferer to stand up before them was doubtless designed to appeal to their feelings of humanity in this respect, but it failed. Matthew includes in his description a further question: "What man shall there be among you, that shall have one sheep, and if it fall into a pit on the Sabbath day will he not lay hold on it and lift it out? How much then is a man better than a sheep?" [19] Luke records this question as having been put on a different occasion, namely, in the house of one of

[18] *Ibid*. iii. 4. [19] Matt. xii. 11, 12.

the chief Pharisees and in the act of healing a man with the dropsy.[20] It is a kind of question which could be put repeatedly without losing force. It elicited no response, for the bigoted onlookers were there, not to pity, but to find an excuse to condemn. Mark adds the dramatic touch, "And when He had looked round about on them with anger, being grieved for the hardness of their hearts, He saith unto the man, Stretch forth thy hand. And he stretched it out: and his hand was restored whole as the other. And the Pharisees went forth, and straightway took council with the Herodians against him, how they might destroy him." [21]

We have already seen that somewhere about this same period, either before or after, some of the fanatical spirits in Jerusalem had begun to think of making an end of Jesus on a similar ground. St. John's report of the matter is that the healing at the pool of Bethesda, being performed on the Sabbath, alone sufficed to stir up the fanatical rage of these people and make them ready to kill the Master; but that His words in relation thereto, "My Father worketh hitherto, and I work" intensified their determination. "Wherefore the Jews sought the more to kill Him, because He not only had broken the Sabbath, but said also that God was His Father, making Himself equal with God." [22] There may have been no connection between the Galilean and Judean developments in the case, but it is more than probable that there was, the danger in the south being greater; in fact

[20] Luke xiv. 5.   [21] Mark iii. 5, 6.   [22] John v. 18.

it was not long before Jesus found it expedient to keep away from Judea for a time and confine His operations to the north.

In Mark's narrative we have here the first reference to the Herodians as a party uniting with the Pharisees with the object of putting Jesus to death. Who the Herodians were is not historically beyond question, but that they were a distinct political party, probably of mixed descent, and pledged for interested reasons to the support of the Edomite dynasty is a reasonable inference. Why they were thus thrown into antagonism to Jesus is not so evident. It could not have been from the same motives as the Pharisees who hated the foreigner and certainly owed no loyalty to Herod. Possibly the Herodians saw in the growth of a popular religious cult an ultimate threat to their own safety; on the other hand, the way Mark's statement is made points rather to a deliberate plot on the part of the Pharisees to get the Herodians to put force in motion to get rid of Jesus. By bribery or otherwise they might induce members of the court party to do what they themselves could not, secure Herod's warrant for having Jesus arrested and treated as John the Baptist had been by the same tyrant, Antipas. Jesus seems to have regarded the danger as of sufficient importance to require care on His part if He were to be permitted to work for any length of time. Matthew says that He withdrew from thence because He knew what was being plotted; Mark says He took His disciples with Him and went to the sea. Where was this? It

could only have been that part of the coast of Syria
to the northwest, which was outside the jurisdiction
of the Galilean province and indeed outside Israelitish territory itself. The Master is now brought
into contact with a community not of Jewish race,
though whether He had any previous acquaintance
therewith cannot be ascertained. It would not be
unlikely. This northwestern shore was easily accessible from the region round about Nazareth, and
even more so from Capernaum.

But here also the work went on. Great multitudes flocked to Him from every part of Palestine
and beyond as well as from the district He had entered itself.[23] The same scenes were enacted as had
characterized the ministry elsewhere. The designation Son of God as applied to Jesus now appears
in Mark for the first time. It is said that the de-
moniacs hailed Him thus, as on previous occasions
they had saluted Him as the Holy One of God.
The evangelist adds, "And He straitly charged
them that they should not make Him known." [24]
The inference is that the evil spirits He was thus
expelling from afflicted persons whom they had possessed knew more about Him than did human beings.

THE COMMISSION TO THE APOSTLES

An impressive intimation is given by St. Luke
alone concerning the important new departure

[23] Mark iii. 8 includes Tyre and Sidon among the places whence
many hearers came.
[24] Mark iii. 12.

which Jesus had now in view. The third evangelist says nothing about this retreat beyond the borders of Israel, but in the same connection as the others, observes: "And it came to pass in those days, that he went out into a mountain to pray, and continued all night in prayer to God. And when it was day, he called unto him his disciples: and of them he chose twelve, whom he also named apostles." [25] Matthew has a perplexing variant of the event. Without assigning it to any specific time or place, he inserts it in his gospel before the episodes above described. This is rather confusing if we look to Matthew rather than Mark for the history of our Lord's doings, which as we have seen can hardly be done. Mark, in less detail than Luke, mentions this ordination of the twelve as taking place at a special session in the hill country. "And he goeth up into a mountain, and calleth unto him whom he would: and they came unto him. And he ordained twelve, that they should be with him, and that he might send them forth to preach, and to have power to heal sicknesses and to cast out devils." [26]

The suggestion here of a somewhat protracted stay in a mountain region corresponds to the statement in Matthew v. 1, introducing the Sermon on the Mount. It would seem to have been on this special occasion—from all indications a memorable one, extending perhaps over several weeks—that Jesus made the first approach to anything like an organization of His followers. The mission of the

[25] Luke vi. 12, 13.   [26] Mark iii. ·15.

twelve (Matthew x. 1, etc.) is plainly a different
and later event. It is curious that Matthew says
nothing about this previous ordination of the
twelve, which finds a place both in Mark and Luke.
He merely begins abruptly with the observation:
"And when he had called unto him his twelve
disciples," [27] and then goes on to give their names.
The second and third evangelists show us that this
sending forth of the apostles to preach had been
preceded by a period of selection and training,
whether long or short we do not know. It is noteworthy that Luke places the original ordination and
his particular version of the Sermon on the Mount
in immediate juxtaposition, thereby strengthening
the hypothesis that this open air summer school
culminated in the solemn setting apart of twelve
men out of the whole company of the disciples for
a special work. Mark tells us definitely what that
work was, and the very word "apostle" implies it.
They were persons sent forth with special authority
from Jesus Himself—authority both to preach and
heal. Their commission is set forth at greater
length in Matthew x, though it is difficult here to
resist the conclusion that some of the words which
the first evangelist attributes to Jesus were spoken
to the twelve at a later period. In this first itinerary they were to announce the near advent of the
Kingdom, and they were endowed with something
of the Master's own power to cure sickness—Matthew also says to raise the dead, but no instance
is given of their having done so.

[27] Matt. x. 1 *ff.*

There is a striking similarity between their bold neglect of ordinary preparation for the needs of the outer man, and the conditions under which the early friars set about their work in Italy in the first flush of their newborn enthusiasm twelve hundred years later. In both cases they were enjoined not to take money or baggage but to rely for the satisfaction of their physical needs upon the good will of the people to whom they were sent. It is nowhere stated that this was their constant practice afterwards; in fact the evidence is to the contrary; the early Christian ministry was not a mendicant one. What Matthew also credits Jesus with saying, that they were sent forth as sheep in the midst of wolves, and would be brought up before governors and kings for their Master's sake; that brother would deliver up brother to death, and the father the child; and that they should be hated of all men for His name's sake, is explicable on the understanding that the evangelist here combines post-resurrection utterances with those specifically relating to the early Galilean ministry. There is no hint of persecution in this first mission of the twelve. They went, and preached, and returned with their report of their reception, a report wholly at variance with the supposition that they had been received otherwise than with interest and to some extent with warmth of welcome. Luke alone records a further mission of seventy disciples who seem to have met with nothing but success, a success which we may presume was accorded to the apostles also. "And the seventy returned again with joy, saying,

Lord, even the devils are subject unto us through thy name." [28] There is no intimation of their having met with hostility.

It is not so easy to understand what Matthew means by the statement: "When they persecute you in this city, flee ye into another: for verily I say unto you, Ye shall not have gone over the cities of Israel till the Son of Man be come." [29] But it is altogether arbitrary to assume, as Schweitzer does, that Jesus expected His own catastrophic manifestation as the Messiah to take place almost immediately, and that He was bitterly disappointed when nothing of the kind occurred. [30] There is not a particle of evidence for this view, nor yet for its corollary that it was because of this disappointment that Jesus made up His mind to die as a means of forcing on the dramatic consummation He desired. On the contrary the narrative implies that the twelve and the seventy were sent out with precise directions and for a specific period, and that when the term was fulfilled they gathered together to Jesus again according to arrangement. No surprise is expressed on either side at the course of events; all was as had been anticipated and is accepted by Jesus as such. He says not a word about any further prospect or that He is dissatisfied with the results. "And the apostles gathered themselves together unto Jesus, and told him all things, both what they had done, and what they had taught. And he said unto them, Come ye yourselves apart

[28] Luke x. 17.
[29] Matt. x. 23.
[30] *Quest of the Historical Jesus*, p. 358.

into a desert place, and rest awhile." [31] The most
obvious explanation of the saying peculiar to Matthew, that they should not have gone over the cities
of Israel before the advent of the Son of Man, is
that it belongs to the great forty days between the
resurrection and ascension of our Lord. Jesus certainly said many things then of which no record ex-
sists save as echoes of them have found their way
into the record of the earlier ministry as in this instance. And the statement is literally true. The
Parousia did take place—that is, a spiritual second
coming of Christ, a universal coming in the life of
the Church as a whole, a perpetual presence of the
Lord in the midst of His own—long before the
apostles had covered all the cities of Israel with
their personal witness to His Messiahship.

THE BAPTIST'S MESSAGE TO JESUS

It is at this point that Mark tells the story of the
arrest and murder of the intrepid Baptist, and the
form in which he tells it shows that in this instance
Matthew follows him closely; for both evangelists
introduce the story by a reference to Herod's apprehension that Jesus might be John risen from the
dead." [32] Evidently John had been dead some time.
All three of the synoptics state, as we have seen,
that it was in consequence of the imprisonment of
His forerunner that the Master originally withdrew
from Judea and made His first appearance as a
public teacher in Galilee. Up to that point He and
John seem to have worked more or less in associa-

[31] Mark vi. 30, 31.   [32] Mark vi. 14; Matt. xiv. 1, 2.

tion. Probably it was not very long. From his prison John watched the progress of Jesus for a time ere he himself was put to death, and Matthew and Luke both indicate that he did not altogether understand the course Jesus was taking. He did not expect a ministry so beneficent, so little accordant with his preconceived idea of the functions either of an Elijah or of the Messiah. Apparently his disciples had constant access to him in prison and kept him informed of Jesus' doings; in fact Luke expressly says so. The Baptist waited, and as nothing further happened along the line of his expectations he presently sent two of his disciples with the direct question: "Art thou he that should come, or do we look for another?" [33] Had we not the fourth gospel's account to assist us we might infer that John and Jesus had not met since the baptism, that the former did not know what the true significance of Jesus' advent was and that his interest had now been quickened by what he heard. But we cannot come to this conclusion with the facts before us. Evidently John was puzzled, and wondered if, after all, he might have been mistaken. We have already noted the probability that he was fully aware of Jesus' Messiahship and even disclosed it to certain of his own disciples. He could not have disclosed it to all, for not a hint is given throughout the gospels that John's disciples in general shared this knowledge. Even in sending this embassy from prison the Baptist maintains his reticence. He does not say whether he regards

[33] Matt. xi. 3.

Jesus as the Messiah or only as the herald of the
Messiah; he hardly goes so far as to suggest the
possibility of His being either. Before making any
reply, Jesus goes on performing works of mercy
in the presence of the messengers, and then impressively observes: "Go and show John again those
things which ye do hear and see: the blind receive
their sight, and the lame walk, the lepers are
cleansed, and the deaf hear, the dead are raised up"
—that is, presumably, the spiritually dead—"and
the poor have good news preached to them. And
blessed is he, whosoever shall find none occasion
of stumbling in me." [34] This was His answer to
John's misgivings. His present mission was as
Savior, not as judge. He had come to declare good
tidings, to bless and succor; it was thus that the
Kingdom of God should be heralded. Let John
ponder these things and not allow doubt to develop
into disapproval.

Following upon this episode—which, as will be
readily understood, conveyed much more to the
Baptist, in accordance with the private understanding between him and Jesus, than it would to any
of those who actually witnessed it—Jesus began to
speak to those about Him in words of highest com-
mendation concerning John. "What went ye out
into the wilderness to see?" He inquires—a plain
reference to the impression produced on the national consciousness by the preaching of the Baptist and to the fact that many of Jesus' present
audience had flocked to the Judean wilderness to

[34] Matt. xi. 4-6; Luke vii. 18 *ff*.

see and hear him. Mark omits this particular encomium, though elsewhere—in his account of what followed the transfiguration—he states like the others that Jesus expressly declared to the inner circle of the apostles that John the Baptist fulfilled the function of the expected Elijah and was His own forerunner. But this is a point which belongs to a later and important development. For the moment it is sufficient to recognize that in His public eulogy of John, which Matthew and Luke report, Jesus declares John to be more than a prophet, namely, the divine messenger foretold in Malachi iii. 1, whose advent was to herald that of the Messiah Himself. He tells His hearers that this is the Elijah of prophecy—not literally, but in the fact that his work has been to prepare the way for a greater advent, the advent of the Messiah-judge—but He is careful not to say that He Himself is that Messiah-judge, nor would His hearers be likely to make that deduction from His words in the circumstances. They would not think of this compassionate teacher and healer, notwithstanding His majesty and force, as answering to the popular expectation of the One who was to bring the affairs of the world to a sudden and mighty issue.

Jesus concludes His testimony to John by the striking statement: "Among them that are born of women there hath not risen a greater than John the Baptist: notwithstanding he that is least (or he that is but little) in the Kingdom of heaven is greater than he." [35] What can this mean?

[35] Matt. xi. 7 *ff.*; Luke vii. 24 *ff.*

If no greater than John had ever lived, then he that was least in the Kingdom of heaven was greater than all the sons of men that had preceded that day and generation; this is the logic of the comparison. The most reasonable explanation of the words is that our Lord referred to the Kingdom as existing in heaven at that moment, and also to its coming establishment on earth. The least among the citizens of the heavenly Kingdom, the sharers of eternal life, as it exists in glory above, is greater than the greatest whose eyes are partially blinded by the shadows and limitations of earth. And Jesus, knowing as He spoke, what no one else up to then could either know or understand, that He had come to bring that heavenly life within reach of men, to introduce in some degree an immediate experience of the life eternal to human hearts; knowing as He must have done that this would mean an entirely new dispensation, a break with the past whose greatness it would be impossible to overestimate, a new start in history, a new quality of life for the individual rooted and grafted in Himself, a new society living by new and higher standards, dared to say with magnificent vision of the future and with perfect truth, that not even John had grasped the implications of the Gospel it had been his work to prepare the way for.[36] John did not understand the mystery of redemption, the new humanity, or the Christian law of love, to go no farther; he was of the old order, not the new.

[36] For a discriminating comparison of the ideals of Jesus and His forerunner, *vide* Bruce: *Kingdom of God,* chap. iii.

Both Matthew and Luke add at this point a remarkable comparison made by Jesus between His own methods and those of the Baptist, but only Luke gives the reason for it. He says that those who listened to His praise of the Baptist were variously impressed according to their nature. "And all the people that heard Him, and the publicans, justified God, having been baptized with the baptism of John" [37]—a remark which shows how extensive that baptism had been, and, therefore, how vast the religious stirring which the preaching of the Baptist had accomplished. "But the Pharisees and the lawyers"—that is, the scribes—"rejected for themselves the counsel of God, not having been baptized of him." We here get a suggestion that very few of the Pharisaic order had undergone baptism at the hands of John, though we have already been told that some of them wished to do so. Was this because John refused to admit them till they had given proofs of sincerity in the matter of moral reformation? It would almost seem so, for the stern preacher had no mercy upon formalism divorced from genuine worth. It would only be natural in such a case that the persons thus repelled should have derided a movement which they could not capture and control. Something of this must have been evident in their demeanor as the Master spoke of John, for He immediately continued: "Whereunto shall I liken this generation? It is like unto children sitting in the markets," etc.[38] He

[37] Luke vii. 29.
[38] Matt. xi. 16 *ff.*; Luke vii. 31 *ff*.

illustrates the reception of His ministry and that of
John on the part of their contemporaries by a reference to what must have been a familiar scene in
any Galilean village. Children trying to get their
fellows to play, propose to imitate a wedding ceremony or a funeral as the case may be, just as now-
adays in our own country boys play at being soldiers and girls at housekeeping. Sometimes their
playmates are churlish and will not take their ap-
propriate parts or respond to any signal. Hence
the expostulation: "We have piped unto you, and
ye have not danced; we have mourned unto you,
and ye have not lamented." John came as an ascetic, a man of austere habits and taking part in
none of the social festivities of his time; and he
was called a madman. Jesus came living an ordinary, natural life, mixing with His fellows on all
ordinary occasions, and the complaint against Him
was that He was a glutton, a drunkard, and a fre-
quenter of bad company—this last, no doubt, an
allusion to the criticisms of His conduct in associating with publicans and sinners at Matthew's table.

It is startling to read that anything as coarse and
vindictive as this could ever have been said about
Jesus or that there could have been aught in His
behavior to lend color to it in the remotest degree.
We have, therefore, a brief glimpse likewise of an
impending rupture with orthodox society at large
in the very places where the Master's work had attracted most attention. It may relate to a somewhat later period, but both Matthew and Luke
suggest that the denunciation was spoken at or

about the time of the sending forth of the twelve
on the mission already specified. It is rather surprising to find Jesus speaking in such scathing tones
of Capernaum and Bethsaida wherein He had done
so much, and apparently up to then been well received. We cannot come to any other conclusion
from the evidence than that the feast in Matthew's
house made an enormous difference to Jesus' standing in the community, and that henceforth He was
treated with ingratitude and contumely and not
made welcome to the synagogue as previously.

How long it was after these events before the
Baptist was put to death is nowhere indicated.
Although Herod had imprisoned John he still paid
him a certain deference, for it is said that "he did
many things and heard him gladly." [39] The
preacher was under restraint, but the tyrant regarded him as a man of God, nevertheless, and paid
some heed to his words until the day came when at
the instance of a wicked woman he reluctantly consented to take away his life. Herodias had never
forgiven John for his bold denunciation of her adulterous union with her brother-in-law, and at last
her opportunity came. Her daughter Salome delighted Antipas by dancing before him on his
birthday in the presence of a great assembly of no-
tabilities, and the king impulsively offered her any
favor for which she might ask. After consulting
with her mother the girl demanded the head of
John the Baptist. Herod was trapped; he could
not withdraw from his promise, greatly though it

[39] Mark vi. 20.

grieved him to keep it. He sent orders accordingly to have John executed and his head brought to Salome. This was promptly done, and the daughter of Herodias carried the ghastly trophy to her mother with her own hands. It is to be noted that in Matthew's version of what followed it is stated that "his disciples came, and took up the body, and buried it, and went and told Jesus." [40] It is evident that this seemed to them the obvious thing to do, and that their master's opinion of Jesus was such that when their tie with the former was broken by this act of assassination they felt that their place was by the side of the latter.[41]

As aforesaid, the story of this tragic episode is introduced by Mark, and following him by Matthew, with the observation that at the height of the Galilean ministry Herod Antipas, hearing of the doings of Jesus, expressed the belief that He might be John the Baptist risen from the dead. Luke states that it was other people who said this and that Herod was perplexed thereby. "John have I beheaded," he declared, "but who is this of whom I hear such things? And he desired to see him." [42] It is not a little curious that it should have been possible at this stage for any large number of people to have identified John and Jesus, seeing that the two had actually been associated in public work in the south, that Jesus had produced a marked impression in Jerusalem while John was still at large, and that later the Galilean ministry was attracting

[40] Matt. xiv. 12.
[41] But, as already observed, this subject is still obscure.
[42] Luke ix. 9.

such widespread attention during John's imprisonment that the Baptist should have sent an inquiry to Jesus in relation thereto, and that multitudes should have flocked to it from every part of the country. That the Baptist and his greater successor were not universally confused in the public mind is plain enough from other references, particularly, perhaps, the remark attributed to Jesus' hearers in the neighborhood of Jordan where John originally baptized: "John did no miracle; but all things that John spake of this man were true."[43] It is apparent from this point that, not only were John and Jesus distinguished from each other in the public mind, but that what the Baptist had said of Jesus was remembered by many who had heard and seen both.

We can but conclude that any mystification which arose on the subject was confined to circles which had hitherto paid little attention to either—namely, the worldly and cynical society of Herod's provincial court, and perhaps also a few isolated centers whose inhabitants were too poor or too indifferent to travel far to listen to the Master or behold His works. And any one who knows how easily the superstitious and ignorant folk of the near East jump to conclusions on a subject of this kind will not be surprised that with the disappearance of John from the scene they should soon have forgotten to ask whether Jesus began to preach before or after the death of His great contemporary. One thing is indisputable, and that is that Jesus had a

[43] John x. 41.

considerable vogue while John was still alive and in prison; but, as will be remembered, He did not begin to preach in Galilee until John's public ministry was at an end. Herod's superstitious fears and guilty conscience are enough to account for the apprehension attributed to him, that perhaps the man of God whom he had slain had returned to life and freedom.

CHAPTER IX

THE CULMINATING PERIOD OF THE MINISTRY

Jesus' Relations with His Family

Several developments occur about this time which require special attention. One of these is that while Jesus was still instructing the twelve in a house before sending them forth, the multitude thronged in upon them in such wise that there was no opportunity for privacy. The summer school in the Galilean hills was now over, but apparently the people were not disposed to lose sight of their teacher. The inference from the text is that the house in question was still Jesus' own or at least the one in which He was accustomed to reside at Capernaum. This being so, the next sentence, peculiar to Mark, is specially striking: "And when His friends"—that is, kindred—"heard of it, they went out to lay hold on him: for they said, he is beside himself." [1] Who were these relations of His who thus took such drastic action? Are we to identify them with the mother and brethren men-

[1] Mark iii. 21.

tioned later in the same chapter as seeking speech
with Him? It may be so, but equally it may not.
The point is worth making, if only that it frees
Mary from the imputation of joining in the attempt
to put physical constraint upon her son. St. John
tells us that at this period His brethren had not yet
come to believe in Him, whatever that may mean.
The remark is made in a connection which suggests
that they believed He had certain supernatural
gifts which might be turned to profit, but not that
He Himself was what His resurrection afterwards
proved Him to be. He and they had other kindred in Galilee; perhaps it was these who, under
the influence or at the bidding of the synagogue
authorities, took measures to have Him sequestered
for a time in order that the dangerous excitement
provoked by His action might die away; they may
have been apprehensive for their own safety with
the authorities if He were allowed to continue unchecked. Did they bring pressure to bear upon
Mary and her stepsons to this end? The latter
may not have needed much pressure, but that it
was made is the obvious explanation of the fact that
Mark leaves a certain interval between the statement that an actual attempt was made to seize Him,
and, that this, presumably, having failed, His
mother and His brethren later tried to obtain access
to Him, perhaps with the object of warning Him
that He could not continue in His present course
without peril to Himself and the family. All that is
said here is that they desired speech with Him and
could not get near Him because of the crowd. It

does not say that they succeeded in reaching Him, nor does it say that if they had done so they would have taken a hostile attitude; that thef were opposed to Him is only an inference from what is stated in John vii and in the Marcan passage above quoted, that His kindred wished to place Him under restraint.

There is, however, another passage which suggests that there was some estrangement at this time between Jesus and those to whom He was allied by blood, and that is the pathetic observation made in answer to a certain scribe who impulsively announced his readiness to follow the Master whithersoever He went. "And Jesus saith unto him, The foxes have holes, and the birds of the air have nests; but the Son of Man hath not where to lay his head." [2] This does not belong to the Marcan tradition, but to the source already referred to as common to Matthew and Luke. It can only mean that Jesus was now cut off from His early home and domestic associations, whether of Nazareth or Capernaum or both. The synagogue may have taken drastic action and compelled this virtual excommunication after the feast in Matthew's house. That Jesus felt bitterly this want of sympathy on the part of those nearest to him in family relationship is unquestionable. Actually He had plenty of places wherein to lay His head; there was no lack of hospitality for Him; but He was spiritually homeless, exiled, outcast, bereft of what was once the background of His life, and He was human

[2] Matt. viii. 20; Luke ix. 58.

enough to be very sad and sorrowful on account of
it. This is one of the many little glimpses in the
gospels that, as time drew on and Jesus' pathway
darkened, He became more and more lonely and
isolated from His fellows. Metaphorically speaking, He had nowhere to lay His head; there was
no one to whom He could go for perfect sympathy
and understanding, and He longed for both as is
evident, for example, and most movingly, in His
request for companionship in His last dread vigil
in Gethsemane. Was it because of this growing
sense of isolation, following upon His expulsion
from synagogue circles and the temporary opposition of His family, that Jesus uttered the saying
reported in more than one connection, "A prophet
is not without honor, but in his own country, and
among his own kin, and in his own house"?[3]

How far did Mary share the family attitude at
this time? There is nothing to show, save this one
intimation that she appeared with the brothers on
the occasion reported above. If these brothers were
really her stepsons they may have persuaded her
to come along with them in order that she might use
her gentle influence to withdraw Jesus from the
course on which He had embarked. No doubt, as
aforesaid, they were afraid for themselves and their
fortunes.[4] She, motherlike, was afraid for her son
and wanted to screen Him from danger. Even this
is more than is explicitly stated, for the evangelists'
bare remark that they wanted to speak to Him is

[3] Matt. xiii. 57; Mark vi. 4; Luke iv. 24; John iv. 44.
[4] So Oskar Holtzmann: *Life of Jesus*, p. 248.

not a definite declaration that they wanted to silence Him: still it is a legitimate inference, especially considering the circumstances, for at the moment of their arrival the antagonism between Him and the religious authorities had become acute.

But His reception of His mother's request sounds harsh and unnatural if we have regard to its face value only. Apparently He paid no heed to it, but instead went on to say with hand outstretched towards His disciples, "Behold my mother and my brethren! For whosoever shall do the will of God, the same is my brother, and my sister, and mother." [5] But we should be doing an injustice to one of the most instructive episodes in the whole gospel story if we were to accept this interpretation as complete and sufficient. These words were no repudiation of relationship but the exact contrary. With that readiness to seize hold of homely and familiar illustrations of spiritual truth which always characterized His teaching, Jesus said in effect: Who is my mother? You all know what motherhood means; how close, how dear, how unforfeitable the relationship between mother and son; many of you know of the love that exists between me and my own mother. What is brotherhood? You know of the special bond it makes, how unbreakable despite all differences of feeling and outlook between those born of the same parents; friendship may fade and perish, but brotherhood cannot be utterly repudiated. Sisters? Is there any man here who would not cherish his sister or feel no sense of obligation for her safety

[5] Mark iii. 34, 35. *Cf.* Matt. xii. 49, 50; Luke viii. 21.

and welfare? Behold then the bond that unites me to all seekers after God. They belong to me and I to them with an even higher affinity than these earthly relationships. They are as brothers and sisters to me; yea, I feel towards the aspiring soul a respect akin to that which I feel for my dear mother. If these domestic ties are so sacramental in their operation, what of the ties between soul and soul on the highest plane of all?

It is indeed perilous to attempt to state in modern everyday phraseology what we may reverently believe to have been our Master's meaning in His use of the words above quoted, but can it have been other than this? Was it not an attempt to convey by means of a felicitous allusion to the dearest earthly relationships some consciousness of what fellowship must be between spirit and spirit in God's eternal Kingdom? Moreover, it is nowhere stated that Jesus here refused to see His kinsfolk or hold intercourse with them. The evangelists do not record the fact one way or the other, for the reason that their interest was centered in the striking saying which all the synoptics preserve and of which this meeting was the occasion.

The Warning against Blasphemy

It is now, as stated above, that the opposition of the scribes and Pharisees to Jesus becomes overt and uncompromising. The evangelists show that it was the scribes who came down from Jerusalem who took the lead in this, and it is noteworthy that it was so. From the first, our Lord's appearances in Jerusalem gave rise to sharp controversy and were evidently followed by visits, more or less continuous, of representatives of the Judean Pharisees to Galilee to keep watch upon His movements, and no friendly watch. It was these men who are said to have declared that He cast out devils through the prince of the devils. Matthew records this saying twice; no doubt it was made many times. On this occasion it drew from the Master the impressive warning: "He that shall blaspheme against the Holy Ghost hath never forgiveness, but is in danger of eternal damnation." [6] This is a saying which has caused much perplexity and not a little misgiving to many simple souls; but its meaning is not far to seek. Jesus here expressly distinguishes between honest opposition to Himself and a malicious hypocrisy which refuses to recognize the presence and working of the Spirit of God. These accusers well knew that what they were witnessing of the fruits of Jesus' healing ministry could not be evil, yet out of their hatred for Him they pretended it was; they knew it was of God, yet willfully declared it to be of the devil. Jesus, therefore, gravely pointed out the danger in which they stood; they were running the risk of quenching the Spirit, their only hope of attaining to God and goodness.

There is nothing arbitrary about the sentence here defined; they were sentencing themselves by their course of action. There is no mystery about the character of the sin against the Holy Ghost.

[6] Mark iii. 29; Matt. xii. 31; Luke xii. 10.

THE CULMINATING PERIOD

No one has ever yet committed it irretrievably who remained in grief and trouble about his spiritual condition thereafter. The truth is that, as Harriet Auber's well-known hymn has it, the Holy Ghost is the source of every good in us:

> And every virtue we possess,
> And every conquest won,
> And every thought of holiness,
> Are His alone.

What then must be the result of resisting the work of the Spirit of God in our hearts? Inevitably that in time He will let us alone. A sinner may suffer from the prickings of conscience for a time, but if he persists in his sin he will become hardened and irresponsive to the monitions of the Spirit. He can commit transgressions by and by without the qualm that at first would have made him wretched in his self-reproach. This is a terrible fact, but is only the operation of a law which is quite understandable. A man who calls good evil and evil good, or deliberately and continuously denies what he knows to be the truth about God's will, is like a traveler going to sleep in the snow; it is the sleep of death. Literally construed, our Lord's words were the enunciation of this law: "Whosoever shall blaspheme against the Holy Spirit hath not forgiveness, but is guilty of (or in peril of) an eternal (or age-long) sin." It is not a question of damnation—the word damnation is not used—but of the sin itself; this *is* damnation.

THE LIFE OF CHRIST

Jesus' Power over the External World

We come now to the consideration of a group of
nature miracles said to belong to this period of the
ministry, and which are full of difficulty to the
modern mind. The first of these is the stilling of
a tempest on the Sea of Galilee, a story which has
its parallel in that of the walking on the sea as recorded, not only by the synoptics, but also by the
fourth gospel. Luke records the former but not
the latter miracle; John has the latter but not the
former; Matthew and Mark give both. Mark says
the occasion was after the deliverance of the parables of the sower and the grain of mustard seed—
on the same day, to be precise—whereas Matthew
places it in a different connection. Jesus, as was
His frequent custom, had been teaching with a
boat for a pulpit, his congregation sitting and
standing on the seashore. At the conclusion of His
discourse He asked those with Him to cross to the
other side of the lake. This was in order that He
might escape the crowd and secure some rest; it was
getting towards evening. Being exhausted with
His labors He fell asleep in the after part of the
boat with His head on some sort of a pillow, furnished doubtless by the solicitude of one of His
followers. Was there a woman's touch here? It
is not a far-fetched inference, for it is in association
with this series of incidents that Luke introduces
a remark not mentioned by the others, namely, that
certain women whom He had healed of various in-
firmities were of the company of His disciples as

He went from village to village preaching, and that these "ministered to Him of their substance." [7] They included some persons of good position such as Joanna the wife of Chuza, Herod's steward. Mary Magdalene was also included in the number, and the evangelist states that there were many others. It is a reasonable supposition that there was a feminine touch about the little attention to His comfort indicated in the addition of a pillow to the furniture of the fishing boat from which He had been speaking all day; pillows were not a feature then any more than now of fishing boats cruising along the lake shore.

While they were still in the act of crossing the lake, one of the sudden and violent storms sprang up for which that peculiar expanse of water is still noted, but so deep was the Master's slumber that it did not awaken Him, notwithstanding the pitching and tossing of the boat. They were in danger of being swamped, for Mark says "the waves beat into the ship, so that it was now full." [8] We gather from the description that all happened very quickly, as is quite probable,[9] and that believing themselves to be in imminent peril of their lives, the men with Him in the boat—who they were is not stated—rushed to Him panic-stricken, and awakening Him cried out: "Master, carest thou not that we perish?" [10] Matthew gives the prayer as "Lord, save us, we perish." [11] The same evangelist adds

[7] Luke viii. 3.   [8] Mark iv. 37.

[9] The Sea of Galilee is noted for the same characteristic to this day.

[10] Mark iv. 38.   [11] Matt. viii. 25.

that His first words were: "Why are ye fearful, O ye of little faith?" There are interesting variations in detail in the several accounts of the synoptics, but all agree on the main facts. This is an instance of the way in which a well-established tradition was reduced to writing from word of mouth. The story was generally accepted in apostolic circles and universally known, hence the mutual independence of the narratives in their mode of relating what happened, and their substantial agreement in essentials. They all state that He rose and stilled the tempest by an authoritative command. Those present do not seem to have expected this or anything like it, for Mark adds that "they feared exceedingly, and said one to another, What manner of man is this, that even the wind and the sea obey him?"

Here we have an occurrence almost incredible from the standpoint of ordinary experience to-day. The healing ministry is admissible with reservations, for we are not unfamiliar with similar phenomena at the present day, but there is no parallel to this exhibition of power over nature.[12] Hence there are many persons, and not wholly among men of scientific training, who would draw sharp distinction between this kind of wonder-working, and, say, the cure of an epileptic

[12] "The force He embodied could hardly be denied a physical expression. It was no more extraordinary to have miraculous power over nature than to have miraculous power over men. Miracles of sense are no more supernatural than miracles of spirit. . . . It had rather surprised us had one whose position is so pre-eminent in man and history been feeble and commonplace in relation to nature and action." Fairbairn: *Studies in the Life of Christ*, p. 158.

by touch and spoken word. It is thought, and with some plausibility, that this class of miracle may be in the main figurative and meant, in oriental fashion, to have a spiritual significance rather than to be a relation of literal fact. And the spiritual use of the incident is obvious. It is that which is commonly made in its Christian associations.

> So, when our life is clouded o'er,
> And storm-winds drift us from the shore,
> Say, lest we sink to rise no more,
>   "Peace, be still."

But a warning needs to be entered against a too ready acceptance of this explanation. The distinction thus noted between the different classes of miracle is not made in the gospels themselves. The utmost that we are entitled to say is that perhaps the narrators were not unconscious of the spiritual parallel that such a story as this at once suggests to modern readers. As we have seen, it is St. John's method to give to every miracle a parabolic use; and to an extent this may have been in the minds of the other evangelists also. But we must beware of concluding that the story itself and others like it are merely metaphorical. Let us not lose sight of the point of view with which we began, that from a transcendent person we may expect transcendent facts. A mighty being, belonging essentially to the supernatural order, must be credited with a mastery over the natural order such as the rest of us, conditioned entirely by the latter, can neither possess nor understand.

But now follows an even more perplexing episode. Arrived at the other side of the lake, in the territory of the Gadarenes or Gergesenes, Jesus healed a demoniac, a raving madman, who lived among the tombs apart from human habitation. Like many madmen, he was possessed of almost superhuman strength. All attempts to put him under restraint had failed; even chains were insufficient to bind him, he had always got away. This weird creature was an object of terror to the neighborhood. "And always, night and day, he was in the mountains and in the tombs, crying, and cutting himself with stones." [13] Matthew says there were two of these dangerous lunatics "exceeding fierce, so that no man might pass by that way;" [14] Mark and Luke only mention one. Possibly one was spokesman and more aggressive than his afflicted companion. What is most striking about the incident is that the poor creature, or rather the evil being possessing him, is said to have saluted Jesus in terms which had not hitherto been employed by any one: "What have I to do with thee, Jesus, thou Son of the most high God?" [15] Matthew adds the question, "Art thou come hither to torment us before the time?" [16] Here again we have the suggestion that evil spirits knew more of the Master's heavenly dignity than did His contemporaries on earth. Another curious feature of the narrative is that Jesus asked the name of this possessing entity and was told that it was Legion, for there were

[13] Mark v. 5.
[14] Matt. viii. 28.
[15] Mark v. 7.
[16] Matt. viii. 29.

many of them. Most remarkable of all was their prayer that if they must be cast out of the human body they had invaded they might be allowed to enter into a herd of swine feeding near by. Jesus granted the prayer, with the result that the swine immediately rushed down the slope into the lake and were drowned. Mark says there were two thousand of them, so the loss to their owners must have been considerable. The terrified keepers of the herd promptly rushed off to the city with the tidings, whereupon the inhabitants flocked out to Jesus in great fear and begged Him to go away out of their land. This was an unusual request so far as Jesus was concerned and no doubt prompted by the general apprehension excited by the destruction of the herd of swine, and is in striking contrast with the welcome said to have been accorded to the Master directly afterwards on the farther side of the lake whence He had come. "And it came to pass, that when Jesus was returned, the people gladly received him: for they were all waiting for him." [17] These people of Gadara, if Gadara it were, could not have known the Master as people did on the Galilean side of the lake, though they must previously have heard much of Him, as is evidenced by the statement that persons from Decapolis were amongst His hearers in Galilee. They acted under the influence of fear in entreating Him to go away, and under the circumstances the fear was not unnatural.[18] The amazing spectacle of the recovered demoniac sitting at Jesus' feet "clothed

[17] Luke viii. 40.   [18] These were a non-Jewish people.

and in his right mind" did not, perhaps, impress them so much as their own personal loss. Be that as it may, Jesus granted their request and, entering again with His followers into the boat, went back to the Capernaum shore. The ex-demoniac begged earnestly to be allowed to accompany Him, but Jesus refused, bidding him, instead, go and tell his friends and neighbors what great things God had done for him. This he did forthwith in all the Decapolis region.

From the advice thus given, as well as from the admission of the twelve, it is apparent that by this time Jesus was at less pains to keep His miracles from public notice. At first it was His habit to request His beneficiaries not to draw attention to what He had wrought on their behalf, but as they generally paid no heed, and as public interest grew in consequence, and many of His most notable works of healing were performed on public occasions and in the presence of the religious authorities, there could be little point in concealing them any longer. His object in doing so at all could have been no other than the wish to avoid the concentration of public interest on the miracles to the exclusion of the teaching. That there was danger of this is evident throughout, but that the teaching also made its due impression is equally clear from what is elsewhere recorded. After the delivery of the Teaching on the Hill there could no longer be any question of the teaching being submerged by the demand for signs and wonders. It is not stated that any miracle was performed during the days, or more probably weeks, during which the open-air school was held in the Galilean uplands. Again and again also the multitudes flocked to hear Him as He taught them by parable on the lake shore.

No miracle has excited such adverse and even scornful comment as this of the destruction of the Gadarene swine. It is the nearest approach in the evangelical narrative to the type of miracle related in the apocryphal gospels, wherein a nonethical and even nonbenevolent motive is frequently suggested. That there is much that is perplexing about it cannot be gainsaid, but in the absence of full information we must be content to leave it a mystery. If demon possession is to be accepted as a fact, and no one who knows the evidence will dispute it, there is no reason to doubt that inferior creatures can occasionally be so possessed as well as human beings. It is less likely, for human beings frequently open the door to this distressing affliction by their own vices, and discarnate spirits would naturally prefer human organisms to those of the lower animals. Wicked and degraded spirits— earthbound as they are called—are said to seek every opportunity of gratifying sensual appetites, and their own means of doing so is to obtain control, partially or completely, of the bodies of beings still in the flesh and whose habits are in affinity with their own. This is a serious danger attending the practice of necromancy, and the principal reason why the Church discourages it. And it is no imaginary danger, as many inquirers into the operation of abnormal psychical and physiological developments can testify. Nor do those who give rein to their passions unchecked generally realize the risk they are running from the same source.[19]

The third of this group of nature miracles is the feeding of the five thousand. Properly speaking, it belongs to a somewhat later period, namely, the return of the apostles from their mission to the cities of Israel, but may very well be considered here. It is full of intense human interest, an interest so closely interwoven with the details of the entire episode that the two cannot be separated, notwithstanding the difficulties of the narrative. The story appears in all four of the evangelists, John, as usual, turning it to spiritual account. It is hopeless to seek to reconcile the several versions chronologically. Mark's, which is followed by Luke, makes the event the sequel to the apostles' report of their doings during their itinerary, and this seems the most probable. John gives it no particular connection at all; Matthew subjoins it to his account of the death of John the Baptist. Mark's, besides being the oldest, is certainly the most suitable setting for the event and is told with an artless verisimilitude which is convincing. Matthew does not actually contradict him, but misses the association of the sequence of incidents with the ending of the mission of the twelve. The second evangelist tells us that the Master, solicitous for the welfare of these friends and workers of His,

[19] R. H. Benson's *Necromancers* illustrates a peril of obsession which is not imaginary. *Vide* Myers' important section on the subject in *Human Personality and Its Survival of Bodily Death*, Vol. II.

bade them come with Him to a desert place and rest awhile; for, he significantly adds, "there were many coming and going, and they had no leisure so much as to eat." [20] Luke emphasizes Jesus' motive in doing this, for this evangelist states that Jesus took them privately into the hinterland of Bethsaida, a piece of rough, sparsely inhabited country some distance behind the city. He knew that they needed rest and refreshment both of mind and body, a fact which ought to be borne in mind by all spiritual workers. To serve the world effectually, we must retire from the world periodically to remake our souls, as it were. There must be a period of taking in as well as giving out; spiritual poverty and fussy activity frequently go together. It is impossible to work effectually for God without being much alone for necessary spiritual infilling. Our Master knew this so well that He was careful to secure His periodical escapes from the wear and tear and exhaustion of His public ministry in order that He might commune in secret with His heavenly Father.

In this instance His benevolent object was temporarily frustrated. He and His followers departed in a fishing boat towards the northeast coast of the Galilean lake, but the multitude observed them going and rushed after them along the shore. In that magical way in which news travels among comparatively unsophisticated peoples, a knowledge of Jesus' advent at once preceded Him into the district whither He had temporarily retired.

[20] Mark vi. 31.

Mark says: "And the people saw them departing, and many knew Him, and ran afoot thither out of all cities, and outwent them, and came together unto Him." [21] What we are meant to understand is that somehow the inhabitants of the territory round about this desert region, being thus informed of the Master's whereabouts, flocked towards Him again. Jesus had not the heart to send them away. The evangelists say that He was moved with compassion towards them, because they were as sheep not having a shepherd; so the teaching and healing ministry went on as before. At length, as the day was drawing to a close, the apostles suggested to their Master that He should send the people away to the farms and villages round about to obtain food for themselves, as they had nothing to eat. To their surprise He answered, "Give ye them to eat." John's version represents Philip and Andrew as taking the lead in the matter, as is natural when we remember the association of these two men with that particular locality. He also gives a different antecedent to the suggestion that Jesus should send the people away. It is the Master Himself who puts the first question, "Whence shall we buy bread that these may eat?" [22] The apostles who belonged to the neighborhood of Bethsaida might be supposed to know whither to direct them or where supplies might be secured. The question seems to have been addressed to Philip merely in order to elicit the reply which followed. Philip answered that it was an impossibility to obtain sufficient food in that remote spot for so large a number of mouths, even if they had the means wherewith to purchase it, which they had not. "Two hundred pennyworth of bread," he observed, "is not sufficient for them, that every one of them may take a little." "There is a lad here," put in Peter's brother Andrew, "which hath five barley loaves, and two small fishes; but what are they among so many?" This is a fuller statement of the facts than the other evangelists give, but amounts to much the same thing. Mark furnishes the additional detail that it was in response to a suggestion from Jesus Himself that Andrew gave this report of their meager resources. "He saith unto them, How many loaves have ye? go and see. And when they knew, they say, Five, and two fishes." [23] Jesus then directed the twelve to make the people sit down in ordered ranks of hundreds and fifties, the better to facilitate distribution. This done, He took the loaves, blessed them, and went on breaking and handing to the apostles, who, in their turn, passed along the ranks, giving the bread to the people. It is said that they ate and were fully satisfied, and that the number thus miraculously fed was about five thousand men besides women and children. There were twelve basketsful carefully collected afterwards of the fragments that remained.

Mark introduces a picturesque detail into this narrative which is absent from the others, namely, that the sitting multitude was so arranged on the

[23] Mark vi. 38.

green grass by the Lord's command as to look like
a vast garden of flowers. This is the force of the
wording of the Greek original in which the story
comes from his pen. [24] It would be a most striking
spectacle, and Mark's figure aptly describes it. So
large an assembly, in the bright, variegated attire
of orientals then as now, so placed in companies of
about equal size as to leave room for the apostles
to pass easily up and down between them, would
look very much like a great garden filled with many-
colored flowers. That the grass was still green, as
Mark alone is also careful to inform us, would add
to the beauty of the setting—a never-to-be-forgot-
ten panorama. Are we not once more listening to
Peter's vivid reminiscences, so characteristic of
the quality of mind of the impulsive apostle as revealed over and over again in the New Testament?

Some difficulty presents itself in respect of the
locality where this miracle could have taken place.
Luke says that it was not far from Bethsaida; Mark
says that the voyage which followed, and which
Luke does not mention, was to have been "unto
Bethsaida." The discrepancy is not serious, however. Both statements could have been literally
correct. What does seem to have happened, in any
case, is that the landing afterwards was not at
Bethsaida, but somewhere farther on, the little sailing boat having been blown out of its course.

The historicity of the miracle has been much discussed, together with that of the feeding of the four
thousand elsewhere recorded. It has been sug-

[24] *Ibid.* 39.

gested that the whole episode is figurative and meant to denote the feeding of the Church with the bread of life, the apostles being the Lord's appointed representatives who take the heavenly food from His divine hands and administer it to His hungering flock. This interpretation receives some support from the synoptic wording of the Master's command, "Give ye them to eat," and is obviously true in the spiritual sense. St. John carries the similitude farther, for he reports a conversation between Jesus and some of His hearers at Capernaum on the subject a little later, in which the Master exhorts them to labor not for the meat which perisheth, but for that which endureth unto eternal life." "I am the bread of life," He added; "he that cometh to me shall never hunger; and he that believeth on me shall never thirst." [25] On the other hand, it should be noted that this is the only miracle related by all the four evangelists, and hence may be assumed to have been regarded in apostolic times as not only one of the most memorable but one of the best authenticated, and there is no suggestion in any of the several narratives from first to last that it was of purely spiritual significance and without historical foundation; at least it would be unwarrantable to assume as much.

Further, the fourth gospel, which gives to it a direct spiritual application, is also careful to distinguish between its literal and spiritual aspects. Thus, the Master is shown as indicating that the very people whom He had thus benefited had

[25] John vi. 35.

failed to appreciate the deeper meaning of His words and works. "Ye seek me," He said, "not because ye saw the miracles"—literally, the signs, not miracles in the strict sense of the term—"but because ye did eat of the loaves and were filled." [26] It was from the standpoint of this rebuke that He proceeded to exhort them to eat of the true bread which came down from heaven, and so perplexing did His words become to their materialistic apprehension that He caused some of them thereby to forsake Him. "Whoso eateth my flesh, and drinketh my blood," He declared, "hath eternal life." [27] "Many, therefore, of His disciples, when they heard this, said, "This is an hard saying: Who can hear it?" They did not understand this spiritual feeding and assimilation, though they had seen and were quite willing to profit by the marvelous power over nature recently exhibited by the speaker in the satisfying of their creature wants. "From that time," adds the evangelist, "many of his disciples went back and walked no more with him." [28] Strange indeed! and clear evidence, if such were needed, that the public saw no necessary association between wonder-working and spiritual eminence. That the apostles were able to see more in Jesus than the rest of His contemporaries is their chief title to respect and justifies their vocation. They were susceptible to His spiritual appeal, and most others were not; it was for this that they adhered to Him as is impressively brought out in this same connection. "Then said Jesus unto the

[26] *Ibid.* 26. [27] *Ibid.* 54. [28] *Ibid.* 66.

twelve, Will ye also go away? Then Simon Peter answered him, Lord, to whom shall we go? Thou hast the words of eternal life." [29] In the authorized version of the New Testament the declaration is added, "And we believe and are sure that thou art the Christ, the Son of the living God." [30] But the rendering of the best Mss. is, "We have believed and know that thou art the Holy One of God," which is not quite so definite. The time for the definite declaration at Cæsarea Philippi already referred to in advance had not yet arrived.

Events developed as follows. From the experiences of this busy and exhausting day it was now evident that Jesus' considerate intention of securing a period of privacy and repose for His weary apostles would be rendered ineffective unless He could adopt some other measures. He had tried to get them away by themselves to rest, and the only result of His effort thus far had been to burden and tax them more than ever. This was no rest; it was continuous and exacting labor. So He adopted a new course to meet the exigency thus created. It is Mark, as usual, who shows us how it was done and gives us a tender and illuminating flash of insight into the Master's sympathetic purpose and thoughtful care for His overworked friends. He says, "He constrained His disciples to get into the ship, and to go to the other side before unto Bethsaida, while He sent away the people." [31] He knew the people would not follow the disciples so long as He was there; He wanted these

29 *Ibid.* 68.   30 *Ibid.* 69.   31 Matt. xiv. 22; Mark vi. 45.

to get away in peace, so He forced them to go and
leave Him to deal with the crowd—such is the implication of Mark's use of the term "constrained,"
and the motive thereof is perfectly apparent. The
sentence is a beautiful sidelight upon the Master's
methods with those about Him and His wise and
watchful solicitude for their needs. Having seen
the little boat off with His friends safely inside it,
He retired by Himself towards a height overlooking the lake, forbidding any one to accompany
Him. He wanted to be alone and pray. The people apparently concluded that they would see Him
again on the morrow; they assumed that He could
not depart from that desolate region without their
knowing it; so no doubt they composed themselves
to slumber under the open Galilean sky, waiting
and hoping for a renewal the next day of the wonders to which they were now becoming accustomed
at the hands of this marvelous being. John says
the miracle of the loaves had convinced them—those
who needed convincing—"that this was the prophet
that should come into the world." [32] He also leads
us to infer that some exciting scenes took place after
the departure of the apostles in their fishing boat—
perhaps even before; a good deal of the narrative
needs to be filled in here. After that wonderful
meal in the desert the enthusiasm of the crowd
mounted high, and it does not require much imagination to picture what ensued. Filled with astonishment, they surged hither and thither over the plain,
chattering, gesticulating, vehemently urging each

[32] John vi. 14.

other on to take some action which would enable them to make the most of the opportunity that had come to them in the person of Jesus. Jesus in the meanwhile was pressing His disciples to depart; they had some distance to go, judging by John's way of relating the event; and as they went down to the sea by one way Jesus began to withdraw by another. Now came some sort of crisis. Some of the bolder spirits in the promiscuous assembly wanted to seize Him and proclaim Him king forthwith, whether He was willing or not. Jesus perceived this, says the fourth evangelist, took His way up into the hills as the shadows fell, leaving His would-be subjects still discussing Him on the ground where the miracle had been performed. They waited, but He did not come back; and when they met Him again—for some of the same company appear to have done so in Capernaum shortly afterwards—it was with utmost curiosity to know how He had managed to transport Himself from one district to another without their being aware of the fact or following His movements.

We may interject a question here. Was it as the sequel of the excited discussions here indicated, culminating in the sudden scheme to put Him forcibly at the head of a revolutionary movement, that Jesus afterwards asked the twelve, "Whom say the people that I am?" [33] which was the immediate occasion of Peter's dramatic confession of His Messianic status? Luke inserts it immediately after the feeding of the five thousand, which would al-

[33] Matt. xvi. 13; Mark viii. 27; Luke ix. 18.

most suggest that the two events had some association. Mark, on the other hand, places it later, and records the second feeding, this time of four thousand, as having taken place in between. The question is worth asking, but little more. There must have been about this period a great deal of animated speculation concerning the problem who or what Jesus was and what mission He had come to fulfill. No one, apparently, outside the apostolic circle thought of Him as the Messiah in the fullest sense of the term. Even had they proclaimed Him king the act would not necessarily have had any Messianic implications. He would not have been the only Jewish adventurer to head a revolt against Roman authority.

But to return to the sequence of events—Matthew and Mark state that when He had sent the multitudes away He withdrew to a mountain adjoining to pray, and was there alone when night fell. This dismissal of the crowd may only have been, as above suggested, a refusal to allow them to follow Him or place Him under any sort of constraint; He sent them from His presence for the time being, and they, perhaps, were content enough to have it so at such an advanced hour of the evening when doubtless all were more or less weary; any plans they might form could wait till daylight for execution. But as Jesus knelt on His solitary eminence overlooking the sea, He became aware that all was not going well with the twelve in their fishing boat. A wind had sprung up and was blowing hard against them. They had low-

ered their sail and taken to oars, and still made
very little progress. It was hard work after such
a tiring day, and to add to their difficulties darkness had descended before they had gone more than
a mile or two. How late it was before they started
we do not know, but at past three in the morning
they were still tossing between twenty-five and
thirty furlongs from the shore whence they had set
out. Instantly the Master's compassion awoke on
their behalf. He must go to them, but how? There
was only one way. He arose and walked straight
towards the point where they lay battling against
wind and wave, passing over the sea as easily as
over the land. Again it is to Mark that we owe
the statement of the motive for this prodigy: it was
because He *saw* them in difficulties that He came
thus unexpectedly to their aid. The evangelist adds
that He made as though He would pass by them [34]
—not that He intended to do so, but possibly to
reassure them by thus revealing His presence in
the midst of the storm. But it had the opposite
effect; they were frightened, supposing Him to be
an apparition, and uttered cries of alarm. "And
immediately He talked with them"—a humanly
suggestive phrase—"and saith unto them, Be of
good cheer"—literally, Courage!—"It is I; be not
afraid." [35] Following upon His words He ascended
into the boat and joined them, and instantly the
wind ceased. John adds the further detail that
immediately the ship was at the land whither they
went.

[34] Mark vi. 48.   [35] *Ibid.* 50.

Matthew records a further touching incident in this connection which greatly increases the interest thereof, and to which the others make no reference. Before Jesus came into the boat, when His voice was first heard out in the darkness and the storm, Peter answered Him and said, "Lord, if it be thou, bid me come unto thee on the water." [36] The Master complied with the suggestion, and Peter leaped from the boat to join Him on the deep. For a brief moment the apostle was able to maintain his footing by virtue of his faith in Jesus, but the raging of the elements speedily daunted him, and, overcome with terror, he began to sink, crying, "Lord, save me." Hardly was the prayer uttered ere Jesus had caught hold of him, saying as He did so, "O thou of little faith, wherefore didst thou doubt?" It is the first evangelist also who tells us that when Peter and his Master had together come into the boat, all on board prostrated themselves before Jesus, saluting Him as Son of God. Here again it should be noted that though the form of address is an acknowledgment of supernatural status on the part of Him thus designated, there is no explicit association of the words with Messiahship. Jesus is here called Son of God in much the same sense as the description was afterwards applied to Him by the Roman centurion at the crucifixion: "Certainly this was a righteous man"; [37] "truly this was a Son of God." [38] We must not read into the term the full significance that it now possesses for Christian faith. It was an indeterminate recognition of the divine

[36] Matt. xiv. 28.   [37] Luke xxiii. 47.   [38] Matt. xxvii.54.

power inherent in Jesus and whose wondrous exercise they had just witnessed.

What are we to say to these nature miracles? They stand on a different footing from the miracles of healing—or so it has often been maintained. To say the least, they are much more difficult of credence, without parallel in our experience at the present day, and at first sight bear a strong resemblance to the many wonder-stories related of mythical personages in various periods. It is quite possible to construe them as having a symbolical meaning, as we have already seen; indeed, we are accustomed so to construe them in our devotional usage. It may be—and there is no special reason to resist the conclusion—that this story of the Master walking on the sea is a beautiful parable of the apostolic age relating to the early experiences of the Christian Church when exposed to persecution and the danger of being destroyed altogether while still but a small and frail bark sailing the sea of earthly life. The Master watches from above and comes to the rescue at the darkest hour. Peter's impulsive action—again so characteristic of the first of the apostles!—in flinging himself into the sea to join his Master in the very heart of the tempest certainly happened in the first heroic age of the Church's life when he took all risks for his Master's name rather than shelter himself by keeping silent as he had been bidden to do by the authorities of his own nation. "Whether it be right in the sight of God to hearken unto you more than unto God, judge ye," he declared, "for we cannot but

speak the things which we have seen and heard." [39]
Here he was leaping into the boiling sea at his
Master's command in very deed, and even inviting
that command. Moreover, tradition has it, that at
Rome during the early days of persecution, in almost the last hour of Peter's life, he suffered himself to be persuaded to seek safety in flight, but
was compelled by a dream, in which he saw his
Master preparing to take His place on the cross,
to change his mind and accept martyrdom. Nor
need we go even as far as this for an explanation
of the miracle in a symbolical sense. All the above
was fulfilled when Peter vehemently protested his
loyalty in the upper room on the night of the betrayal—"I am ready to go with thee both into prison
and unto death" [40]—and then failed his Lord when
the testing time came, but was afterwards recovered
by the tender grasp of that mighty hand which he
had abandoned to the cruel nails.

This, we repeat, may be the true interpretation
of this suggestive miracle, and there would be nothing lost by accepting it as the only one. But is not
the truth rather to be sought in a combination of
the literal with the metaphorical? It is not the
fourth gospel only that employs historical facts
for the purpose of enforcing a spiritual lesson; the
other gospels do it also, particularly the first; in
fact, they could hardly help doing so with what is
here so felicitously implied. And, what is more, it
seems to the present writer that this was one object
with which Jesus performed His miracles in the

[39] Acts iv. 19, 20.   [40] Luke xxii. 33.

first place. Were not many of them, perhaps most of them, acted parables? Did He not look ahead and see the day coming when the spiritual bearing of much that He was doing would be remembered when His visible presence would be with His own on earth no more? It seems impossible to come to any other conclusion with the facts before us. But this is very different from saying that there was no historical foundation for these nature miracles, and, oddly enough, in this instance it is the fourth gospel which refrains from giving the story a spiritual application; as that had already been done by Matthew, by implication at least, the writer probably thought it unnecessary to follow suit: he contents himself with recording the actual event like the others. We are meant to understand that it certainly took place, that the physical body of Jesus did walk the waves of the sea of Galilee and entered the storm-tossed fishing boat in which His disciples toiled and feared, just as in all the years ensuing His spiritual presence has been with His Church on the stormy sea of human life.

Nor is such a miracle as completely without parallel in the modern world as is commonly taken for granted. This was an example of the phenomenon known as levitation, a phenomenon as fully attested as any of the supernormal manifestations of human faculty. The ascension was another, as we shall see in due course. Let those who doubt the possibility of levitation acquaint themselves with the evidence. It is a proved fact, not only of certain saints in an ecstatic condition, but of some in our own day who are not credited with being saints.[41]

It is worthy of note that, whereas the disciples had set sail towards Bethsaida, according to Mark —that is, perhaps a comparatively short distance from where they embarked—John says towards Capernaum, which was farther on. But Matthew and Mark both say that they landed on the coast of Gennesaret, which was farther on still. Apparently the storm had carried them out of their course, so that Jesus' intervention was not without good reason and may have been necessary to save their lives. The dwellers in that region immediately knew Him and flocked to Him in crowds, as was now usual everywhere, bringing their sick on beds that He might heal them. John adds an interesting variant to which we have already made reference. He says Jesus was soon missed by the multitude He had left on the scene of the miracle of the loaves. They had seen the disciples go away in the only boat, and, knowing that Jesus was not with them, they expected to find Him there in the morning when He came down from His place of solitary retirement. When they learned that He was gone they were bewildered. The only boat there had been that in which He came;[42] it had departed without Him; and as far as they knew He could not get away otherwise without their knowledge, and yet He was not there. Other boats presently began to arrive from Tiberias,[43] which was some distance south of Capernaum on the western side of

[41] Note the authentic testimony regarding the phenomena of D. D. Home, especially that of Sir William Crookes and Lord Dunraven.
[42] John vi. 22.   [43] *Ibid.* 23.

the lake, and we may assume that they brought tidings of Jesus' presence on the coast of Gennesaret. A considerable number of the crowd which had followed Him into the wilderness around Bethsaida now took passage in these boats towards Capernaum in the hope of coming in contact with Him again.[44] At the same time Jesus and His disciples were making their way along the coast northward, so that presently the two companies encountered each other in Capernaum itself or near to it. "Rabbi, whence camest thou hither?" [45] inquired the astonished representatives of the five thousand whom He had fed the day before many miles away. All thought of taking Him by force to make Him a king seems to have been dropped forthwith; this was manifestly not a person to be compelled to do their bidding in this or any other way. For answer, as we have seen, Jesus exposed their selfish and materialistic motives and then proceeded to enforce the lesson of the stupendous miracle whereof they had yesterday been the beneficiaries.

St. John indicates that, as was now frequently the fact, some Jews were present in the synagogue at Capernaum where this discourse was delivered, and that they took strong objection to His calling Himself the bread which came down from heaven. "And they said, Is not this Jesus, the son of Joseph, whose father and mother we know? How is it then that he saith, I came down from heaven?" [46] Here we have the same allusion to His earthly origin which is stated to have been made on other oc-

---

[44] *Ibid.* 24.   [45] *Ibid.* 25.   [46] John vi. 42.

casions. But who are these "Jews" who are here credited with making it? Either the writer of the fourth gospel, writing for Gentile Christians, designates the inhabitants of Galilee as well as of Judea by this term, or else He means us to understand that Jesus' family was known in Judea as well as in the north. The latter would appear to be his intention, for in the opening verse of the next chapter he says: "After these things Jesus walked in Galilee; for He would not walk in Jewry because the Jews sought to kill Him." Here, therefore, we have another undesigned indication that Joseph and Mary were of Jewish and not of Galilean antecedents. Much of the rest of the discourse may be, as all the long speeches attributed to Jesus in this gospel suggest, the author's very free reproduction of the substance of what the Master actually said. The most notable point in connection with it is that it marks a crisis. A change of feeling set in regarding Him on the part of some who had hitherto counted themselves among His followers. From this time forward we shall find this opposition growing and deepening. The period of overwhelming popularity draws to a close; [47] henceforth there is a party which openly desires His destruction; it may have consisted mainly of the Pharisees and their immediate supporters, but John's words would suggest that the hostility was not confined to these, but that some of the Master's own immediate adherents now began to turn against Him.

[47] His denunciation of Capernaum and other centers for their spiritual unresponsiveness may have been partly due to their readiness to accept Him on other grounds.

Here, too, we get the first hint of the defection of Judas Iscariot. When Peter made his confession of loyalty on behalf of all, Jesus' reply was: "Have I not chosen you twelve, and one of you is a devil?" [48] As we shall see later, Judas' change of front, which may have begun from now, can be accounted for partly on the hypothesis that, like these others who "walked no more with Him" henceforth, he was genuinely disappointed in Jesus and found Him other than he had expected and hoped. Judas was from the south, the only one of the apostolic band who did not come from Galilee, and there is good reason to believe that what he wanted was primarily a politico-religious leader to vindicate Israel against the foreigner. He and the other discontented ones now saw plainly that Jesus was not that, whatever else He might be. Were these and Judas the prime movers in the effort to seize Jesus the day before and proclaim Him king? The supposition fits in with the annoyance and disgust with His proceedings which we are now told supervened. Not only did Jesus refuse to conform to their plans of violence and insurrection but He was now using mystical language utterly incomprehensible to their prosaic minds. They put Him down as an unpractical dreamer, a half-madman, perhaps. Here He was calling Himself the bread of life, exhorting them to eat His flesh and drink His blood, calling God His Father, declaring that He had come down from heaven to bring life to the

[48] John vi. 70.

world, and so on. This was not at all what they wanted or understood.

From this discourse in Capernaum, therefore, following upon the feeding of the five thousand, we may date the beginning of the second period of the Master's ministry, the period of persecution and malevolent hatred culminating in His betrayal and death.

JESUS AS TEACHER

This is a suitable point at which to pause and consider the much discussed question whether Jesus can rightly be accounted a teacher or not—whether indeed He thought of Himself as such, and if so whether He can be credited with having enunciated a new and original rule of life or merely spoke in terms of the best that was being thought and said around Him in the Palestine of His day. We have already had occasion to observe that He Himself was the most truly original factor of the new divine revelation that produced Christianity; in a manner of speaking, He was the authoritative divine word, not only to His own age, but to all ages to come. This much we are justified in affirming from the witness of history if nothing more. But to say so does not exclude His actual teaching from the field of our interest, little though there may be in the content of that teaching for which a parallel cannot be found somewhere. It is almost startling to come upon sentences in the Testaments of the Twelve Patriarchs which breathe the very spirit of Jesus, and to remember that He might very well have read them. Thus (Zebulun's Exhortation to His Sons): "Have, therefore, compassion in your hearts, my children, because even as a man doeth to his neighbor, even so also will the Lord do to him"; or (Daniel): "Love the Lord with all your life, and one another with a true heart"; or, most striking of all perhaps, the passage attributed to Gad: "Love ye one another from the heart; and if a man sin against thee, speak peaceably to him, and in thy soul hold not guile; and if he repent and confess, forgive him. . . . But if he is shameless and persisteth in his wrong-doing, even so forgive him from the heart, and leave to God the avenging." The parable of the Last Judgment contains phrases which recall passages from the Testament of Joseph: "I was sick, and the Lord visited me; I was in prison, and my God showed favor unto me." Dr. Burkitt discerns a similarity or connection between this parable and I Enoch lxii, but it is much more likely that the parable was a piece of apocalyptic writing already known to Jesus' hearers and deliberately modified by Him in its moral significance. The introduction of the figure of the Messianic king into the picture at once suggests this view. The outline is current Jewish eschatology, including the reference to the fate of the wicked; the emphasis upon the ethical motive—inasmuch as ye did it, or ye did it not—language, perhaps, partly derived from the Testament of Joseph just quoted—is consonant with all that we know of the mind of Jesus and may represent the sole element introduced by Him to a dramatic story His hearers already knew quite well. He may have followed this method on many occasions, taking proverbial sayings as He found them or even conventional aphorisms, and giving them an unexpected turn. Sometimes this would be a wiser and more effective thing to do than to utter complete sayings which no one had ever heard before, either in form or substance. But, taken on the whole, there is not very much to be found in contemporary apocalyptic that can even plausibly be regarded as the direct source of any considerable portion of the teaching of Jesus. The present-day tendency to ascribe to apocalyptic the credit for the bulk of the ideas attributed to Jesus in the gospels is not borne out by the facts. There is not much in apocalyptic, after all, so far as can now be discovered, from which Jesus may be said to have borrowed.

But one thing He certainly did, and that of set purpose. He used the mental symbols or categories for the conveyance of His message which were those of His age and race and on everybody's tongue. From a study of Q we learn that His mental horizon was not confined by Galilee and Judea, nor was His teaching hampered by the belief that a catastrophic divine judgment was at hand. If in other parts of the gospels, and especially towards the end of the ministry, He is shown as using language which, like apocalyptic, stresses this view of the immediate future, we must take care not to misinterpret the fact. He spoke in the metaphors His hearers knew best and there is no smallest indication that He Himself was dominated and circumscribed by these modes of speech. Many difficulties in regard to the content of the teaching of Jesus could be removed by bearing this one principle in mind: His thought ran in the molds prepared for it by the Jewish mentality of the time, but it was the molds and not the thought that for the most part His contemporaries knew beforehand. It would be hard to say what was not symbolic in the phraseology Jesus habitually adopted in His public discourses. No one seems to have been surprised that He so constantly spoke of God as Father. Evidently it was not unfamiliar. The invading pagan cults of which there were evidences on every hand would be sufficient to acquaint people in general with the idea of associating deity with paternity; but who would deny that in the mouth of Jesus the word had a new ring? The close spiritual and ethical relationship presumed in His use of the term has made all lower views of the divine nature impossible since His day. He was not the first to speak of sonship to God either, and it is not too much to say that this particular figure of speech—for it is nothing more, even in the creeds—is more truly Hellenic than Jewish in origin and associations. It has received a special connotation in Christianity, but as first employed by Jesus it may have been adopted from the current speech of Galileans as daily influenced by intercourse with the many Greek-speaking inhabitants of northern Palestine. We need not be afraid of admitting this, but neither should we allow ourselves to be misled

by it. It appears to have been Jesus' consistent
method to accept the prevailing symbology of His
time as He found it, and even to some extent the
ideas conveyed thereby, and then to have trans-
formed and added to the latter as He chose. He
was never deceived into thinking the symbol more
than a symbol, but merely used it as a means to
help His hearers to a better apprehension of the
truth He had to declare. Thus if He called God
Father, the Heavenly One, He was careful to explain when occasion called for it that this Heavenly
One was omnipresent Spirit. He was never at
any time so theologically minded as to call Himself
Son of Man to emphasize His kinship with the
human race on one side of His personality, and Son
of God as an expression of His divinity on the
other. Son of Man and Son of God were alike
derived from current phraseology, especially that
of apocalyptic, and He did no more than charge
them with an intenser significance as a self-designation. As we have seen, the very terms Messiah
and Kingdom of God were useful, perhaps indispensable, symbols and no more. He employed
them for want of better, just as He would have employed any other symbols characteristic of the
thought and speech of the period had it been necessary so to do. He knew they were only of local
and temporary value and that His word was not
restricted to them, though a careful scrutiny of the
evangelic record compels us to the conclusion that
He was the only person who did fully know this or
was able to stand above and outside the preposses-

sions of His time while declaring in terms thereof that which was for all time.

There is then no great mystery about the teaching of Jesus. Profundity does not exclude simplicity, and its very simplicity is its most outstanding feature. He knew Himself to be in His person and the spiritual ideal He had come to declare the supreme fulfillment of the spiritual aspirations of all preceding ages. He had to announce a new law, but not because the old was false. The Law and the prophets had but found their goal in Him; what He was and had come to reveal had been implicit in them from the first, and all the stumbling efforts of past and present towards the understanding of a perfect good were now explained.

There is no sign of development in His teaching nor in His mind except, perhaps, the growing consciousness that His own death was inevitable as part of the price to be paid before the great consummation could come to pass. In what He says about the Kingdom from the very first He is thinking of the ideal state of life which is presently to be realized by those who listen; He is not thinking of the gradual improvement of human society in order to make room for it, or of the gradual assimilation of human rules of action to this standard. Many are the attempts which have been made to apply in theory the principles of the Sermon on the Mount to human society as at present constituted. Such attempts are not wholly vain, but it should be understood that this is not what Jesus contemplated. He is speaking all the time about an ideal order which already is, and only in a secondary sense of the spirit of that ideal order as taking possession of individuals on earth and finding expression through them as best it can. The eternal Kingdom is already theirs who are humble, simple, unpretentious, single-minded, inoffensive, earnest in their desire for goodness, spiritual in thought and aim, with gaze fixed on eternal values rather than on temporal. The law of the Kingdom rules the heart rather than the outer man, or the latter only because the former. Charity and magnanimity of spirit are counseled in all relationships; the children of the Kingdom are they in whom a spirit of brotherly kindness is ever manifest. They are to keep no grudges, to hold the treasures of this world lightly, to avoid anxiety, to live as naturally by the bounty of God as the birds of the air and the flowers of the field. They are never to be censorious or to give any countenance to oppression and cruelty. They are always to do to others as they would be done by—an all-comprehensive rule of life. Jesus lays much stress upon faith as necessary for spiritual life and as the natural attitude of the soul to God. This is one of the most distinctive features of His teaching and has been much misunderstood. Faith in His sense of the word is not intellectual assent to a number of propositions, but the exercise of spiritual instinct. He says nothing about the antithesis between faith and reason, so familiar at the present day; He rather assumes that faith in God—a trustful, humbly confident reliance upon a heavenly Father's bounty and care

—is, or should be, as native to the soul as a child's instinctive confidence in the love of father or mother; indeed, He does not hesitate to illustrate the former by the latter. There should be no need to argue it; it requires no proof any more than belief in the admirableness of any good requires proof.

It is because of this point of view that He attaches so much importance to prayer, and nothing is more remarkable in what He has to say on this great subject than the absence of all qualification of its efficacy. There is no doubt, no hesitation, no warning not to expect too much. Prayer is the communion of the soul with God, and also the statement of all our creature wants in the full and simple confidence that they will be supplied. "Ask, and it shall be given you; seek, and ye shall find; knock, and it shall be opened unto you: For everyone that asketh receiveth; and he that seeketh findeth; and to him that knocketh it shall be opened." [49] "What things soever ye desire when ye pray, believe that ye have received them, and ye shall have them." [50] At a later stage in the ministry He taught His followers to ask in His name—that is, in such a way as they believed He Himself would ask or approve—and promised that such prayers would be certain of their answer. He added, "If ye shall ask anything in my name, I (myself) will do it." [51] But along with this wealth of benediction He also insists upon the most utter and complete self-abnegation. Those who would join them-

[49] Matt. vii. 7, 8.   [50] Mark xi. 24 (R.V.).
[51] John xiv. 14. Gore: *Prayer and Lord's Prayer*, chap. ii, "Praying in Christ's Name."

selves to Him are to enter in by the strait gate of self-renunciation which leads to true life; they are to deny themselves daily, to lose their lives in order to find them. People who pray from such a standpoint as this are not likely to pray selfish prayers. Never was a Master so tender and compassionate to human frailty as Jesus, never a leader who made such a demand upon His followers; He exacted everything they had to give, and would be satisfied with nothing less.

It is sometimes said that His ethic involved despair of the world, as, in fact, did that of early Christianity as a whole which remained true to His precepts; and that His counsel to remain carefree and not to heap up treasures upon earth could only have reference to what He believed to be the comparatively short time remaining before the sudden and catastrophic advent of the Kingdom of God. But in that case why did He warn His followers of coming persecution and of the divisions that His name would cause in the world? "Ye shall be brought before governors and kings for my sake, for a testimony against them and the Gentiles. . . . And the brother shall deliver up the brother to death, and the father the child; and the children shall rise up against their parents, and cause them to be put to death. And ye shall be hated of all men for my name's sake." [52] There seems no good reason for setting these words aside as representing rather the experience of the infant Church in after

[52] Mark xiii, 9, 12; but also in an earlier connection, Matt. x. 18, 21

days than the actual utterance of its founder, for
in the same connection appears the mysterious sentence: "Verily I say unto you, Ye shall not have
gone over the cities of Israel, till the Son of Man
be come." [53] There is no evidence whatever
that Jesus was disappointed in this or that He
expected the Parousia in His lifetime; the evidence of the immediate context, as we have just
seen, is quite the other way. He looked ahead and
foresaw a severe testing time for His faithful ones
before the end came. He professed ignorance of
whether this time would be long or short. "Of that
day and hour knoweth no man, not the Son, but
the Father only." [54] The statement that they would
not have evangelized the cities of Israel before His
return is by no means obscure to those who have
eyes to see. It was literally true; He was thinking
of the new dispensation when He would be spiritually present with His own, of that spiritual
Parousia which took place on the day of Pentecost
and continued from that time forward. "Lo, I
am with you alway, even unto the end of the
world" [55]—or rather, the consummation of the age,
the end of the existing order of things. The consummation is not yet, but the former promise in
anticipation thereof has been faithfully kept.

The lengths to which a preconceived theory will
carry acute critics is nowhere better illustrated than
in regard to the perspective taken in the teaching
of Jesus. It is plain enough to ordinary common

[53] Matt. x. 23.   [54] Matt. xxiv. 23; Mark xiii. 32.
[55] Matt. xxviii. 20.

sense that He did contemplate a period of proba-
tion, during which His disciples would have every
opportunity to put into practice the principles He
laid down. It is denied that there is any indication
that He called the twelve in order to train them to
continue His work when He was gone. Why, then,
did He explain so much to them privately, as we
are told was His consistent custom? What did it
mean to say that He would build His society upon
Peter?—which again has proved to be historically
true, Peter being the first to be summoned to His
side, the first openly to acknowledge His Messiahship in the higher sense, and the spokesman and
leader of the apostolic Church in its first public
appearances after the descent of the Spirit at Pentecost. The plain and simple interpretation of the
teaching of Jesus is that it was intended for the
new society He was calling into existence, and
which has to live its life in the world as at present
organized but by the law of a higher and better
world. Admission into this society was not to be
accorded to a certain order of mind, but to a certain quality of heart. Jesus may or may not have
known of the pretensions of Greek culture, with its
emphasis upon intellect and its contempt of the
uninstructed—probably, as we have seen reason to
conclude, He did know something of it at first hand,
seeing that Palestine had become so extensively
Hellenized—but He made it plain to all that no
such barriers of privilege would be allowed to bar
out the simple from the heavenly Kingdom. On
the contrary, He warned His hearers that trust in

intellect as well as trust in riches might both operate as a disqualification by introducing a certain artificiality into the outlook of those who were thus burdened. And we all know how true this is; it requires no small measure of grace to escape the distorting influence of either. "At that time Jesus answered and said, I thank thee, O Father, Lord of heaven and earth, because thou hast hid these things from the wise and prudent, and hast revealed them unto babes. Even so, Father: for so it seems good in thy sight." [56]

There are some indications of esoteric teaching in what is preserved to us of the Master's words, and the striking saying just quoted is one of them, introducing, as it does, the still more impressive utterance: "All things are delivered unto me of my Father: and no man knoweth the Son but the Father; neither knoweth any man the Father, save the Son, and he to whomsoever the Son will reveal Him." Luke gives it in connection with the return of the seventy from their mission, and adds: "And He turned Him unto His disciples, and said privately, Blessed are the eyes which see the things which ye see," etc.[57] It would be difficult, indeed impossible, for popular gatherings to understand this saying about the relation of the Father and the Son unless some further explanation were forthcoming. It might not be startling to hear the speaker refer to Himself as the Son, for that was not unprecedented and had none of the theological implications we are now accustomed to import into

[56] Matt. xi. 25. [57] Luke x. 23.

the term; but to hear Him make such exclusive claims regarding it was another matter, and from what we are here told it seems reasonable to conclude that the words were spoken to a limited circle, the circle He was daily instructing in the nature of the Kingdom of God. That they would be prepared to admit His own special spiritual authority can hardly be questioned. Peculiar to Matthew is the beautiful subjoined utterance: "Come unto me, all ye that labor and are heavy laden, and I will give you rest. Take my yoke upon you, and learn of me; for I am meek and lowly in heart: and ye shall find rest unto your souls. For my yoke is easy, and my burden is light." [58] It is an accurate commentary upon Jesus' whole teaching, and no doubt a reference to the contrast between it and that of the scribes and Pharisees. Theirs was a heavy and galling yoke; the toilers and the simple-minded were unable to bear it, could not fulfill its requirements, and yet, like suffering humanity in all ages, they needed the light and rest of God. Only One has ever proved Himself able to satisfy that hunger, and wise are they that know it.

Jesus' teaching on nonresistance to evil has been variously construed, but it is clear that the apostolic Church never understood it to mean that the State had no right to use force for the suppression of wrongdoing, and if it has this right within its own borders it has the same right to resist oppression beyond its own borders when occasion calls—nay, the duty so to do. St. Paul says that the

[58] Matt. xi. 28-30.

executive of the State "beareth not the sword in vain" and is "the minister of God, a revenger to execute wrath upon him that doeth evil." [59] In this, as in other things, it may be presumed that the primitive Christians knew the mind of their Master; they could not have thought that Jesus' words about nonresistance to evil contradicted those of the great apostle or the fact would speedily have been pointed out. Moreover, it is evident that Jesus Himself believed in the consecrated use of force. It was only up to a point that evil was to be tolerated; beyond that point He taught that heaven would interfere to destroy it with a strong hand. He did not teach that the world would finally be put right by moral suasion alone; on the contrary, He distinctly affirmed that it would not and that a day of reckoning would come for those who were living in defiance of the laws of God. Most impressive of all, perhaps, in this connection is His statement that He Himself would be the agent in bringing the nations of the world to judgment and passing sentence upon them by and by— so it is apparent that in His thought there was to come a time when He Himself would employ force to secure the ends of righteousness. His counsel about turning the cheek to the smiter is meant for the individual; He does not say that we are to turn any one else's cheek to the smiter, which is what is involved in refusing to protect the weak against the violence of the strong. We are not to resent personal injuries or repay unkindness in a like

[59] Rom. xiii. 4.

spirit. And in this respect the teaching of Jesus has been vindicated with the lapse of time. We do not now think any man admirable who is quick to avenge insults directed against himself; we rather admire him who ignores personal affronts and indignities, but is ready to stand up for high principles and causes from whose vindication he may derive no personal advantage.

This was very far from being the ethical standard of the society in which Christianity first arose, and was described by the exponents of rival systems as slave morality. It is not universally accepted even yet, but it is on the way to being. The type of character which is most respected is the character which approximates to this ideal of superiority to personal considerations in one's bearing towards others and acceptance of responsibility for the welfare of the community as a whole. The rule of action thus laid down is the one which every Christian is expected to obey so far as he can. But there is a balance of duties; our various relationships have to be adjusted to each other in proper and reasonable order. To hand one individual over to ill-usage or affliction rather than to put restraint upon the power of another to do evil is nowhere enjoined or implied in the words of Jesus. What is ideally right is that at which we are bidden always to aim in this as in other things, but it may have to be modified by force of circumstances, so that what is practically right at one time in such an unideal world as ours may not be what an enlightened soul would wholly desire or what would obtain in a truly

Christianized society. This is a distinction of some importance and should never be forgotten by interpreters of the Master's words.

There are several other special sayings in this period of the teaching to which attention should be drawn. There is, for example, the strong saying about plucking out the right eye or cutting off the right hand if these become an occasion of stumbling, rather than having the whole of one's members to be cast into hell. This appears in the Sermon on the Mount, and again in the later period of the ministry; it is quite probable that it was uttered more than once. Mark's version of it is the more elaborate and uncompromising. The meaning is obvious once we understand the metaphor. The sinister valley of Hinnom outside Jerusalem was the scene of public executions. Criminals were there stoned to death or otherwise made away with. Worms preyed upon the dishonored and decaying bodies, and fires were lighted to consume the putrefying flesh and carry away the stench. Jesus' hearers all knew of this. Would it not have been better, He says in effect, that these men who have thus incurred such a fate should have plucked out the eye or cut off the limb rather than have yielded to the temptation which has brought them to destruction? And it is as true of the spiritual sphere as of the natural. There is a judgment of God to be reckoned with even if the judgment of man passes a sinner by unscathed. Better mortify any natural inclination than allow it to master you to your spiritual undoing; better restrict and deny a thing innocent in itself than allow it to become the gateway of evil suggestion. More than this the words do not convey. Any attempt to interpret them literally as relating to the mode of punishment that awaits an impenitent sinner after death is quite unwarrantable. The worm and the fire are both figures of speech, and both suggest the gnawings of remorse rather than any other form of torment.

Another point that may be singled out for special mention is the repeated declaration that there is nothing covered that shall not be revealed, that the secrets of all hearts are to become known. This accords with probability. Here in the flesh what a man is may not be fully evident to those about him or even to himself; nay, we may be sure it is not; but in another state what we are and what we seem shall be one. There is a gracious as well as a stern side to this intimation, too. When all that is now hidden in human motive and aim come to light, there will be some beautiful things to be revealed as well as ugly ones; if we find some persons to be worse than we thought, we shall find others to be better.

The high that proved too high, the heroic for earth too
    hard,
The passion that left the ground to lose itself in the sky,
Are music sent up to God by the lover and the bard;
Enough that He heard it once: we shall hear it by and by.

Jesus teaches, too, that some sort of purgatorial conditions await us in the hereafter, and His words on this subject are full of solemn warning. "Agree with thine adversary quickly," etc. "Verily I say unto thee, Thou shalt by no means come out thence till thou hast paid the uttermost farthing." [60] "With what measure ye mete, it shall be measured unto you again." [61] If these sayings stood alone, they would seem to be an uncompromising assertion of the law of measure for measure, the merciless exacting of retribution for sin. But happily it is not so; there is a place for the operation of free grace likewise; the law of measure for measure has to give way to the love that blots out iniquity on repentance. But there can be no leap from a state of sin to one of holiness, though there may be an instant passing from a state of alienation from God to one of contrition and reconciliation. Jesus bids us know that one evidence of that state of grace is the banishment of all grudge from our own hearts. "If ye forgive not men their trespasses, neither will your Father forgive your trespasses." Again and again the Master insists by parable and otherwise that such forgiveness on the part of God is full, complete, and without reserve and has not to wait to be earned, provided repentance and the consciousness of need are equally deep and sincere.

[60] Matt. v. 25, 26.   [61] Matt. vii. 2; Mark iv. 24; Luke vi. 38.

N.E.

CHAPTER X

LAST PHASE OF THE MINISTRY

DEFECTIONS AND PLOTTINGS

THE great crisis in our Lord's ministry is the discourse in Capernaum noted above. His popularity had never been so great as immediately previous to that event; but henceforth, as we have observed, a certain amount of dissatisfaction begins to show itself on the part of some who had hitherto been counted among His supporters. "From that time many of His disciples went back and walked no more with Him." [1] These are significant words and indicate a great deal more than at first sight might be inferred.

To what was this change of feeling due, and how far did it extend? Was the falling away general or was it confined to a comparative few? We are not in a position to answer these questions very confidently, but it would seem from the various hints on the subject given in all the gospels that the defection was serious and widespread, and that

[1] John vi. 66.

Jesus knew it and took measures accordingly. The populace that would have put Him at the head of a revolutionary movement because of His wonder-working powers was speedily disenchanted by His firm refusal to lend Himself to any such project and by the withering terms in which He rebuked the sordid motives underlying it. He had already antagonized the powerful Pharisaic party, and its representatives were now able to work upon popular prejudice to His detriment; they pointed to His own words as at once indicative of blasphemous claims and of unwillingness to honor the national aspirations. It should be kept in mind that in the south, especially in the capital and its neighborhood, there had never been the same friendliness to Jesus and His methods as in the north; there may also have been more animosity displayed thereto by the Pharisees and scribes of the south than those of Galilee. From this time forward the whole body of Pharisees, scribes, and priests begin to act together in south and north alike, and to make use of Herod's party to compass their ends. They sink their own differences for the time being in their mutual fear of the influence of Jesus. It does not follow from all this that the entire Galilean public now turned against the Master; there is evidence to the contrary; but that He was bitterly disappointed with the spiritual results of the Galilean ministry is apparent from the stern language He employs with reference to it. The very places with which His associations have been closest hitherto now fall under the ban of His solemn censure.

"Then began he to upbraid the cities wherein most of his mighty works were done, because they repented not: Woe unto thee, Chorazin! woe unto thee, Bethsaida! for if the mighty works, which were done in you, had been done in Tyre and Sidon, they would have repented long ago in sackcloth and ashes. But I say unto you it shall be more tolerable for Tyre and Sidon in the day of judgment, than for you. And thou, Capernaum, which art exalted unto heaven, shalt be brought down to hell: for if the mighty works, which have been done in thee, had been done in Sodom, it would have remained until this day. But I say unto you, That it shall be more tolerable for the land of Sodom in the day of judgment, than for thee." [2]

Such grave words as these could only have been provoked by a sense of the comparative failure of the spiritual effort put forth in the very region of the speaker's greatest popularity. Jesus saw with ever-increasing sorrow that His value to the majority of His hearers consisted only in the material benefits they hoped to derive from Him. His self-constraint in the exercise of His miraculous powers, and the care He had taken to hinder their publication in the earlier stages of His work, were now seen to have been fully justified. The people thought of little else and had no desire for aught higher. It was but a few individuals, after all, that had succeeded in perceiving His spiritual eminence and preferred the words of eternal life to the loaves and fishes. And had there been no change in the

[2] Matt. xi. 20 ff.

demeanor of the Galileans towards Him when they realized that He did not intend to comply with their worldly wishes, it is unlikely that He would have taken leave of them as we are now made aware that He did. The crisis was no small one. Soon after the Capernaum discourse on the bread of life, He retires from Galilee altogether and after a period spent in adjoining territories, takes His way southward for the final scene.

Retirement to Foreign Soil

What is chiefly remarkable about this intervening period of retirement is that the first part of it was spent in the heathen land of Phœnicia. It has already been noted that people from this territory had come into Palestine to listen to Jesus, but He could not have been personally known to the bulk of the inhabitants there. His object in going was to obtain some measure of rest and quiet before entering upon the next and hardest stage of His mission. Mark says, "He arose and went into the borders of Tyre and Sidon, and entered into an house, and would have no man know it, but He could not be hid." [3] One wonders whose house this was that was thus honored with the august presence of the Son of Man. It is not said to have been in either Tyre or Sidon, but rather on the seaboard between them. Here the weary Savior finds a welcome asylum within sound of the waves of the Mediterranean. Perhaps one of the many friends whose

[3] Mark vii. 24.

existence is hinted at throughout the gospels, and
who were not numbered in the apostolic band, furnished it. Was he Jew or Gentile? We do not
know, and have no information to guide us, but
what followed would almost suggest that he was
of non-Jewish race—a most interesting fact if it
could be established. Jesus had hitherto restricted
His activities to His own countrymen, feeling, no
doubt, that in the short time before Him it was important to proclaim His Gospel of the Kingdom to
the only people whose antecedents had prepared
them for hearing it. If the Gospel could not be
established on Jewish soil, there was small hope for
it anywhere else; it was broad-based upon Jewish
religion and upon that alone; it was a revelation
that presumed a previous special revelation and a
long preparation in history. But that Jesus had
no intention of restricting His benefits to those of
His own nation is evident from several of His most
important utterances. "Many shall come from the
east and west, and shall sit down with Abraham,
and Isaac, and Jacob, in the Kingdom of heaven.
But the children of the Kingdom shall be cast out
into outer darkness; there shall be weeping and
gnashing of teeth." [4] "The Kingdom of God shall
be taken from you, and given to a nation bringing
forth the fruits thereof." [5] In sharp contra-distinc-
tion to the rabbinical teaching of His time, Jesus
emphatically taught that the Jewish nation as such
had no monopoly in the things of God.

This attitude is exemplified in the touching story

[4] Matt. viii. 11, 12.   [5] Matt. xxi. 43.

of the Syro-Phœnician woman, who, learning of
His presence on the coast, now came to solicit His
aid in the healing of her daughter's madness. "Let
the children first be filled," was the seemingly harsh
reply; "for it is not meet to take the children's
bread, and to cast it unto the dogs." [6] This repulse
of a sorrowful, pleading mother can only have been
intended as a trial of her sincerity, though quite
consonant with the Master's usual reluctance to extend His ministry beyond the limits He had for
good reasons marked out. The humble rejoinder,
"Yes, Lord: yet the dogs under the table eat of the
children's crumbs" was quite sufficient for the compassionate One thus addressed. It is not Mark but
Matthew who gives the reply in its tender fullness:
"O woman, great is thy faith; be it unto thee even
as thou wilt." [7]

This is only one of several recorded occasions in
which our Lord came into contact with foreigners
and willingly helped them. The healing of the centurion's servant is, perhaps, the most striking of
these and elicited from Jesus the impressive encomium, "I say unto you, I have not found so great
faith, no, not in Israel." [8] But this took place
at a much earlier stage in the ministry and on Israelitish soil; the incident we have just examined belongs, as we have seen, to the period immediately
following the close of the Galilean ministry, and
the miracle of healing was performed for the benefit of a heathen woman in a heathen land.

[6] Mark vii. 27.   [7] Matt. xv. 28.   [8] Matt. viii. 10.

Returning from this probably not very prolonged period of rest and retirement, Jesus passed through Galilee once more on His way to Decapolis, a district in which He had not hitherto exercised any public activities. It does not seem likely that He did more than touch upper Galilee on this occasion; He would appear to have avoided the plain of Gennesaret, the principal scene of His former labors and the center in which He had made His home. Whether He said or did anything notable in Decapolis, the evangelists do not expressly say; but on His way north again He performed two notable miracles at the Sea of Galilee—the healing of a deaf and dumb man and the feeding of four thousand people in the same manner as the feeding of the five thousand shortly before. There is some difficulty in placing these events, especially as in Matthew's version they were preceded or accompanied by a great amount of healing activity in a mountain overlooking the great Galilean lake. There is a want of precision in the narrative of these doings which renders it difficult to understand; but on the whole it is unlikely that any of the works recorded were performed on the old familiar ground of Capernaum and the neighborhood. Many critics take for granted that this second miraculous feeding is a variant of the first, that the two stories relate to one and the same tradition. But as against this view is the fact that Mark records both as having happened very near together. In the former case, as we have seen, important developments followed which led to a change in the whole venue of the ministry; in the second case nothing of the kind is mentioned, but a suggestive conversation is added which definitely presumes the historicity of both feedings. Mark says that on this second occasion He took ship after He sent the multitude away and came into the parts of Dalmanutha and that the Pharisees of that neighborhood instantly came forth and began to question Him, demanding a sign from heaven. Where Dalmanutha was nobody knows, but if, as seems likely, it was on the Galilean side of the lake, then the feeding of the four thousand must have taken place on the other side near to Decapolis. After refusing the sign Jesus embarked again and went away, a proceeding which supports the hypothesis that it was no longer easy for Him to make any public appearance in Galilee and that He had no intention of doing so. We gather from the way in which the story is told that He was scarcely on the shore before He was attacked by the Pharisees and that He and His companions forthwith returned in the same boat to the eastern side of the lake whence they had just come. "A wicked and adulterous generation seeketh after a sign," He declared; "and there shall no sign be given unto it but the sign of the prophet Jonas" [9]—that is, the summons to repent which was its own attestation, an appeal addressed to conscience.

This episode would appear to have disturbed Jesus greatly, for Mark says, "He sighed deeply in His spirit," a sympathetic descriptive touch

[9] Matt. xii. 39.

which bears the impress of first-hand testimony. On the return voyage, which He thus felt Himself compelled to take to avoid these unpleasant encounters, a strange and suggestive incident occurred. In the hurry of their departure, the disciples forgot to take bread with them. It may have been in order to obtain bread that they had touched on the western shore at all. Mark adds the detail that they had only one loaf in the ship. Jesus, sitting deep in thought about what had just happened, suddenly observed, half in meditation, half in warning: "Take heed, beware of the leaven of the Pharisees, and of the leaven of Herod." [10] The simple men made no direct reply, but, seeing in the remark a reference to the verbal encounter from which they had just departed they jumped to the conclusion that their Master was bidding them not to accept bread from the Pharisees or their associates: in other words, to avoid relations with them for the future. They whispered this to one another. "It is because we have no bread," they said. Jesus, knowing this, corrected their matter-of-fact interpretation of His words, asking them if they had forgotten the two miraculous feedings in the wilderness and the baskets of fragments remaining over from the banquet in each case. "How is it that ye do not understand?" He asked. Mark does not explain what it was they were to understand, but Matthew adds: "Then understood they how that He bade them not beware of the leaven of the bread, but of the doctrine of the Pharisees and of

[10] Mark viii. 15.

the Sadducees." [11]   Mark's substitution of "Herod"
for "Sadducees" is not unimportant.   It indicates
that the Master meant the ideals of living of poten-
tates like the cynical Antipas on the one hand and
of the hypocritical and self-righteous religious leaders of Israel on the other.

WANDERINGS IN THE NORTH: THE SCENE AT CAESAREA PHILIPPI

Still keeping to the eastern side of the lake, Jesus
and His few companions disembarked somewhere
near Bethsaida (perhaps Bethsaida Julius), where
He healed a blind man. The only notable fact about
this healing is that it is an isolated incident on this
journey and that, in keeping with His policy of
avoiding any more public appearances in that neighborhood, Jesus asked the man to go quietly to his
own home and not to enter the town or tell of the
miracle to any who dwelt therein. Obviously, His
intention was to keep His movements secret for
the present; He had no mind to reopen His Galilean ministry; that was now definitely at an end.
The final chapter of His earthly history was beginning.

Passing on northward He came to the territory
of Herod Philip, and halted somewhere in the district surrounding Caesarea Philippi. It is not
stated that He entered the city itself, Philip's capital. Indeed, judging from the silence of the gospels, it would seem that Jesus deliberately avoided

[11] Matt. xvi. 12.

all foreign cities in His itineraries throughout Palestine; He had no love for their pagan atmosphere and never attempted to deliver His message therein. But on this occasion, with His faithful companions —perhaps the apostles only—He sought retreat in some of the villages hereabouts and remained for some time. And it is during the seclusion thus obtained that He puts to His disciples the momentous question, "Whom do men say that I am?" [12] Several answers were given—John the Baptist, Elijah, Jeremiah, or one of the old prophets risen again. But, pressing the inquiry, He continued, "But whom say ye that I am?" The question was addressed to all, but only Peter replied. "The Christ of God," he said—or, more simply, the Messiah. The synoptics each give a different version of the memorable utterance, but the variations are unimportant. If Peter's own recollection of the words is to be regarded as the most exact, we have it in Mark's rendering: "Thou art the Christ." Matthew subjoins to this avowal the amplifying phrase, "The Son of the living God." It is the first evangelist also who preserves the Master's impressive reply upon which so much ecclesiastical controversy has since turned: "Thou art Peter, and upon this rock will I build my Church; and the gates of hell shall not prevail against it. And I will give unto thee the keys of the Kingdom of heaven," etc.[13] The words which follow concerning the power of binding and loosing are reproduced elsewhere in

[12] Matt. xvi. 13 *ff;* Mark viii. 27 *ff;* Luke ix. 18 *ff.*
[13] Matt. xvi. 18, 19.

the same gospel and also in St. John xx. 23, where they are said to have been spoken to the whole company of the disciples present in the upper room at Jerusalem immediately after the Resurrection. There is some difference in phrasing, but the meaning is substantially the same. Whatever our Lord may have intended by this specific commission to the apostle, it cannot be legitimately held to cover all that is claimed by the Bishops of Rome at the present day. So far as the New Testament evidence goes, Peter himself never either claimed or exercised the functions of universal bishop, the vicegerent on earth of the risen and exalted Lord. But Christians outside the Roman communion need not disavow the distinctive significance attaching to the words here quoted. That Peter did exercise a certain leadership in the primitive Church is as undoubted as that no proof exists that he ever exacted unquestioning obedience from his fellow apostles or regarded them as his subordinates.

More difficult of interpretation, perhaps, than the emphatic declaration to Peter here given is the definite announcement which Jesus couples with it that there were those then present among His hearers who should not taste of death till they had seen the Kingdom of God come with power. It is a saying which can only be understood in strict connection with its antecedents. That the Master had now determined upon taking the apostles more fully into His confidence with regard to the future is the explanation of this private conference with them at Cæsarea Philippi. He had not hitherto acknowledged His Messiahship even to them for reasons to which we have already referred. That they on their part, were prepared to admit it as a possibility is apparent from the testimony of the fourth gospel, but by this time it must have become clear to all of them that if Jesus really were the Messiah, He was such a Messiah as no one had hitherto anticipated; He did not fit in with popular expectation at all. That He should now explicitly disclose His identity to them in these terms was to open up a vista of possibilities, not, indeed, free from perplexity, but full of marvelous promise for the future of mankind. Henceforth they would have to identify the Galilean teacher and wonder-worker with the hope of Israel and the world—how they did not at present understand, but would have to wait for the revealing.

In the view of the present writer, however, even this was not the main point of the discussion recorded. It was not Jesus' Messiahship that was in question here and now so much as the association of that Messiahship with suffering and death. He had brought them there to tell them that. He first got them to acknowledge the Messiahship, binding them to keep it secret yet a little longer, and then went on to teach them "that the Son of Man must suffer many things, and be rejected of the elders, and of the chief priests and scribes, and be killed, and after three days rise again." [14] It was in order to reveal this that He had introduced the subject of His Messiahship at all; from now onward they

[14] Mark viii. 31.

were to think of the two in conjunction a hard task, if not an impossible one, for minds constituted as theirs were. A prophet being put to death they could understand, but that such a fate would be reserved for the Messiah was incomprehensible. Again Peter voiced the feelings of the rest by impulsively exclaiming, "Be it far from thee, Lord; this shall not be unto thee." Apart from their unwillingness to think of their Master as having to submit to such ignominy and disaster, there was this new factor to be disposed of: how could the Messiah be treated thus? The Messiah would not come to suffer but to conquer, and if Jesus were the Messiah soon to be declared He would inevitably carry all before Him. A tragical finish to His present work could not be assimilated to such a consummation. It may be that the idea that Jesus was the Messiah had often been discussed between the members of this little group; there is nothing to show that it was not. Perhaps Peter's public confession of it was only an avowal of the conviction at which they had unanimously arrived already. Perhaps they had been more or less of that opinion all the way through, and were only waiting till Jesus should see fit to confirm or correct their view. If this be so, there is no disagreement even in emphasis between the three earlier gospels and the fourth on this difficult subject. The Messiahship of Jesus may have been tacitly assumed by His intimates from the first, but not discussed because of His reticence in regard thereto. He had now admitted that they were right in their assumption, that was all; but to go straight on with the declaration that He must suffer rejection at the hands of the representatives of the chosen people and be put to a shameful death was an amazing anticlimax. How could the two things be fitted together? If He were the Messiah, how could He perish; if He were to perish, how could He be the Messiah? That this was the dilemma present to their minds is shown by Peter's protest.

Swiftly and sternly the Master turned upon him. "Get thee behind me, Satan," He exclaimed; "for thou savorest not the things that be of God, but the things that be of men." [15] In other words, Peter's previous utterance had been by the direct inspiration of God; this one was the plea of mere worldly wisdom. The rebuke sounds unnecessarily harsh till we perceive what the word Satan indicates. It was, indeed, the old adversary whom He had vanquished in the wilderness who was now tempting Jesus once more through the lips of His faithful follower bidding Him turn aside from the somber path of sacrifice which was marked out for Him to tread. And the vehemence of the repudiation is understandable enough if we recognize that the Master's own human nature shrank from the pain and sorrow ahead and was already on the side of Peter's spontaneous exhortation to spare Himself this fearful ordeal. Here we enter the shadow of a mystery which deepens till Calvary is reached. We do not know what it means any more than did these simple Galileans. All that is plainly stated is

[15] Mark viii. 33.

that Jesus now knew, may have known from the beginning, of His public work, and chose the moment to impart to those most closely associated with Him, the dreadful fact that He, the Messiah, the chosen of God, the world's deliverer, must pass through shame and death to the fulfillment of His mission and the triumph of His cause. His glorious advent could only be made possible by His passion. No explanation is offered: the bare fact is disclosed and we are left to ponder it. It is not so very wonderful that the apostles should be represented as failing to understand.

It is in this connection that Mark inserts the saying about losing the life to find it, a saying which appears in several different settings in the gospels. No doubt it was repeated more than once, together with the companion saying about taking up the cross and following after Jesus. Some scholars have thought it unlikely that Jesus should thus definitely have spoken of the cross before He Himself came to it, but the likelihood is all the other way. The melancholy processions of condemned prisoners, bearing their own crosses to the scene of execution, were all too common at that period under the Roman occupation, and the eyes of Jesus and His friends may have compassionately rested upon them on occasion. The Master could hardly have been under misapprehension concerning the nature of the death He would have to die when the time came. The mystery is not in that, but in the fact that He should have had to die at all. What the inner meaning of the Passion is we are no nearer understanding to-day than were the humble Galileans to whom Jesus first foretold it; nor do we know why it was the indispensable preliminary to the establishment of His Kingdom. If we did know we should know at the same time the meaning of all the world's pain and sorrow.

THE TRANSFIGURATION AND ITS SEQUEL

It has been suggested that the transfiguration —which Matthew and Mark state to have taken place about eight days after the events at Cæsarea Philippi—Luke says eight—was the fulfillment of the prophecy that some of those present should not taste of death till they had seen the Son of Man coming in His Kingdom. This is hardly likely, however. The prophecy would have taken another form had its fulfillment been so near; there was no need to mention death in such a connection; and, moreover, the transfiguration does not answer to the conception of the glorious advent of the Son of Man as present to the minds of His hearers. The Messianic advent, as we have seen, had a fairly well-defined significance to our Lord's Jewish contemporaries; at the very least, it could only be held to mean an event from which human history would make a fresh beginning.

Neither is it warrantable to conclude with extreme critics of the gospel sources that this is an instance in which Jesus or His reporters, or both, were mistaken in their outlook upon the future. If the Master really did expect the wind-up of the existing dispensation and His now triumphal return to take place within the lifetime of some of the members of the little company then listening to Him, it is plain that He was deluded, tragically so; and in that case His authority would have counted for little with His disillusioned followers in after days. It seems strange that more allowance should not have been made for this by upholders of the theory that Jesus built all His hopes upon a speedy second coming and drastic reconstitution of human society with Himself as Messianic king. If it were so, then the confidence of the primitive Church in Him would be inexplicable. Nowhere is it either stated or hinted in the New Testament that He held out expectations to His adherents which were not fulfilled. These very words were not recorded until many years after they were spoken, and no suggestion is offered by the evangelists that they were considered to be either mysterious or disappointing in their effect. What then do they mean? The most reasonable explanation of them is that they are an allusion to the spiritual second coming —a true coming of the Son of Man in His Kingdom—which ensued at Pentecost, following upon the passion and resurrection. It was the beginning of a new era, the end of one age and the opening of another, the dividing line between ancient and modern civilization, between paganism and Christianity with all that the distinction between those two has since signified to the destinies of the human race.[16] That Jesus should have known this is almost more impressive than that He should have foreseen the tragical ending to His own present ministry. There is no other example in history of a master of men being convinced that he would be more truly present with his followers after his departure from earth than before, and surely there is no more convincing evidence of the unique greatness of Jesus than that He should have calmly and confidently affirmed this of Himself in relation to the ideal for which He stood and the work He had come to do.

But, although the transfiguration cannot rightly be regarded as the fulfillment of the prophecy relating to the glorious coming of the Son of Man, it certainly has a bearing upon it. The incidents of this short sojourn in the neighborhood of Cæsarea Philippi are all linked together. The veil is now lifted slightly and the Master's intimates are shown a little of the close touch which He constantly maintained with the transcendental world. Only Peter, James, and John were privileged to see it. The evangelist's record tells us that Jesus took them up into a high mountain apart by themselves—tradition says Mount Hermon, some distance to the north of Cæsarea Philippi—and that there something happened, the like of which they had never witnessed before. A great and supernatural change passed over His customary appearance. Matthew says His face shone as the sun; Mark adds the

[16] H. J. Holtzmann: *Synoptic Gospels,* p. 409, distinguishes three several second advents, one at the end of the world, one at any great historical crisis or period of fresh beginnings, and one in the hearts of believers.

striking detail that "His raiment became shining, exceeding white as snow: so as no fuller on earth can white them"; [17] Luke has it that as He was praying "the fashion of his countenance was altered, and his raiment was white and glistening." [18] The synoptics differ in their phrasing while agreeing upon the facts. It would seem that in this instance, at any rate, they draw severally upon a definite and uniform oral tradition concerning a phenomenon which had deeply impressed the imagination of the apostolic circle. Each of the evangelists contributes some vivid particular to the description of a scene which bears every mark of being authentic.

Here again psychical research comes to our aid. The statement that the three disciples were heavy with sleep is accordant with what we now know of certain supernormal phenomena of a psychical character; it suggests a trance condition, a condition in which superphysical vision is made temporarily possible. All the rest of the description fits in with this hypothesis. Two supernatural beings appear upon the scene, conversing with Jesus. These are said to have been Moses and Elias, but we are not told how Peter and his companions knew this. Once again comes the Voice which is said to have been heard at special crises in the Master's brief career: "This is my beloved Son, in whom I am well pleased." [19] A dazzling radiance surrounds Jesus and the heavenly visitors, and a bright cloud

[17] Matt. xvii. 2; Mark ix. 3.
[18] Luke ix. 29.
[19] Matt. xvii. 5.

overhangs the entire assembly. Luke says that Jesus and the two super-earthly beings who were thus revealed held conversation: "they spake of His decease which He should accomplish at Jerusalem." [20] The three watching Galileans were in great fear as was not unnatural; they felt themselves to be transported into the midst of awe-inspiring verities. Peter, as usual, burst forth into unconsidered speech, offering to erect three booths for Jesus, Moses, and Elias, respectively—his own later version of the occurrence, as given by Mark, being that he did not know what he was saying. The three of them trembling fell down on their faces, and, Matthew says, Jesus walked over to them and touched them, bidding them not to be afraid. This sympathetic consideration for the human susceptibilities of those about Him is one of Jesus' chief characteristics, as is illustrated frequently in the gospel narrative.

Lifting up their heads, they found that the vision had passed and that Jesus only stood beside them, looking just as they were accustomed to see Him from day to day. Coming down from the mountain He charged them not to say anything about what they had seen until He was risen from the dead. Luke says they "kept it close" in consequence, but often wondered what the rising from the dead would mean. They had never been taught to expect that the Messianic Son of Man would have to pass through death to reach His throne. The first evangelist continues that they questioned

[20] Luke ix. 31.

Jesus on the point. "Why then say the scribes that Elias must first come?"—that is, as the herald of the Messiah. In reply Jesus definitely told them that John the Baptist had filled this office, and that John the Baptist's fate must be shared by the Messiah Himself.

It cannot be too frankly stated and admitted that all these supernatural occurrences—clairvoyance, clairaudience, photism, the white cloud, levitation—are quite credible from what we know of lesser beings. They are well attested facts, as any one can discover for himself who takes the necessary trouble to follow up the subject. That three Galilean fishermen, utterly ignorant of the results of modern scientific inquiry into suchlike happenings, should have told their story in such a way as to accord fully with what we now know of psychical phenomena is the best testimony to its genuineness. The very artlessness of their witness has its value from this point of view. All that they thus say with the simplicity of a child describing a unique experience without attempting to explain it, is strikingly true to what trained observers have long been accustomed to note and classify concerning certain supernormal states of consciousness. The transfiguration, or something very like it, has been affirmed of others than Jesus in the centuries intervening between that day and this. That the Master admitted Peter, James, and John to the privilege of witnessing it in this instance was no doubt to impress upon them the outstanding importance of the double disclosure made at Cæsarea Philippi and the new departure it betokened. They now knew Him as a supernatural being, one not of earth, but of heaven, though sharing human nature and wearing human flesh; they knew He was the Messiah who had yet to be revealed in glory, and they had now glimpsed that glory; and they also knew, mysterious and baffling though the announcement were, that the full manifestation of that glory was somehow bound up with His coming submission to shame and death. Henceforth His face was turned towards the cross, and they could but wait to see what this awe-inspiring revelation portended.

From this point the narrative runs very clearly for some distance. We learn that while Jesus with Peter and the two sons of Zebedee had been absent on the summit of Hermon or wherever the transfiguration took place, the rest of the apostolic band and those who journeyed with them remained on the plain at the foot. When He came down He saw that a great multitude had assembled round them and that a company of the scribes was busily engaged in interrogating them, presumably in a hostile spirit. Luke says this was on the next day after the vision, so apparently the Master and His three principal apostles spent some time together conversing on what had happened before returning to those they had left. No sooner did the crowd catch sight of Him than they rushed towards Him greatly excited and began tumultuously to tell Him what had been going on. Jesus turned quietly to the scribes and asked what they were questioning His disciples about—a further example of the way in which He is repeatedly represented as standing between His friends and possible danger, the most striking instance of this being, as we shall see, at the very moment when He Himself was about to fall into the hands of His foes.

The story is a very human one. Before these local doctors of the Law could answer, one of the multitude, falling down on his knees, broke out into supplication. Hearing that Jesus was in the neighborhood, he had brought his lunatic son to Him in the hope of a cure, and not finding Him had entreated the disciples to see if they could effect it, but in vain. Even while the afflicted father spoke, the boy fell into a paroxysm at Jesus' very feet. Mark's graphic description causes the scene to pass vividly before us. For a moment the Master stood gravely regarding the sufferer and then, turning to the father, inquired, "How long ago is it since this came to him?" "Of a child," was the reply, followed by a painful summary of long years of bitter, hopeless sorrow and grief. "If thou canst do anything," he cried in conclusion, "have compassion on us and help us." "If thou canst!" was the swift rejoinder. "All things are possible to him that believeth;" whereupon the father instantly cried out with tears, "Lord, I believe; help thou mine unbelief." [21] Jesus paused no longer but, seeing the crowd rapidly increasing from all directions—a development He had no wish to encourage at that particular juncture—He expelled the unclean

[21] Mark ix. 23, 24.

spirit from its victim and lifting the child up placed him in his father's arms.

It must have been difficult to get away from the crowd after this, and how it was done is not stated. The text would almost suggest that Jesus and His disciples went for a little while into the house of the family to which father and son belonged, for we are now told that "when He was come into the house, His disciples asked Him privately, Why could not we cast him out?" Matthew says they came to Jesus apart and put their question, but there is no necessary discrepancy between his account and Mark's; it is he who supplies us with the discourse which follows, given to them alone, and of which we may reasonably suppose Matthew to have been an actual hearer, concerning the power of faith to remove mountains, which is surely true. The same figure of speech appears in other connections as would be likely enough.

Leaving this abode, they continued their way southward, Jesus explaining to His disciples *en route* that though they must pass through Galilee He did not wish the public to know it, and then for the second time He declared to them, almost in the same words as at Cæsarea Philippi, that the end of His ministry was approaching and that it would be a tragic one to be followed by resurrection. Again we are told that they were unable to understand the saying and were afraid to ask what it meant. The intimation is so worded in this case as to suggest that Jesus now regarded it as unsafe for Him to make any more public appearances in Galilee. His life was threatened there as well as in the south, and if He were to die He intended that it should be in the capital. As He remarked with sad irony, "It cannot be that a prophet perish out of Jerusalem." [22] The wording of St. Matthew's version suggests that He went to and fro for some time between Galilee and the heathen lands to the northwest. It is in this connection also that Mark and Luke tell of the strife among the apostles on the question who should be the greatest. Notwithstanding the impressive announcement of the coming Passion to which they had just listened, and which the first evangelist says had made them "exceeding sorry," they began to strive among each other for precedence while they were yet on the road. They had failed to grasp the significance of this secret journey, for such it was. From Mark's account, the inference is that Jesus was walking some distance apart from His friends, wrapped in His own thoughts; they may have dropped behind a little and were vigorously disputing among themselves in low tones, thinking that He did not hear. Their awe of Him is evident in that they abstained from wrangling in His presence. He gave no sign that He had noticed anything amiss until they had reached His old quarters in Capernaum where He startled and confused them by abruptly asking, "What was it that ye disputed among yourselves by the way?" [23] As they preserved a somewhat shamefaced silence He sat down and called them

[22] Luke xiii. 33.   [23] Mark ix. 33.

round Him—such is the force of the language employed to describe the scene—and taking a little child on His knees taught them the much needed lesson that precedence in the Kingdom of God was accorded to the qualities of humility, simplicity, unpretentiousness, and willingness to love and serve. If we were not now so accustomed to this view of the nature of moral excellence—little though we conform to it—its striking originality and beauty, indeed uniqueness in either the ancient or the modern world, would be evident at a glance. It was Jesus who first taught the world to see the charm and sweetness of child life, as it was Jesus who first among religious teachers insisted on the high respect due to womanhood. Whether it was now or later that the touching episode occurred of His reception of the little children who were brought to Him by their mothers and whom the disciples would have driven away is not ascertainable. According to Matthew the incident in question took place, not in Galilee, but in the parts of Judea beyond Jordan, which in the circumstances is more probable as it was a public event.

There is a flash of affectionate humor in the story which Matthew relates in conjunction with this private visit to Capernaum, of a conversation between Jesus and Peter relative to the tribute money due from both for Temple expenses. What followed —the obtaining of a stater from a fish's mouth— may not have been a miracle; it is not recorded elsewhere and is on quite a different footing from the works of benevolence of a miraculous character

(1) I personally object to many of R. J. Campbell's
interpretations especially of the Miraculous. he seems to want
to hang with the orthodox & yet destructive critics, this epoch
in whole Book. This last interpretation is very Blatant —

LAST PHASE OF THE MINISTRY

which all the evangelists attribute to the Master. It
may only have been a playful way of saying that
as neither He nor Peter had any money He would
have to rely on the apostle to go and catch enough
fish to sell and discharge the obligations for both.
This, at least, seems a reasonable way of interpreting the incident, which is not without spiritual suggestiveness on other grounds.

In this same connection also—perhaps on the
same occasion as the rebuke administered to the
warring little company after the unnoted return
to the Master's house at Capernaum—a further
conversation took place which incidentally throws
some light on the fiery and impulsive character of
the sons of Zebedee. They state that they had seen
a man casting out devils in their Master's name and
that they had forbidden him because he was not of
their company. In gently deprecating this ready
intolerance Jesus added: "He that is not against
us is on our part" [24]—a saying antithetic to that
elsewhere preserved: "He that is not with me is
against me." [25] There is no contradiction between
the two. In the one case a man was casting out
devils in Jesus' name because he believed in the
power of that name; in the other the malignant opponents of Jesus were declaring that He cast out
devils by the power of the prince of the devils.
There was all the difference in the world between
the two situations.

There is a good deal of doubt about the meaning

[24] Mark ix. 40.
[25] Matt. xii. 30; Luke xi. 23.

of the name Boanerges,[26] but perhaps the interpretation "sons of thunder" does convey something of the impression made by these two men upon their associates. That they were ambitious to a degree and somewhat explosive in temper is more than hinted at by what is narrated of them in the gospels and also by the witness of tradition. That these qualities should have gone along with other and more admirable ones is not psychologically impossible; they are consistent with whole-hearted devotion to the person of the Master, as, indeed, is indicated by the very form in which this confession was made; it was because they conceived that an indignity was being done to Jesus in the illegitimate use of His name that they had interfered. A nature essentially lovable and sweet could exhibit these same traits, and it is evident that Jesus regarded John with the affection of an elder for a younger brother. That the son of thunder should afterwards have become the apostle of love was one fruit of this association.

No doubt it is because of the mention of James and John at this point that Luke here inserts the further story of their wish to call down fire from heaven to consume the Pharisees who would have hindered Him from proceeding to Jerusalem. How Jesus and His inner circle of disciples managed to get in and out of Capernaum and along the shores of the sea of Galilee without public notice being taken of Him on this occasion must remain a mystery. The news of His presence in the

[26] But *vide* Rendel Harris: *Boanerges* for another interpretation.

neighborhood would have caused the greatest excitement had it become known, but apparently it did not and He and His friends were careful that it should not. He did not stay long; as Luke says, "He steadfastly set His face to go to Jerusalem"; [27] He was moving calmly and deliberately towards the final consummation, and would not wish to delay in Galilee any longer than He could help. If this house in Galilee were His own, as seems not improbable, this was His farewell to it; He perhaps left His mother therein with the thought in His heart that she, too, would have to find some other shelter ere long. How Jesus had maintained this home up to the present we do not know and there is no means of finding out. It may have been, as, in fact, seems most likely, that some persons of substance attached themselves to Him during His public ministry and contributed to His maintenance and that of His little band of followers. We are expressly told by St. Luke that there were some women of rank among these, and there would be nothing undignified on His part in accepting such help. Other public teachers did the same, and do still in the East, as is illustrated by the remarkable Bahai movement of our own day.

EVENTS IN THE SOUTH

The several narratives of this progress towards Jerusalem are full of unsolved problems. The pilgrims need not have gone through Samaria to get

[27] Luke ix. 51.

into the region beyond Jordan where we next hear
of the Master exercising a teaching and healing
ministry; but the information furnished is too
meager to enable us to form a very clear idea of
the course actually followed. There is nothing like
the continuous residence anywhere which Jesus had
hitherto maintained in Capernaum; He has now no
fixed abode, but moves from place to place without
any plan or purpose which can be traced. Perhaps
the journey from Galilee in the first instance was
undertaken in order to be present in Jerusalem at
the feast of Tabernacles. This is the simplest explanation of His movements. The feast of Tabernacles fell in September after the Day of Atonement so that there would still be six months or more
before the feast of the Passover, at which Jesus was
arrested. The best and most convenient route from
Galilee to Jerusalem, of course, lay through Samaria, but pilgrims going up to the feasts were
chary of taking it because of the hostility of the
Samaritan people to Jewish religion. These did
their utmost to put hindrances in the way of any
who might be thought to be going up to worship
at Jerusalem; pilgrims were frequently maltreated
by them and sometimes killed. On the occasion here
referred to Jesus and His friends approached a
Samaritan village, seeking accommodation for the
night, but it was discourteously refused on the
ground that they were obviously proceeding to
Jerusalem for the feast of Tabernacles. St. Luke's
restrained narrative gives the barest description of
the manner in which this refusal was conveyed, but

we can well imagine that it would be with fanatical insult and contumely. It was not hostility to Jesus personally that dictated this action on the part of the inhabitants of this unnamed village; it is more than probable that they knew nothing of His identity; they were influenced solely by religious bigotry and race prejudice. Filled with anger at this churlish conduct, James and John, in keeping with the temper already manifested in the instance cited above, would have had their Master call down fire from heaven and destroy the offenders. "Ye know not what manner of spirit ye are of" was the grave rebuke; "for the Son of Man is not come to destroy men's lives but to save them." [28] The evangelist adds that they went to another village where, judging from the absence of any statement to the contrary in the record, they were differently received.

It is here, too, that Luke gives the episode of the would-be adherent who enthusiastically declared, "Lord (or Master), I will follow thee whithersoever thou goest," [29] and to whom Jesus returned the pathetic answer already noted. Matthew, with more verisimilitude, places this at a much earlier stage of the ministry, namely, soon after the Sermon on the Mount. The companion incident of the disciple who asked to be allowed to go and bury his father before giving up all to follow the Master is also recorded by both the first and third evangelists, but is more in place in the former than the latter gospel. It appears in that portion of St. Luke which, as we have seen, is mainly derived from some

[28] *Ibid.* 55, 56.   [29] *Ibid.* 57.

special source and inserted abruptly at this point without apparent regard for chronological sequence. In Luke's version an important turn is given to the story by the statement that it was the Master who first asked this disciple to follow Him and not the disciple who spontaneously proffered to do so. Here then we have an instance of a man who had an opportunity of becoming an apostle of Jesus Christ and rejected the privilege. Or did he reject it? Perhaps not; it is not so stated. "Follow me," was the Master's uncompromising comment, "and let the dead bury their dead." [30] The seeming harshness of this utterance disappears when we realize that the whole point, both of the excuse and the reply it elicited, was that this man's father was not dead. The son's observation meant that he wanted to remain at home as long as his father was alive in order to make sure of his share of the inheritance, but this Jesus would not tolerate; it was too much of the earth earthy. "No man, having put his hand to the plough," He declared, "and looking back, is fit for the Kingdom of God."

It is on this great southward journey again, according to St. Mark, that the impressive meeting with the rich young ruler occurs. It is one of the most interesting and memorable in the entire evangelistic record, and one of the best attested, for with unimportant variations it appears in detail in all three of the synoptical gospels and serves as the introduction to a special discourse on riches and also on spiritual rewards which is of the greatest value.

[30] Luke ix. 60.

Tradition has had much to say about the personality of this young man. Some have identified him with Lazarus, but for that there is little warrant, seeing that by this time, if Mark's order be reliable, the friendship with the family at Bethany must have been well established, whereas the rich young ruler in question is evidently not personally known to the Master. If he really were Lazarus, then it is gratifying to think that there was another and later chapter to this story. What is chiefly remarkable about it, as given here, is that it is the only instance in the gospels in which it is definitely stated that Jesus smiled; for this is the meaning of the beautiful expression of St. Mark, "Jesus, beholding him, loved him." [31] In other words, He tenderly smiled upon the young man, while at the same moment making the hardest demand upon him that could possibly have been made just then. There must have been something ingenuous and attractive about one born to high estate who could thus humbly kneel down on the road before a wandering preacher and ask to be shown how to inherit eternal life. The phrase "eternal life" is noteworthy as suggestive of the fourth gospel rather than the others, and shows that it was in use concurrently with "Kingdom of God" to signify the supreme good. Perhaps it was more of the south than of the north where the Kingdom was more commonly spoken of, but both were much on the lips of those whom Jesus addressed throughout Palestine.

Considerable attention has been directed to Jesus'

[31] Mark x. 21.

repudiation of the title "good Master" on this oc-sion. "Why callest thou me good?" He de-manded; "there is none good but one, that is, God." Elaborate critical theories have been built upon it but in the present writer's belief most of them are based upon a misconception. The conventional compliment was unthinkingly paid in this instance as it might have been in a hundred others. The young man would have addressed almost any rabbi in the same way. Jesus wanted no such lip service and, therefore, deprecated the idle use of an epithet which should have been reserved for God or only for His servants as deriving from Him any good-ness they might possess.

Why did Jesus tell this young man to sell all his goods and give them to the poor? It is clear that He did not make the same drastic demand of all those with whom He was on terms of friendship. Was it not in order to demonstrate to the ques-tioner the unreality of his professions? It was as though to say: You claim to have kept all the com-mandments, to love God and your neighbor, neither to steal nor to defraud any, and yet here before your eyes every day are people suffering from want and misery, and you hug your wealth and do nothing to help them.[32] Jesus struck hard at this young man's weakest spot, his love of riches. He was not pre-pared for a sacrifice so complete as was thus re-quired of him, and went away sorrowful.

The sequel to this parable is equally remarkable in its way. Jesus, gazing with commiseration and

[32] *Ut sup.*, p. 94, *Gospel According to the Hebrews.*

something of sadness in His own demeanor, after
the retreating form of one who had come so near to
the heavenly Kingdom and yet rejected it, began
to discourse gravely on the spiritually disabling effect of great worldly possessions. This seems to
have caused much astonishment among His hearers, for Mark makes the illuminating observation
twice over that they were amazed, even beyond
measure, at the Master's words. Clearly it had
never occurred to them before that the possession of
wealth should be regarded as a hindrance to membership in the Messianic Kingdom when it came.
Why should it? they thought; surely it ought to be
an advantage rather than the contrary; and would
not entrance into the Kingdom carry with it the
acquirement of an abundance of all the things
usually counted necessary to complete a happy life,
and would not that mean wealth? They had not
yet begun to shake off their preconceptions of the
material nature of the Kingdom; they thought of
it as a good time coming here on earth, much as
Irish peasants talked of Home Rule years ago as
in some magical way to supply every Irishman with
an abundance of gold without much need for work.
The apostles were not materialists or Jesus would
never have chosen them to witness for Him in the
world; He chose them because of their moral earnestness and spiritual susceptibility; but they were
as limited as their contemporaries in their ideas of
the Kingdom of God. If it was to be a Kingdom
of righteousness it was to them to be also a Kingdom of plenty; it was to be a restored Kingdom of

Israel. Hence the force of Peter's question which immediately followed: "Behold we have forsaken all, and followed thee; what shall we have therefore?" [33] If riches were not to count in the new Kingdom, what sort of gain would be theirs who had adhered to the Messiah long ere the world knew Him as such? Peter honestly thought, and so did the rest, that they merited some special reward from Jesus for having espoused His cause thus early. Would they not be persons of special importance and consideration in the new order?

The reply is quite surprising. Instead of correcting Peter's crude expectation He seems to endorse it. In the very same breath as the drastic demand which He had made upon the rich young ruler to strip himself bare of everything He tells this humble Galilean peasant that riches and splendor await him as the reward of his fidelity. "Verily I say unto you, That ye which have followed me, in the regeneration when the Son of Man shall sit on the throne of His glory, ye also shall sit upon twelve thrones, judging the twelve tribes of Israel. And every one that has forsaken houses, or brethren, or sisters, or father, or mother, or wife, or children, or lands, for my name's sake, shall receive an hundredfold, and shall inherit everlasting life." [34]

We can imagine the half-smile, at once gracious and baffling with which Jesus would accompany this mysterious utterance. There was grave humor in it. He knew He was bewildering these simple-

[33] Matt. xix. 27.   [34] Matt. xix. 28, 29.

minded auditors; but the time would come when
they would understand. And the time did come
when this prophecy was seen to be literally true,
only by that time their whole outlook had changed.
The time came when, careless of all earthly possession, taking every risk for the sake of their vocation, counting nothing dear to them, without
homes of their own or fixed abode, they found
themselves welcomed everywhere as their Master's
representatives. Wherever the Church went they
were honored guests; all houses were open to them;
they had a thousand friends where formerly
they had one, and they were bound to these
by the ties of a charity the like of which the world
had never known before, a mutual loyalty in the
fellowship of Christ which burst all barriers of race
and nationality and made them one in the joy of
the Lord. And no prophecy has ever been more
truly fulfilled than that which placed these men on
twelve thrones judging the twelve tribes of Israel.
That is exactly the position they occupy to-day,
owing to their association with Jesus. No Israelite
of old has ever meant so much to the world as these
lowly fishermen of Galilee who first carried the gospel from Jerusalem to the nations of the earth.
Israel's past only has meaning as consummated in
them and their work; it is they who have revealed
it, and through them has its spiritual dignity become manifest.

The events of this period, as placed in juxtaposition in the synoptics, hang well together; for
again the sons of Zebedee appear upon the scene.

Influenced apparently by the striking promise to which we have just given consideration, they approached the Master with the request that they might be allowed special positions of honor in His Kingdom, one to sit on His right hand, the other on His left. Mark says they made this ambitious solicitation themselves, Matthew that they got their mother to do it. Both versions might literally be true. As was not unnatural, their fellow apostles were very angry with James and John, feeling that these two brothers were trying to steal a march on their companions by getting their mother to secure from Jesus a promise which would be to the disadvantage of the rest. Again, however, Jesus is represented as surprisingly acquiescent. Instead of rebuking the presumption of James and John, He merely asks them if they are able to drink of His cup and be baptized with His baptism. They reply confidently that they are, and His solemn rejoinder is that they shall indeed have this privilege, but that to sit on His right hand and on His left is not His to give, but is for those for whom it is prepared of the Father. In other words, as He gently told them, they did not know what they were asking. Spiritual eminence is not a matter of arbitrary precedence, but of lowly goodness and of the love that seeketh not its own; no man has won to the highest until he is utterly willing to be identified with the lowest, though of a directly contrary spirit. Jesus knew these two men better than they knew themselves. He knew them capable of the uttermost of self-sacrifice, and knew that the day would

340

come, was indeed not far ahead, when they would share His cup of pain and baptism of sorrow to the full, counting not the cost, but willingly and joyfully accepting it as His will for them and asking no higher reward than to be the witnesses of His holy love to mankind.[35]

While the others were venting their indignation upon the two brothers for what they esteemed their selfish request, Jesus intervened to complete His lesson. "Ye know," He said, "that they which are accounted to rule over the nations of the world exercise lordship over them; and their great ones exercise authority upon them. But so it shall not be among you; but whosoever will be great among you, shall be your servant; and whosoever of you shall be the chiefest, shall be servant of all. For even the Son of Man came not to be ministered unto, but to minister, and to give His life a ransom for many."[36] Luke's version of the same saying adds a piece of quiet irony. "They that have authority over them," the Master observes, "are called benefactors."[37] There is a versimilitude about this saying which stamps it as a genuine utterance of Jesus, and it is absolutely true to the facts. We do talk even to-day, as much as in any other day, as though those in high secular position or the controllers of great stores of wealth were the benefactors of their fellow creatures in virtue of the fact that so much material power is placed in their hands. But they may be deserving of no special

[35] Bruce: *Training of the Twelve*, pp. 276-279,
[36] Mark x. 42-45.
[37] Luke xxii. 25.

credit for its use; those only are the benefactors of the race in whom the spirit of service has suppressed all desire for self-aggrandizement and is moved and motived by the love of God.

It should be noted that in Mark's order of events the foregoing is preceded by a passage in which the commencement of the last journey to Jerusalem is indicated, but from what point is not stated. It is a very vivid piece of description. "And they were in the way going up to Jerusalem; and Jesus went before them: and they were amazed; and as they followed, they were afraid." [38] The scene is brought sharply before us—the Master walking in front, the disciples following full of awe and something of dread at what they observed in His demeanor. They felt that some great crisis was at hand, but could not understand what. There was an exaltation, a remoteness, a suggestion of firm resolve, of unusually tense emotion in the Master's manner which disquieted them with a vague apprehension. Read in conjunction with the fourth gospel, this uneasiness of theirs is perhaps to be accounted for on other grounds as well. They were reluctant to go to Jerusalem for the good reason that of late violence had been offered to Jesus therein, and there was every likelihood that it would be so again. Turning to them as they conversed upon the prospect which had thus filled them with foreboding, Jesus began once more to tell them explicitly "what things should happen unto Him." [39] He left them in no doubt concerning the outcome.

[38] Mark x. 32. [39] Mark x. 32.

He knew, and was going to Jerusalem in the full knowledge, that betrayal and death were to be His portion; He calmly reviewed the events of the passion, and concluded by once more predicting His resurrection on the third day. It is not said that they understood Him on this occasion any better than on the others, though this time it might be supposed that there could be no room for misconception in their minds. To some critics this obtuseness is inexplicable, but it may be questioned whether it would have been greatly different with any other group of persons under the special circumstances. Considering their prepossessions concerning the functions of the Messiah and the nature of the Kingdom that they believed He would inaugurate, considering, too, how much there was in the utterances of Jesus of late which was to them mysterious and perplexing, it is not altogether wonderful that they should have failed to grasp the full implications of what He was now impressing upon them. They were afraid to venture into Jerusalem, but how it could be true that the Messiah should have to submit to such a fate as He had just described was to them incomprehensible. Either Jesus could not be the Messiah, after all, or such things could not happen to Him. Hence it was in a mood of very considerable perplexity and disturbance of spirit that they approached the neighborhood of Jerusalem on this occasion.

This, as aforesaid, is probably the journey referred to in the eleventh of St. John, of which the raising of Lazarus was the immediate objective.

This striking event is not mentioned in the synoptics, nor its bearing on the determination of the Sanhedrin to have Jesus apprehended before the feast of the Passover. But that there had been some previous visits to Jerusalem after the close of the Galilean ministry is shown by what is recorded in chapters vii to x inclusive of the fourth gospel. It is evident that from the date of the discourse on the bread of life in the synagogue at Capernaum Jesus was not left long unmolested anywhere; His life was continually being threatened.

An incidental corroboration of the synoptical account of the definite ending of His public work in Galilee is afforded by the statement in St. John vii. 10, that He went up secretly to the feast of Tabernacles, to which reference has already been made above. That He was living in retirement, perhaps somewhere in the neighborhood of Nazareth, is also suggested by the form of the narrative here in which Jesus' brethren are represented as urging Him to go up to the feast of Tabernacles. "There no man that doeth anything in secret, and He Himself seeketh to be known openly. If thou do these things show thyself to the world." [40] The evangelist subjoins the comment that "neither did His brethren believe in him." This may not mean as much as has usually been read into it. There is no indication that these brethren of the Master's were deliberately rejecting His claims to Messiahship or even that they knew of them; such claims are not mentioned in the connection. "Neither did

[40] John vii. 4.

his brethren believe in him" may simply mean
that He had not yet been presented to them as the
Messiah. Their advice to Him to go up to the feast
was a, perhaps, not disrespectful deprecation of
His policy of withdrawal from the public gaze. It
must have seemed to them a puzzling thing that
He should act as if His mission were at an end.
If, indeed, He had a mission, as His past activity
had seemed to demonstrate, it was surely His duty
to show Himself to the world.

We should, therefore, not be justified in assuming that there were strained relations between our
Lord and the other members of His family at this
time or, indeed, at any other time; the form of St.
John's narrative suggests that the brothers were
asking Jesus to go with their caravan. This He
excused Himself from doing, telling them to go
without Him, as He did not deem the moment for
the journey a suitable one so far as He was concerned. The story is very well told. Jesus did not
wish to rush unnecessarily upon danger, and there
was now great danger in making a public progress
to Jerusalem. He was living in comparative privacy; His brethren evidently knew His whereabouts, as did His disciples, but not the general
public. In response to His brothers' suggestion,
therefore, that He should come out into the open
again by accompanying them to Jerusalem and
continuing His work there, Jesus tells them that
they could go without risk at any time, whereas He
could not, and that He intended to choose His own

time for whatever public appearances He might make in the future.

As we have already noted, He waited till the ordinary caravans of pilgrims had set off from Galilee, going perhaps by the Perean route, and then with a little group of friends He also made towards Jerusalem, "not publicly, but as it were in secret," [41] taking the road through Samaria. We now see why He took this road; it was because He was less likely to meet Jewish pilgrims upon it at feast times than upon the other, and He wanted to avoid notice.

He arrived after the feast had begun. St. John says the Jews were looking for Him everywhere and disputing about Him when suddenly He appeared and went boldly up to the Temple and taught. This was a dangerous proceeding, indeed, for it is evident from the context that His death had been determined upon. "Why go ye about to kill me?" [42] He asks, and makes a specific reference to His last visit when He had excited hostility by healing an infirm man at the pool of Bethesda on the Sabbath day. Many were astonished at His daring to appear in public at all. "Then said some of them of Jerusalem, Is not this He whom they seek to kill? But, lo, He speaketh boldly, and they say nothing unto Him. Do the rulers know, indeed, that this is the very Christ? (or, that this is in truth the Christ). Howbeit we know this man whence He is: but when Christ cometh, no man

[41] *Ibid.* 10.   [42] *Ibid.* 19.

knoweth whence He is." [43]   Discussion of the possibility of His being the Messiah is now apparently quite overt. With great emphasis Jesus replied in a loud tone: "Ye both know me, and ye know whence I am; and I am not come of myself, but He that sent me is true, whom ye know not." It is to be observed that He says nothing about Messiahship, but in striking language points out what any spiritually-minded man ought to have recognized, that His earthly origin is not in question, but His right to speak in the name of God. When the Messiah actually comes, said some of those who heard, will He do more wonderful things than this man? It is improbable that the expected Messiah was ever thought of as a worker of miracles in the sense that Jesus now was, so this exclamation can mean no more than that people in general were conscious of the transcendent power and impressiveness of Jesus' personality and of the evident tokens of God's presence with Him. Their question in substance was a demand to know whether any one could reasonably expect the Messiah to be a more wonderful being than this prophet of Nazareth.

The sequel is interesting. The Sanhedrin determined upon His arrest and sent officers for that special purpose. Why they did not execute their commission at once is not stated, but for some reason they delayed. When they reached the Temple where He was discoursing they stayed to listen and fell under the spell of His influence. Somehow they felt that could not arrest Him, though there

[43] *Ibid.* 25 *ff.*

was a division among the people because of Him. Some were emphatically declaring Him to be the Christ; others as vehemently maintained that Christ ought to come out of Bethlehem the city of David, not from Galilee, and to be of David's seed. It would seem, therefore, that Jesus' Davidic descent and birth at Bethlehem were not known to the people He was now addressing. Presently the officers returned to those that sent them—no doubt they were a band of the Temple police acting under the orders of the Sanhedrin, and, therefore, orthodox Jews—saying in excuse for their failure to lay hands upon Him, "Never man spake like this man." [44] This is one of the most illuminating touches in the gospels relating to the effect of Jesus' personality upon His hearers.

For the sequence of events in this closing period of the ministry we are almost wholly dependent upon the fourth gospel, and many of the details given in connection therewith suggest an eyewitness; the local coloring is correct in every particular. The controversy with the Jews—presumably resident in the capital—is represented as continuous, though without any definite testimony to show how much of it took place during the feast of Tabernacles. It should be noted that in more than one instance the Master now explicitly states that He is returning to Him that sent Him, whither His opponents cannot follow Him. This saying greatly perplexes His hearers, whereupon He publicly declares on at least one occasion: "Ye are from

[44] John vii. 46.

beneath; I am from above: Ye are of this world; I am not of this world." [45]   Nothing could be more definite as a revelation of His consciousness of belonging to an altogether higher order of things than that of earthly existence.   That those to whom it was made regarded it as such is shown by their further inquiry, "Who art thou?"   If He were not of this world what was His super-earthly status; whence and how had He come into this world and for what purpose?   But Jesus refuses to answer further than that He had told them all along that He was one sent of God.   This was all He chose to reveal thus far, but it was quite sufficient to suggest to many minds, taken in connection with His marvelous words and works of power, that He must be the Messiah.   It did not follow that the Messiah was a supernatural being, but as many persons thought of Him as such, in accordance with popular apocalyptic views, the suggestion was inevitable that Jesus might be He if His account of Himself were to be believed.   "When ye have lifted up the Son of Man," He continued, "then shall ye know that I am He." [46]   In the light of after developments we have in these words a veiled reference to the crucifixion and ascension, but also, after the manner of the fourth gospel, the saying has a spiritual significance which could not then have been apparent.   He further calls Himself the light of the world, and concludes a daring discourse with the striking affirmation, "Before Abraham was, I

[45] John viii. 23.
[46] Or, "What I Am": John viii. 28.

am." [47] What His hearers could have made of this it is difficult if not impossible to say, and they seem to have regarded it as intolerable and attempted to stone Him for it, but by some means not stated He got away into safety. A dramatic, nonmiraculous escape may be indicated in the laconic passage: "But Jesus hid Himself, and went out of the Temple, going through the midst of them, and so passed by." The better authenticated Mss. of the gospel merely have it that He concealed Himself and withdrew from the Temple; there is no hint of the marvelous about His manner of doing so; all that is conveyed in the narrative is that violence was offered and that Jesus thereupon terminated His discourse within the Temple precincts and retired from the scene, perhaps assisted by His friends and disciples. How often He came and went between Jerusalem and His place of retreat during these last months is nowhere stated, but, reading between the lines, we may infer that He was now more or less constantly on the move. His familiarity with the home at Bethany justifies us in concluding that this was one of His favorite resting places whence He could easily reach Jerusalem when He wished to do so or remain in privacy in the intervals. All that is recorded in chapters vii to x of St. John's gospel may have taken place in a comparatively short time and with few public appearances. Moreover, we may judge from our Lord's general way of conducting Himself at this period that He had made up His mind not to accept death

[47] *Ibid.* 58.

until the feast of the Passover, partly because that was the great religious gathering of the year which persons of Jewish race attended from all over the Roman empire, and partly because He was conscious of the fitness of inaugurating the new dispensation by an act of sacrifice as the old had been. He was Himself to be the victim, the paschal lamb, as it were, whose sprinkled blood should cause the destroying angel to pass by the habitations of God's people. That this is no fanciful interpretation of the Master's motives is apparent from the entire gospel record. Hence these withdrawings in the midst of storm and tumult and ever-increasing rancor; hence, too, the comparative secrecy of Jesus' movements from day to day.

To this phase belong the story of the healing of the man born blind and the discourses in which Jesus describes Himself as the Door and the Good Shepherd. It is noteworthy that to the erstwhile blind man, who had bravely defended Him against the calumnies of the Pharisees and been cast out of the synagogue for his fidelity, He revealed Himself as the Son of God. Perhaps it is to this self-designation that reference was made shortly afterwards at the feast of the Dedication. The blind man may have told others of it and thus it became known. The episode of the woman taken in adultery is inserted here as part of the story of the events grouped around the feast of Tabernacles, but whether it belongs to it or not, or, indeed, ought to find a place in the fourth gospel at all, is, of course, questionable. It has all the marks of authenticity, and the attitude said to have been adopted by the Master on the occasion accords with what we might expect of Him; it is part of the general apostolic tradition; but it is impossible to refer it confidently to any one specific period in the ministry. All through the feast of Tabernacles and the discourses appertaining thereto, Jesus is consistently represented as being assailed by His adversaries in public disputation with the utmost bitterness and animosity. That He knew the end was near is apparent from some of His own utterances in reply to them. "I lay down my life," He declared, "that I might take it again. No man taketh it from me, but I lay it down of myself." [48] And the sharp division of parties concerning His personality and mysterious but astounding claims grows more and more intense. Had Jesus not withdrawn His presence from the capital the tragedy of Calvary would almost certainly have been anticipated by some months.

In St. John's version of the events of this period it is not said that He left Jerusalem at all between the feast of Tabernacles and that of Dedication; it merely states that He was present at both. Luke leaves room at this point for more, and adds a description of a visit to Martha and Mary at Bethany, which may reasonably be regarded as corroborating what has been said above that Bethany was His place of retreat while He was in the neighborhood of Jerusalem.

At the feast of Dedication above mentioned the

[48] John x. 17, 18.

Jews—that is, the same set of hostile inhabitants of Jerusalem as before—surrounded Him as He walked in the Temple in Solomon's porch (a descriptive touch which suggests a vivid recollection of the scene on the part of the narrator) and put to Him the abrupt question: "How long dost thou make us to doubt? If thou be the Christ, tell us plainly." [49] Once more in reply the Master without either affirming or denying His Messiahship declares that He is heaven-sent and that His mission is spiritual, but concludes with a more startling claim than any He has yet made regarding His relationship to God. "I and my Father are one," [50] He says. Again the attempt is made to stone Him, this time for making Himself God, and it is in this connection that Jesus defends Himself by asserting on the authority of the Psalmist the divine quality of all messengers of the word of God. "If He called them gods unto whom the word of God came," He asks . . . "say ye of Him whom the Father hath sanctified and sent into the world, Thou blasphemest; because I said I am the Son of God?" [51] As He is not reported to have said so previously except to the blind man whom He had healed at or soon after the feast of Tabernacles, the observation is arresting. Apparently it was because they knew of this that they interrogated Him on the subject of His Messiahship, and it would seem that they understood the phrase Son of God in a Messianic sense, which it did not necessarily bear. The immediate result of this avowal,

[49] *Ibid.* 24.   [50] *Ibid.* 30.   [51] *Ibid.* 35, 36.

however, was that they at once attempted to seize
Him, and again He had to make His escape, this
time going away beyond Jordan—Bethabara?—to
the place where John had originally baptized. He
appears to have fixed His dwelling there for some
time, many people going out to see and hear Him
as they had formerly gone out to see and hear the
Baptist.

It is to St. Luke that we have to refer for fuller
details of this Perean ministry which lasted till near
the feast of the Passover. For one thing Jesus'
life is now threatened from a new quarter. Some
of the Pharisees warned Him to flee out of the
district because Herod intended to have Him put
to death. "Go ye, and tell that fox," He intrepidly
answered, "Behold, I cast out devils, and I do cures
to-day and to-morrow, and the day following: for
it cannot be that a prophet perish out of Jerusalem." [52] These words are strongly confirmatory of
the opinion expressed above, that Jesus was now
deliberately waiting for the feast of the Passover
to come before delivering Himself into the hands
of His enemies and submitting to the fate which
He saw to be in store for Him. "O Jerusalem,
Jerusalem," He concludes in mournful apostrophe,
"which killest the prophets, and stonest them that
are sent unto thee; how often would I have gathered
thy children together, as a hen doth gather her
brood under her wings, and ye would not! Behold,
your house is left unto you desolate: and verily I
say unto you, Ye shall not see me, until the time

[52] Luke xiii. 32, 33.

come when ye shall say, Blessed is He that cometh in the name of the Lord." [53]

It is to Luke's special source that we are indebted for such slender details as we possess relative to this Perean ministry, mentioned elsewhere only by inference. It is not so clear that we ought to refer to it the various works and discourses which occupy this part of the third gospel. A more probable view is that some of these at least are inserted here out of their due chronological order and might belong to any period of Jesus' public activities. We have already seen reason to suggest that chapter xv, with its three beautiful parables, is a report of a discourse delivered on a much earlier occasion, namely, the feast in Matthew's house, and the same may be true of much else that is inserted here, such as the healing on the Sabbath day of a man afflicted with dropsy. The three parables of the great supper, of the unjust steward, and of Dives and Lazarus may be on a different footing, however. The first-named may be an allusion to the Messianic banquet of popular apocalyptic belief; indeed, it probably is so, and, therefore, the warning of rejection which it contains is more in place at the end of the ministry than it would have been at the beginning. Matthew's parallel to it, the parable of the marriage of the king's son, has the same bearing though widely different in detail. The point of the story of Dives and Lazarus, as of the unjust steward, is that the use of earthly possessions is a matter of grave responsibility of which men must

[53] *Ibid.* 34, 35.

give account in the world to come. There is some ground also for referring to the general circumstances of these last few weeks or months the parable of the Good Samaritan, if it be a parable, and that of the rich fool. The former would gain additional force from the fact that Jesus had recently been inhospitably treated on His way through Samaria. Was it now also that, as Luke suggests in contradistinction to Matthew, our Lord uttered the pathetic saying that He had not where to lay His head? for it would be literally true of these last wanderings. He had said good-bye to Galilee and was more or less of a fugitive and in hiding, moving from place to place without settled abode. It is Luke again who tells about Martha and Mary and the one thing needful, and Luke's special source also (chapter xi) is the Christian classic on the subject of prayer. Luke, as we have seen, is always anxious to preserve sayings that reflect upon the rich and show sympathy with the poor, and he also shields the reputation of the apostles where he can. Thus we get the parable of the rich man who wanted to pull down his barns and build greater. It is Luke also who tells about the fruitless fig tree which was spared a little longer, and the miracle of the woman bowed with a spirit of infirmity—another Sabbath day healing. All these emphasize the compassionateness of Jesus.

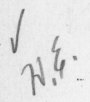

CHAPTER XI

THE PASSION, RESURRECTION, AND ASCENSION

Events Antecedent to the Last Passover

While Jesus was absent in Perea for the reasons above stated, His friend Lazarus, of whose home He had been an inmate not long before, fell ill and the good sisters, Martha and Mary, sent to tell their Master so in one of the most beautiful messages that ever fell from human lips: "Lord, he whom thou lovest is sick." [1] We are not told how the message was conveyed, but apparently the senders thought it would instantly be heeded. But no overt response came; Jesus allowed His friend to die and be buried before He made any move to help the mourners or to show that He cared about their sorrow. Perhaps they hardly expected Him to come in person to their aid; they must have known, as everybody now knew, how perilous a journey to Judea had become for Jesus; in fact, the apostles remonstrated with Him for proposing to return on this occasion. "Let us also go that we

[1] John xi. 3.

may die with Him" was the way in which one of
their number summed up the probabilities if Jesus
were resolved to venture as near as Bethany to the
headquarters of the deadliest opposition He had to
encounter. Nevertheless He went. Lazarus is said
to have been dead four days by this time. "Lord,
if thou hadst been here my brother had not died" [2]
was the gentle reproach with which both the sisters
greeted Him on His arrival. The house was filled
with mourners, including some of the Pharisees
from Jerusalem, a fact which suggests that Lazarus
and Mary and Martha were persons of some social
importance, associated, perhaps, by relationship
with the Pharisaic order. St. John says that "many
of the Jews had come to Martha and Mary, to con-
sole them concerning their brother." Was there an
inner tragedy here? Was Judas another brother
of the family? We shall see ground presently for
inferring that this may, indeed, have been so, and,
therefore, that there was a direct connection between the raising of Lazarus and the death of
Jesus; the one was the immediate occasion of the
other. The Master's emotions overpowered Him
at the grave, and He wept—not for him who lay
within and whom He was about to restore to the
two bereaved women whose hearts He would glad-
den by the wondrous act, but for all that would
presently accrue therefrom and for the world's burden of sorrow, for the dead He would not raise that
day and all the stricken homes He would not comfort, for the long, long tale of human suffering

[2] *Ibid.* 21, 32.

throughout the ages, the appalling total of man's
wickedness and woe. That was why He wept as
He would weep to-day before the bloody battle-
fields and devastated homes of Europe.

It is not to be denied that the silence of the synoptics concerning this amazing miracle is very strange.
They, especially Luke, give considerable space to
the events leading up to the arrest of Jesus in Jerusalem in holy week and yet omit all mention of this
crowning exercise of His wonder-working power,
notwithstanding the fact that the fourth evangelist
emphatically avers that it was because of it that the
chief priests and the Pharisees held the council at
which it was formally determined to have Jesus
put to death as soon as they could lay hands upon
Him. Their avowed reason for this proceeding is
said to have been that if they let Him alone He
would sweep the whole nation after Him and that
the Romans would in consequence deprive them of
such remnants of self-government as they yet possessed. They were afraid that Jesus, with or without His own consent, would become the center of
an insurrectionary movement which would lead to
the suppression of Jewish nationality by the Roman
military power. As we have seen, however, the
Sanhedrin had another reason for wishing to get
rid of Jesus, and that was that He was imperiling
their own authority with the people.

But what of the miracle itself? Is it credible?
Three times our Lord is said to have raised the dead
—in the case of Jairus' daughter and of the widow's
son at Nain, as well as of Lazarus—and the ordi-

nary man at the present day would naturally deny
the possibility of such occurrences if he were now
hearing of them for the first time or in connection
with any other person than Jesus. But this is a
subject in which we shall have to reëxamine our
prepossessions. There is reason to believe that the
trance state, which so closely resembles death as to
be all but indistinguishable therefrom in many instances, is prolonged for a short time even after
death. Most of those who pass over to the other side
of life are said to remain in a state analogous to
sleep for a certain period, long or short, as the case
may be. It is also asserted that the spirit or discarnate self of the deceased person usually remains
for a few days after the severance effected by death
in the neighborhood of the body; separation is not
entirely complete. There is nothing gruesome in
this idea. The disembodied spirit might be quite
unconscious of being held captive in any degree by
the fleshly tenement it had just quitted, as, indeed,
of everything else for a time, and in any event the
connection is a very loose one and cannot last long:
it would naturally cease with the commencement of
corruption. Had Jesus waited longer than the four
days specified, the spirit of Lazarus would have
been finally freed from all attachment to the body
and begun to adjust itself to new conditions; as it
was it was not too late to recall the whole being to
the world of sense. This was not well understood
then, nor is it now, but in the light of modern ex-
perimental knowledge of the mysterious borderland
between life and death, all that is recorded in the

New Testament regarding Jesus' power to raise the dead is perfectly credible. In every instance that power was exerted within a short time after death or what seemed to be death: it may have been trance, but if the view just advanced be correct there is not much difference between the two.

It should not be overlooked, however, that with this as with all other miracles it records, the fourth gospel gives a parabolic turn to the marvel. "I know that he shall rise again in the resurrection at the last day" says poor sorrowing Martha: "I am the resurrection," [3] is the Master's impressive reply. Here again, too, Martha is shown as confessing that she knows Jesus to be the Messiah. There is nothing wonderful in this. As Jesus had now definitely revealed His consciousness of Messiahship to the twelve, there is no reason to suppose that He would conceal it from other trusted and intimate friends.

St. John says that Jesus knew what was being plotted, and, therefore, did not stay long in the neighborhood of Jerusalem on this occasion, but went back into the wilderness region for safety, staying with His disciples for a short time in a place called Ephraim, the locality of which it is now impossible to determine. We cannot be certain about the sequence of events from this point. It is not very likely that He returned northward through Samaria, and yet Luke mentions (xvii. 11) the healing of ten lepers either in Samaria or in Galilee. This healing may have taken place on the southward journey through Samaria already men-

[3] John xi. 25.

tioned. The parable of the unjust judge and of
the Pharisee and the publican is placed here in
Luke's special source, together with the blessing of
little children. Perhaps the parable of the laborers
in the vineyard, which is peculiar to Matthew,
should be assigned to this short period of retirement in the Judean wilderness. Its application is
that those entering late into the service of God are
at no disadvantage as compared with the earlier.
There is in this an evident allusion to non-Jews
whom the gospel message had not hitherto reached,
and who in response to the inquiry "Why stand ye
here the day idle?" could honestly say "Because
no man hath hired us." [4]

Last Journey to Jerusalem

We come now to the Messianic crisis and the
close of our Lord's earthly life. There is substantial agreement in all the gospels on the preliminary
facts. The Passover drew near, and many who
went up to prepare for it speculated on this occasion, as at the feast of Tabernacles not long before,
whether Jesus would dare to come to the feast, the
chief priests and Pharisees having given orders that
if any man knew where He was he should disclose
it in order that they might seize Him. For the last
time Jesus predicts His coming passion to the few
disciples who shared His retirement—though apparently with so little effect that James and John
now made the ambitious request referred to above.
Moving towards Jerusalem He passes near Jericho,

[4] Matt. xx. 7.

healing blind Bartimæus on the way. Here again
Matthew mentions two persons while Mark and
Luke say one. The noteworthy thing about the
incident is the blind man's salutation: "Jesus, thou
son of David." [5] How did Bartimæus know that
Jesus was of Davidic descent? No information is
given on this point, but we may reasonably infer
from the silence of Jewish opponents thereon in
later days that the fact that Jesus was of the seed
of David was unquestioned by those who knew His
origin. That there were some who did not know it
during His public appearances in Jerusalem is
equally evident.

The beautiful incident of Jesus' visit to the house
of Zacchæus, the publican, here finds a place in
Luke's narrative. There does not seem to be sufficient reason for identifying Zacchæus with Matthew as some have attempted to do. It would throw
Luke's chronology completely out if we were to
place this dramatic meeting at the beginning instead of the end of the ministry, and it is not without significance that the parable of the Pharisee
and the publican is represented as having been
spoken about the same time. The parable of the
pounds may have been uttered on this occasion or
it may not. Luke says the Master addressed it to
those who "thought that the Kingdom of God
should immediately appear." [6] It is a close parallel
to the parable of the talents recorded by Matthew,
but there are important differences also.

[5] Mark x. 47. *Cf.* Matt. xx. 30 and Luke xviii. 38.
[6] Luke xix. 11.

Events now move rapidly. A few days before the Passover Jesus came to Bethany once more—or Bethphage, as two of the evangelists have it. Then follows the triumphal entry into Jerusalem, a proceeding on the part of Jesus which must have been deliberate and undertaken with a solemn purpose in view. He abandons all concealment and openly challenges the constituted authority which He knows to be resolved upon His death. Why is this; and what does the public welcome given to Him signify? Did the acclamation of the multitude, "Hosanna to the Son of David," etc.,[7] mean that they recognized Him as the Messiah? Perhaps the best answer to the question is the one they themselves gave when interrogated on the subject, "This is Jesus the prophet of Nazareth of Galilee."[8] They acclaimed Him, not as the Messiah, but as a prophet, a prophet whom they regarded from His own words as declaring the near advent of the coming Kingdom. John, however, distinctly states that some saluted Him as the king of Israel coming in the name of the Lord; but he also adds that His disciples did not understand the complete significance of the event—that is, apparently, did not take the apostrophe literally. Still there must have been some who remembered that He had already been desired as king and were quite willing to proclaim Him as such. Jesus' action in riding upon an ass's colt may have been designed to draw attention to His Messianic claims or at least to set

He was accused of such a claim —

[7] Matt. xxi. 9, 15.   [8] *Ibid.* 11.

people thinking about them in accordance with the well-known prophecy in Zechariah. The facts are best explained on this hypothesis. The hour was near when He meant to declare Himself, but to declare Himself at the very moment when He was making the supreme act of sacrifice, so everything He did beforehand had reference to the consummation He had so long foreseen. John says a crowd of people went out to meet Him with palm branches in their hands, and that what mainly influenced them in doing so was the stupendous miracle of the raising of Lazarus shortly before.

The authorities were completely nonplused and knew not what to do. They had meant to arrest Him at the first opportunity; but this astonishing and unexpected public appearance in the very midst of the crowded city took them unawares. "The Pharisees, therefore, said among themselves, Perceive ye how ye prevail nothing? behold, the world has gone after him." [9] There could be no public attack on Him now or there might be a tumult; they must change their tactics and get Him into their power quietly if that were possible. They decided to put Lazarus to death also—possibly because they believed him to be a confederate with Jesus in palming off on the public an imposture in the shape of his supposed death and resurrection. If they could have him slain the imposture would be exposed and Jesus discredited. It is not said whether they ever succeeded in this plan; it would not be easy to secure the requisite consent of the

[9] John xii. 19.

Roman governor in the case of Lazarus, as no specific charge could be preferred against him. In any event the destruction of Jesus would be enough for the gaining of their ends.

The fourth evangelist tells us that Jesus had been six days at Bethany before this triumphal entry which excited such commotion, and that Lazarus and his sisters prepared a supper for Him. This would appear to have been in presence of a large company, for the comment is added that "much people of the Jews, therefore, knew that He was there; for they came not for Jesus' sake only, but that they might see Lazarus also, whom he had raised from the dead." [10] This suggests that Jesus no longer wished to conceal His movements; the crisis had come, and He had come to meet it; there was no further point in keeping out of the public view.

It was at this supper that Mary is said to have anointed His feet with costly ointment and wiped them with her hair. And herein arises a problem of no small complexity, but capable of a solution of much suggestiveness for a right understanding of the situation now developing. Matthew, Mark, and John record this particular scene in terms which are not inconsistent with each other. Luke does not, but tells of another very like it as having occurred earlier in the ministry. Roman Catholic tradition identifies these two narratives; Protestants for the most part sharply discriminate between them. On the former theory it has to be

[1] *Ibid.* 9.

admitted that Mary of Bethany and the woman that was a sinner—otherwise identified with Mary Magdalene—were the same person, and perhaps the reluctance to concede this has somewhat influenced Protestant judgment in the matter. Catholics, on the other hand, would see no difficulty, rather the contrary, in affirming that a harlot might become a saint and attain to the closest spiritual intimacy with Jesus. Still, despite the similarities in the two stories, the chronological difficulty remains. What are we to say about it; and how account for Luke's beautiful and touching version of an incident which seems to have been repeated almost on the eve of Jesus' arrest?

To the present writer it appears the more probable conclusion that there were, indeed, two anointings as so many Protestant exegetes contend, but that the Catholic view is the true one concerning the identity of the woman in question. Tradition has it that Simon the Pharisee and Simon the leper were the same person. He is said to have been present at the first anointing, but not at the second. Why? Because in the latter case he could scarcely have been sitting at meat with a promiscuous company; a leper, even a wealthy one, would have to be kept apart from others more or less—certainly at meal times. Mary is said to have been enticed away from home in the first instance by a young Greek centurion serving in the Roman army, who afterwards deserted her in Galilee. She was not a bad woman; like so many others, she sinned for love's sake, for her proud Pharisee father would never have consented to her marriage with a foreigner and an oppressor of God's chosen people. Thus left alone in Galilee and driven to despair, she may have sunk into a life of shame. The statement that seven devils were afterwards cast out of her implies as much, for this was only another way of saying that she was a woman of abandoned life who had been recovered from her evil courses. Somewhere she must have met with Jesus and heard His word. Then, possibly by arrangement, she followed Him to her old home in the hope of being forgiven. This is the only explanation which will fit the facts of the first anointing. Jesus sat at Simon's board waiting for the latter to show some sign of relenting towards his daughter whom he had cast off for having wrought folly in Israel. The sign was not forthcoming, and the poor penitent began to weep with grief and shame as she stood behind the only friend who had shown her sympathy and understanding. As her tears fell upon His sacred feet she stooped and wiped them with the hairs of her head and anointed them from the alabaster box of ointment she carried with her. The hard Pharisee remained unmoved, saying only to himself that if Jesus were a prophet He ought to have known the character of this erring daughter of a pious household before admitting her to the number of His disciples. Jesus knew what was passing in the man's mind, and with rising indignation rebuked his self-righteousness, declaring that this woman merited forgiveness if only because "she loved much," [11] but that there

[11] Luke vii. 47.

was little love in the heart of the discourteous host who had omitted all warmth of welcome from his reception of the wandering teacher and the group of friends who journeyed with Him, of whom Mary was one.

Who was this Simon? If Simon the leper of Matthew and Mark were the owner of the house (as these two evangelists say he was) in which the second anointing took place, it must also have been the house of Lazarus, Mary, and Martha. John clearly suggests this, although he does not expressly state it. He gives us to understand that Lazarus was host on the occasion and tells us that Martha did the serving. Then he goes on to describe Mary's action which was almost a precise repetition of the earlier anointing described by Luke. Was it a repetition designedly made to recall the former? Was it not in the same house? And she was intimate enough with the Master to know—her loyal affection for Him and womanly sympathy would make her aware of what others failed to see—that she was, indeed, anointing Jesus to His burial.

A further point of considerable importance emerges here. St. John tells us that Judas Iscariot raised strong objection to the waste of ointment on the ground that it might have been sold for three hundred pence and given to the poor. Matthew and Mark mention his objection, but do not specially associate Judas with it. Here, therefore, we have another instance in which the fourth gospel throws light upon a situation which would otherwise have remained obscure. John says Judas spoke as he did because he was a thief and had control of the common purse; but is there not something deeper behind the incident, a sad and tragical story? Was Judas also a brother of the inmates of the home at Bethany? If so, it would explain a good deal. It is noteworthy that he is said to have been Simon's son. Simon was a common enough name, but it would hardly have been mentioned in this connection—as John mentions it twice—except to draw attention to the name. Here is a supper in Simon's house, and here is an apostle who was Simon's son. What can this mean but that Judas belonged to the family? He was the only apostle who came from the south; all the rest were from the north. He and his Pharisee father may at first have seen in Jesus the possible hope of the deliverance of Israel, though they may never have thought of Him as the Messiah. It may have been through the connection with Judas that Jesus ever came to be a guest in Simon's house. Now that the Pharisees had definitely turned against Jesus, Judas sided with his father's party and betrayed to them the secret of Jesus' claim to be the Messiah. This, as Schweitzer says, was the real betrayal.[12] The restoration of Mary and the friendship with Lazarus and Martha, so far from pleasing Simon, especially after the public rebuke at the first anointing, would be likely to make him all the more the enemy of Jesus, and through Judas he and his Pharisaic associates now determined to put an end to Jesus' power with the public. No doubt Judas

[12] *Ut sup. Quest of the Historical Jesus,* p. 389 *ff.*

was genuinely disappointed with the outcome of the ministry thus far. Jesus would seem to him a mere dreamer whose ideas of benefit to Israel bore no relation to the national hope in which he had been trained. Further than that, he had now become aware that Jesus saw through him, and, as generally happens in such a case, he hated the Master both for His discernment and the spiritual greatness that made it possible; to be constantly in the presence of one so utterly superior to himself was galling to his bad heart. He may honestly have persuaded himself also that if he could destroy this disturber of the public mind, this scathing critic of the national religion and its authorized exponents, he would do a good thing. So he entered into an understanding with the chief priests and the scribes to betray Jesus into their hands.

EVENTS OF PASSION WEEK

After the triumphal entry, Jesus proceeded to the second cleansing of the Temple, and for some days appeared to be master of the situation, teaching daily within the Temple precincts, the Temple authorities being unable to forbid Him. His denunciations of Pharisaic religion now became increasingly stern, and His prophecies of coming doom to Jerusalem increasingly explicit. He foretells the destruction of the Temple, and dwells much upon the catastrophic nature of the divine judgment which is to take place before the end. It is not easy to interpret this collection of sayings to mean other than that the Kingdom in its fullness was to come catastrophically and as a drastic wind-up to the existing order of things and the beginning of another. He Himself, as the Son of Man from heaven, was to be revealed in glory as the agent of this consummation which had yet to take place. To some extent we can interpret this forecast metaphorically, but not entirely so. John presents a rather different picture, dwelling less upon the world crisis to come than upon the life eternal which is Jesus' precious gift to His own.

The Pharisees and Herodians tried hard to en-tangle Him in His talk in order to have something wherewith to accuse Him, such as in the question about paying tribute to Cæsar. A doctor of the Law questioned Him about the great command-ment, and Mark says that the questioner was greatly impressed and acknowledged the truth of the answer he received. This seems to have been followed by a question addressed by Jesus Him-self to the Pharisees, "What think ye of Christ?" [13] All three of the synoptists give this, which evidently was full of meaning. It was an attempt to evoke in their minds the thought that the person of the Messiah had greater significance than merely that of Davidic descent. Then follow the denunciations and woes of which Matthew's gospel is the principal repository. Jesus was careful to say that He Himself did not know when all these things would be accomplished; that knowledge was reserved for God the Father alone. All the parables spoken

[13] Matt. xxii. 41 *ff;* Mark xii. 35 *ff;* Luke xx. 41 *ff.*

in this final phase of the ministry are eschatological in their bearing. Matthew records that of the ten virgins, and in the same connection that of the man traveling in a far country who left his servants in charge; Mark's version of this is very short. Luke has the same idea in the parable of the pounds said to have been uttered earlier. It is Matthew again who records the parable of the last judgment, perhaps (as we have seen reason to infer) an altered Jewish apocalypse with its figure of the Messianic king as judge; but no orthodox Jew would have given it the universal application that Jesus does or made the judgment turn upon purely ethical issues.

Events now proceed in the following order. Two days before the feast of the Passover a meeting of influential members of the Sanhedrin was held at the house of Caiaphas, the high priest, wherein it was decided to have Jesus arrested, but not during the feast. Judas arranged to lead the Temple police to a point where they could succeed in obtaining possession of Jesus' person quietly without interruption from the mob. It is Mark who tells the beautiful story, confirmed by Luke, of the way in which the upper room was obtained where Jesus meant to eat the Passover with His disciples. We gather from the facts as given that the owner of this room was one of the fairly numerous unnamed friends of Jesus of whose existence we have many scattered hints throughout the gospels, and that he and the Master had already settled that the latter was to have the use of the room for the paschal meal. The synoptics and the fourth gospel are apparently at variance with each other concerning the hour when the Last Supper took place and what its character was. The critical difficulties are very serious, and perhaps it is impossible with our present data to arrive at a full and final conclusion concerning them. Was the Lord's Supper, as Christians call it, a Passover supper, or was it not? Some critics hold that the fourth gospel deliberately corrects the others here, but there is nothing to prove that that is so, nor is the discrepancy between them as absolute as at first sight appears. The first three gospels represent Jesus as eating the Passover with the apostles; Luke says that the Lord Himself described it as a Passover. John, on the other hand, has it that His accusers some hours later refused to enter Pilate's judgment hall lest they should be defiled as they had not eaten the Passover. It would seem, therefore, that the meal which Jesus and His disciples had together in the upper room was only figuratively a Passover; in instituting the Lord's Supper Jesus deliberately intended to impress upon the minds of His followers that the old dispensation was henceforth to be superceded. There is no mention of any lamb as there naturally ought to have been if the meal in question was the regular Jewish Passover; Jesus was Himself the lamb that was about to be slain. The Passover lambs were killed by the priests in the late afternoon of the fourteenth Nisan and eaten in the early hours of the fifteenth. Jesus was actually dead before the hours arrived between which the paschal lambs must be consumed, so we can only conclude that the meal which He ate with His disciples was the occasion of the institution of the Christian Passover, the Lord's Supper, but was not, and was not intended to be, even by anticipation an observance of the Jewish Passover.

All the synoptics are agreed about the fact of Jesus' intimation of the impending betrayal and of Peter's defection, but it is to the fourth gospel that we must look for the most detailed information here: only an eyewitness could have furnished descriptions so minute in certain particulars and withal so illuminating and so impressive in their verisimilitude. Thus we gather that the position was around the table. The company reclined in the usual oriental fashion, each person on his left side with feet outward and with the right hand free to reach to the dish placed in the center. The head of each member of the company would thus lean towards the right breast of the person on his left, though, of course, without actually touching it. From John's narrative it is apparent that he himself was placed on the Master's right and Judas on the left. John, the youngest member of the party, was privileged to take the affectionate liberty of lying so close to Jesus that he could lay his head on the latter's bosom as he ate; Jesus' arm might thus have to pass around John's neck in order at certain moments to touch the table. It was a custom also as an occasional courtesy for one person to hand a choice morsel to another as the meal proceeded, and this also is alluded to in the story in a very touching way. When the Master made His announcement

THE LIFE OF CHRIST

that one of those present at that very board was
about to betray Him to His enemies, consternation
followed together with the appeal from every one
individually, "Lord, is it I?" [14] This seems a
strange question for any intimate of Jesus to ask,
especially under the circumstances, and it is only
to be accounted for on the hypothesis that they
thought it applied to the future, not the present,
and that no such conspiracy existed as Judas had
already entered into. Each member of the apostolic band was anxious to be assured at once that
under no temptation could He ever play his Master
false.

We can only understand the succeeding developments, as given even in the synoptics, from the Johannine particulars indicated above. Peter, placed
near John, seems to have whispered to the latter
to ask Jesus directly who the betrayer was. It was
easy for John to do this without being heard by
the others, and easy for Jesus to make the low reply: "He it is to whom I shall give a sop, when I
have dipped it." [15] Thereupon Jesus reached for a
piece of bread, dipped it in the center dish, and
handed it to Judas. It was a last appeal to the
heart of the betrayer. Their eyes met as the little
courtesy was rendered; then those of Judas hardened; "Satan entered into him"; and the Master
gravely and solemnly added, "That thou doest do
quickly." They understood each other, though, as
John states, no one else knew of the moral tragedy

[14] Mark xiv. 19.   [15] John xiii. 26.

that was taking place, but supposed that Judas was being instructed to go out and buy what was required for the paschal feast. Rising instantly, he went, Jesus alone knowing upon what sinister errand.

But before this somber moment was reached, Jesus had done an unexpected and impressive thing. He had risen from supper and gone round the table washing the disciples' feet despite their protests that it was unseemly that He should perform an office so humble. It is worth remembering that Judas was still present when this was done and, therefore, present when it was explained. The mutual rivalries of these simple men, as Luke tells us, continued even into the upper room. James and John had not been forgiven for their self-seeking attempt to steal a march on the others. All were full of the recollection of the triumphal entry and the great things it seemed to portend: Peter especially, we may fairly assume, judging by the vehemence of his protests a few moments later, was jealous of his privilege as the appointed leader of the rest, the rock on which the Church was to be built, whatever that might mean. "Thou shalt never wash my feet," he declared, but immediately recanted when told, "If I wash thee not thou hast no part with me." [16]   Not for the first time, but by means of this acted parable more impressively than ever before, Jesus now reminds these wondering men that precedence in the things of God is won by humility of heart and willingness to serve. "Ye

[16] *Ibid.* 8.

call me Master and Lord; and ye say well, for so
I am. If I then, your Lord and Master, have
washed your feet; ye also ought to wash one another's feet. For I have given you an example,
that ye should do as I have done to you." [17] The
new commandment, to love one another, was uttered
as soon as Judas left the room. At the same instance the Master announced His coming withdrawal from their midst. "Lord, whither goest
thou?" [18] was Peter's prompt inquiry, and it is in
this connection that the fourth gospel places the
protestation of loyalty which drew from Jesus the
terrible announcement, "The cock shall not crow
till thou hast denied me thrice." [19] There is a slight
variation in form between this version of the prophecy and that of the earlier gospels, but its effect is
the same. Mark's account suggests, and is sustained by Matthew, that this colloquy did not take
place till they had left the upper room and gone
out of the city towards the Mount of Olives, and
that the introduction to it was Jesus' announcement that they would all desert Him that same
night. Luke comes nearer to John: "And the Lord
said, Simon, Simon, behold, Satan hath desired to
have you, that he may sift you as wheat: but I have
prayed for thee that thy faith fail not; and when
thou art turned again, strengthen thy brethren.
And he said unto him, Lord, I am ready to go
with thee, both into prison, and to death. And he
said, I tell thee, Peter, the cock shall not crow this

[17] *Ibid.* 13-15.   [18] *Ibid.* 36.   [19] *Ibid.* 38.

day, before that thou shalt thrice deny that thou
knowest me." [20]

On the whole it would seem more probable that
the order as given in the fourth gospel is correct,
for the beautiful discourses contained in chapters
fourteen to seventeen depend closely upon the conversation just mentioned. For example, words of
Thomas are quoted to the effect that as they did not
know whither He was going they could not know
the way. For answer Jesus went on to prepare
them for the removal of His bodily presence and
the inauguration of a spiritual fellowship, closer
and more intense than that which was now coming
to an end. He tells them they will have to suffer
and endure much evil in the world, but that in Him
they will overcome. And then He significantly
adds: "These things have I told you, that when the
time shall come, ye may remember that I told you
of them. And these things I said not unto you at
the beginning, because I was with you. But now I
go my way to him that sent me; and none of you
asketh me, Whither goest thou? But because I
have said these things unto you, sorrow hath filled
your heart." [21] The fact is they were utterly dismayed; this was not at all what they had expected,
as we have already seen. They had *begun* by inquiring, "Whither goest thou?" but as the discourse
proceeded their misgivings deepened until they
quite forgot their original question, the one thought
uppermost in all minds being that in some fell way

[20] Luke xxii. 31 *ff*.   [21] John xvi. 4-6.

they were about to lose their Master; they were not ready to talk about any higher relationship as compensating them in any degree for the ending of the fellowship they had enjoyed for the past two or three years and which had been more precious to them than they yet realized. In gentle deprecation of their gloom the Master suggests that they ought to press their question, "Whither goest thou?" For that was the whole point. If they could be got to understand that the coming passion was not the last word, but that there was a glory beyond and a triumph to be won which would transcend their highest imaginings of the future, it would save them from grim depths of sorrow and despair. In words of tender exhortation He bids them be of good comfort. "These things have I spoken unto you, that in me ye might have peace. In the world ye shall have tribulation. But, be of good cheer; I have overcome the world." [22] The valedictory discourse closes, as indeed seems fitting, with the beautiful prayer in the seventeenth chapter, and the synoptics say, with a hymn, after which they went over the brook Kidron to the Garden of Gethsemane.

To whom the Garden of Gethsemane belonged cannot now be ascertained. That it was on or near the Mount of Olives, and on the further side of the brook just mentioned, is evident from the statement of all four gospels. The traditional site may be correct. John says that Jesus often resorted thither with His disciples, and, therefore, that Judas knew the place. Some friend of the Master must have

[22] *Ibid.* 33.

afforded Him this place of retreat where He could
obtain rest and quiet after His exhausting labors
and controversies in the city without His having
always to go out as far as Bethany. It may have
belonged to Lazarus, but, judging from one brief
passage in Mark's story of the arrest, there seems
some probability that it belonged to Mark's mother
who, as we learn from the Acts of the Apostles, was
a lady of some substance whose house in Jerusalem
afterwards became a rendezvous for members of
the infant Christian Church.

Leaving the other members of the apostolic band
in one part of the garden, Jesus took Peter, James,
and John to another and more retired spot that He
might prepare Himself by prayer for the coming
trial. Nothing is more pathetic in the whole gospel record than the Master's craving for sympathy
in this hour of dreadful waiting. He turned to
these three intimate friends for it, but they failed
Him. He asked them to watch, possibly lest He
should be taken by surprise when the betrayer and
the officers came, and then He withdrew from them
about a stone's cast and, falling on the ground,
poured forth His soul in agonized entreaty to His
Father in heaven, praying that He might be spared
the bitter cup of shame and horror which He had
now to drink. Three times He came and went
between this place of solitary anguish and the three
apostles, and each time He found them asleep.
What a strange lack of understanding of the extremity to which their beloved Master had been reduced! Gently He reproached them with their

failure; they had promised many things; could they not at least have watched by Him for one single hour? Luke says they were sleeping for sorrow—a strange expression which may have a little truth in it; it cannot be supposed that the period of anxiety and strain through which they had all recently passed had left these men untouched and altogether uncomprehending. They did not know what was coming, and apparently Jesus did not tell them, but they were full of grief at the prospect of separation from Him, and tired nature at last yielded to the strain and they slept. There was no sleep for Jesus. It was not merely the prospect of a shameful death that daunted Him; there was the whole mystery of the seeming collapse of His hopes and of His mission to the world. Perhaps there is a deeper depth still in this dread experience which human wisdom cannot fathom. His previous utterances show that He knew of the ultimate triumph, as well as the present passion, but apparently in the latter He was compelled for a time to lose sight of the former. He could do no more than submit without understanding, and this at length He did. "O my Father," He cried, "if this cup may not pass away from me except I drink it, Thy will be done." [23] "Watch and pray," was His warning to the sleeping disciples, "that ye enter not into temptation," compassionately adding in the same breath, "The spirit indeed is willing but the flesh is weak." [24] Perhaps this last sentence referred to Himself as much as to them.

[23] Matt. xxvi. 42.   [24] *Ibid.* 41.

RESURRECTION AND ASCENSION

Hardly was it uttered before Judas and the Temple police arrived, a strong band of men with lanterns and torches and weapons. The signal of identification was to be a kiss. The kiss of Judas has now become a proverb, but that it could be given as though customary shows the terms on which the Master stood with His intimate followers. "Comrade!" was His only comment in this instance, "wherefore art thou come?" [25]—an address which ought to have pierced the traitor's heart, and perhaps did. Peter offered some show of resistance, but Jesus forbade it, healing with a touch the servant of the high priest whom he had wounded. The panic-stricken disciples waited for no more, but instantly fled. Peter and John, together or separately, recovered themselves sufficiently to follow the procession at a safe distance, and presently, through some influence which the younger man possessed with the high priest, were able to come into the palace itself to observe what happened to their Master who was now so strangely helpless in the hands of His foes.

A point to which attention should be directed suggests itself here. Who heard the threefold prayer in Gethsemane and witnessed the mysterious agony which has since so impressed the imagination of Christendom in all ages? It could not have been Peter and the two sons of Zebedee, for they are said to have been asleep. We cannot easily picture Jesus Himself as the narrator after the resurrection. Yet here is some one who observed closely

[25] *Ibid.* 50.

and sympathetically what He did and remembered what He said likewise. Who could it have been but the young man with a linen cloth cast about his naked body whom Mark describes as present at the final scene and following so closely that the Master's captors tried to arrest him, too, and he only escaped by leaving the linen cloth in their hands and fleeing naked into the night? There could be no purpose in inserting this in every little detail had it not possessed a special interest for the writer. Was it not Mark himself? If so, he alone in history was privileged to watch by Jesus while others slept and to listen to the words wrung from His tortured lips in the moment of His greatest human need and most solitary conflict. The context suggests that the young man was in bed and asleep on the premises when Jesus and His disciples entered the garden, and having awakened he arose, feeling that something unusual was afoot, and, throwing a loose garment around him, stole softly through the trees in the direction of the little group. Standing amid the shadows he saw and heard everything; a vigil never to be forgotten to his dying day. It is to him that we are indebted for what would otherwise never have been told.

Concerning the sequence of events on that dreadful night, John is our best authority. Jesus was taken first to the house of Annas, father-in-law of Caiaphas the high priest; Annas without delay sent Him bound as He was into the presence of Caiaphas. Here, while He was being interrogated, Peter stood warming himself at a fire kindled in

the courtyard. One of the maids of the high priest
and, the fourth gospel says, a kinsman of the servant Peter had assaulted in the garden, became sus-
picious of Peter's identity and accused him of being
associated with Jesus, which he vehemently denied.
His Galilean accent, however, made them press the
question, and they continued to do so until at length
with cursing and swearing he denied all knowledge
of the accused, whereupon Jesus turned and looked
at him and the cock crew. That look was more than
the poor cowardly fisherman could bear. A flood
of recollection swept over him, regarding his braggart professions in the upper room and Jesus' striking prophecy of what he would actually do when
the testing time came. With bursting heart and
overwhelmed with shame he instantly made his way
outside and wept in hopeless sorrow. His humilia-
tion was as deep as his repentance was sincere, and,
so far as he knew then, it must have appeared certain that he would never have an opportunity to
retrieve his fall or take his place again by the side
of the being he loved best on earth.

Jesus Put to Death

During the rest of the night Jesus remained in
the high priest's house exposed to insult and ill-
treatment at the hands of the palace retinue. A
hastily summoned session of the leading members
of the Sanhedrin was convened—it is improbable
that it was a formally constituted assembly of that
important body—and in their presence the high

priest examined Jesus on the various counts in the
indictment brought against Him. It is remarkable
that no witnesses could be produced who could sub-
stantiate any charge worthy of the capital sentence.
They contradicted one another, and twisted the
Master's words about destroying the Temple so as
to give them a sinister application, but no definite
accusation could be framed. Had it not been for
Jesus Himself they would have been utterly without any tangible ground on which to bring Him before the Roman governor with a request for his execution, and without the sanction of the Roman
authority they could not have put Him to death.
But Jesus supplied the evidence they wanted. He
remained silent on all the minor charges, but when
at length the high priest suddenly sprang the question upon Him whether He were in truth the Messiah He boldly acknowledged it and went on to
affirm that they should yet see Him coming in
power and glory to judge the world. This was
all the high priest wanted, and it is evident that he
was somehow already acquainted with the facts,—
probably through Judas, as stated above. Rising
in pretended consternation at what he called this
blasphemy, he declared that no more witnesses were
necessary for the culprit was now condemned out
of His own mouth. The rest of the council agreeing with him, it was determined to bring Jesus
before Pilate without delay as a dangerous fomen-
ter of sedition against constituted authority. They
had to give a political turn to His pretensions in
order to induce Pilate to take cognizance of them.

RESURRECTION AND ASCENSION

Messiahship must be construed as a claim to secular kingship in insurrection against the Roman power.

As early as possible in the morning this was done, and the method of procedure was somewhat curious. As this was the day of preparation for the Passover, the accusers would not enter into the judgment hall lest they should be ceremonially defiled and, therefore, precluded from eating the paschal meal in the evening. Pilate had to come out in front of the prætorium to listen to the accusation, but he seems to have questioned Jesus in private within the hall itself. It did not take him long to realize that the ostensible ground of accusation was not the true one. Priests and scribes would not have been so venomous in their opposition to a real rebel against the Roman power or pretender to the throne of Israel, there must be something else. In reply to the governor's demand to know if He were indeed a king the strange prisoner unhesitatingly avowed it, but added that His Kingdom were not of this world. Pilate was so deeply impressed by Jesus' demeanor that he tried hard to save Him, first sending Him to Herod to get Him away from the rancorous Temple priesthood and their allies, and then when that failed offering in accordance with custom to free either Jesus or some other prisoner as a compliment to the Jews on the occasion of their great national feast. The alternative he suggested was Barabbas, a brigand and murderer who was awaiting execution. He supposed there could be no question which would be desired, but he was soon undeceived. The mob, at the insti-

THE LIFE OF CHRIST

gation of the priests, demanded Barabbas. Herod
had long been desirous to see Jesus, and as he happened to be in Jerusalem just then, Pilate, on the
plea that Jesus belonged to his jurisdiction, suggested that he should take Him away and judge
Him, but the priests and scribes were determined
not to lose sight of their victim. They pursued
Him with their accusations before Herod also, and
that crafty potentate, after mocking and scourging
his silent prisoner, sent Him back again to Pilate
who then weakly consented to allow Him to be
crucified.

Once again before passing sentence in the teeth
of his own convictions, the Roman governor tried
to excite the compassion of the fanatical rabble by
bringing Jesus out to them after He had been
scourged and maltreated by the brutal Roman soldiers in the judgment hall. This scourging was
one of the most dreadful punishments ever invented,
the victim's body being lacerated in the most sick-
ening manner by thongs and rods. In mockery of
His supposed claims to royal dignity, Jesus was
clothed in a purple robe and a crown of thorns was
plaited and hammered down upon His head. A
forlorn and ghastly spectacle, indeed, was that of
the suffering Savior as Pilate led Him forth in
view of the multitude. "Behold the man!" [26] he said.
"Crucify Him, crucify Him!" [27] was the instant and
savage response. Pilate's last attempt had failed.
Taking a basin of water he washed his hands be-

[26] John xix. 5.   [27] *Ibid.* 6.

388

fore them, exclaiming "I am innocent of the blood of this just man, see ye to it." [28] "His blood be on us and on our children" [29] was the awful rejoinder, a self-invoked judgment fulfilled to the last degree upon the guilty nation in days to come.

That Pilate had had many misgivings concerning the piece of wickedness he was now permitting to be perpetrated, and for which he in vain tried to divest himself of responsibility, is perhaps illustrated by his wife's dream. What the dream was is not stated, but that it filled her with terror and foreboding is evident from her message to her husband entreating him not to have anything to do with the murder of one so holy. Did she know anything of Jesus personally? It is not impossible. Herod's own foster brother was one of the earliest Christian converts, and other members of the court are said to have been of Jesus' immediate following. But it is at least equally probable that Pilate had not concealed from her his uneasiness at the course events were taking and his contempt for the malicious gang who were engineering it for their own wicked ends. The matter so preyed upon her mind that night that some warning of the enormity of the contemplated crime came to her in sleep and, in consequence, she vainly endeavored to stand between her husband and its commission. Pilate's symbolical hand-washing was the result. This dream must have been in the day rather than the night, for Jesus was brought before Pilate early in

[28] Matt. xxvii. 24.   [29] *Ibid.* 25.

the morning and was dead before the next night came.

The question has sometimes been asked, What had now become of the multitude that had welcomed Jesus to Jerusalem with hosannas only a few days before and on account of which the Temple authorities had been afraid to seize Jesus openly? How was it that the only multitude of which we hear anything from the moment of His arrest is one that is savagely hostile to Him? Had the same mob that had acclaimed Him now turned against Him, or what? We need not go far for the explanation. It is fully in accordance with mob psychology that as long as a person is powerful and master of the movement of events he should be visited with every species of homage and applause, but let him show himself vulnerable and at once he becomes an object of popular execration. It is a strange and saddening phase of human nature this, but undeniable as history abundantly testifies. Nevertheless, we may be perfectly sure that there were many, especially among the Galileans, who had come up to Jerusalem for the Passover and of those who had witnessed or become acquainted with the miracle of the raising of Lazarus, who never turned against the Savior in His hour of dereliction and woe, but, like the disciples themselves, were dismayed and taken by surprise. The priests and Pharisees had calculated rightly. Once Jesus was in their power there was no more to fear; His friends had no leader and no rallying center; the blow struck and the Master condemned, there

was no one strong enough to act on His behalf.
How could they? It would be acting against all-
powerful Rome. Besides, much of the very public
confidence in Jesus sprang from a feeling that He
was superior to every ill that could be devised
against Him. When this was proved not to be so
all who wished Him well would conclude that His
cause was irretrievably lost.

The dreadful procession took its way towards
Calvary, a hillock outside the city whereon criminals were crucified. Jesus, as was the custom with
those condemned to this sort of punishment, was
compelled to bear His own cross, but faint from
anguish and loss of blood He sank under its weight
and a passer-by named Simon, from Cyrene in
North Africa, was laid hold of by the soldiers and
made to carry it in His stead or along with Him.
The form of Luke's narrative would suggest that
they supported it together, Simon following behind
the sufferer. Mark says this Simon was the father
of Alexander and Rufus, two members of the apostolic Church, and there is an early tradition that he
was himself a Christian. Why was he forced into
this sad service, a service which yet will be his peculiar glory to the end of time? Was it that his
captors saw in his face some compassion for the
condemned; did he venture to express it; was he,
pilgrim from a distant clime though he might be,
himself a disciple and friend of the Master? Perhaps; we do not know.

Arrived at the place of death, Jesus was stripped
and stretched upon the cross; there were those who

followed Him to the last, principally women, some
of them of cruel Jerusalem itself, who openly wept
in pity for His fate; and at the cross His mother
stood, the sword of which Simeon had spoken in
the Temple long before piercing through her an-
guished heart as her august Son hung in torture
above. Over the sufferer's head was affixed the reason of His condemnation, in three languages, by Pilate's order: "This is Jesus the king of the Jews." [30]
No doubt Pilate intended this as a gibe at the representatives of the nation which had thus worked
their evil will upon one worthier than themselves,
and they are said to have protested against it.
There is some discrepancy between the synoptical
gospels and the fourth on the question of the actual
hour of the crucifixion and how long it was before
the end came, but perhaps the method of calculat-
ing is different in each case. Bitter were the taunts
leveled at Him, meanest of all the cry: "He saved
others, Himself He cannot save." [31]   Two highway
robbers were crucified with Him, one on either side,
and it is said that these also joined in the mockery
with which He was assailed, but that presently one
of them repented of this and rebuked the other.
"Lord, remember me when thou comest in thy
Kingdom," [32] he prayed. The prayer was a vague
one, but it shows that the speaker thought it quite
possible that Jesus might yet do what His enemies
taunted Him with being unable to do, come down
from the cross and thus demonstrate to them all that

[30] Matt. xxvii. 37; Mark xv. 26; Luke xxiii. 38; John xix. 19.
[31] Matt. xxvii. 42.
[32] Luke xxiii. 42.

He was the chosen of heaven; it could hardly mean more. All the sweeter and more comforting, therefore, to one with a spark of good in him was the promise in reply, "To-day shalt thou be with me in paradise." [33] Paradise was the place of the departed, not heaven, but not a place of torment either, and what was reassuring in this word spoken to the penitent robber was that he and Jesus would be together there. Whatever happened, therefore, on that mysterious farther side of death, it would be well.

Other words the dying Master spoke before the end came. He complained of thirst, and there were those present who would have given Him a stupefying drink prepared by some compassionate ladies of Jerusalem who were accustomed to endeavor to assuage the sufferings of the victims of this horrible mode of public execution. But Jesus shook His head; He would not die drugged. Hour after hour He hung there enduring the inconceivable agonies to which He was subjected and of which the victims often died raving mad. Six hours after the crucifixion began He suddenly cried with a loud voice in the Aramaic tongue, "Eloi, Eloi lama sabachthani,"—"My God, my God, why hast thou forsaken me?" [34]—apparently a quotation from the twenty-second Psalm which rose to His lips in this dread hour. The bystanders thought He was calling for Elijah as the Galilean dialect suggested, and some of them seem to have imagined it possible

[33] *Ibid.* 43.
[34] Mark xv. 34; Matt. xxvii. 46.

that the great prophet whose advent was popularly expected to precede that of the Messiah might, indeed, appear to save Him. But no such dramatic deliverance took place, and soon after Jesus cried with a loud voice, "Father, into thy hands I commend my spirit," [35] and bowed His head and died. Mention has already been made of the divine sufferer's last thought for His mother. From the cross He committed her to the care of the beloved disciple in words which most certainly identify this disciple with St. John. How John dared to be at the cross when the other Galileans were in hiding is not explained; perhaps it was due to his acquaintance with the high priest.

It was the cruel custom to break the limbs of crucified criminals in order to put an end to them if they were too long in dying. The Jewish authorities asked that this might be done in the case of Jesus and His fellow-sufferers in order that their bodies might not remain hanging on the cross on the Sabbath day, and this was done in the case of the two thieves, but was found not to be necessary in the case of Jesus, as He was already dead, though in order to make sure that He was not only in a swoon one of the soldiers pierced His side with a spear. The water which flowed from the wound, in addition to blood, is said to demonstrate that our Lord died from a ruptured heart as is easily conceivable after all He had gone through in the space of twenty-four hours.

Certain portents are said to have accompanied

[35] Luke xxiii. 46.

His passing, which are worthy of note—three hours
of phenomenal darkness which, as is often the fact,
appears to have been connected with seismic dis-
turbances, the rending of the veil of the Temple
from probably the same cause, and the appearance
of a number of apparitions of persons long dead.
This last is recorded by Matthew alone, but it is
far from being incredible. Moved, perhaps, in
some degree, by these abnormal happenings, but
still more, no doubt, by what he had observed of
the demeanor of Jesus throughout His trial, the
centurion in command of the execution, a man foreign to Jewish ways, was sufficiently impressed to
declare in the hearing of the assembled multitude
that they had crucified an innocent man and probably a divine being—for this is the force of the
double ejaculation, "Certainly this was a righteous
man: truly this was a son of God."

His opinion was shared even by members of the
Sanhedrin, as betokened by the action of Nicodemus and Joseph of Arimathæa who obtained per-
mission from Pilate to inter the sacred body with
respect. It was laid in Joseph's own tomb, one of
the many rock-hewn tombs of the neighborhood,
and the like of which still abound in Palestine.
John says it was in a garden hard by, and he describes in detail the hasty yet loving burial. All
that the forlorn little group could do was done in
view of the fact that the Sabbath was so near; it
was expected that some of them might come again
later and perform more carefully the last offices of
anointing the body with sweet spices. The heavy

stone that fitted the opening of the sepulcher was rolled into position for the time being, and the sorrowful mourners went their way.

Perhaps some of the Pharisees witnessed the interment and heard the resolve expressed that some of the women should come again after the Sabbath with proper unguents for completing the preparation of the body for the grave. At any rate, they determined to make sure that there should be no tampering with the tomb without their knowledge, for they seem to have been quite aware of the Master's prophecy that He would rise again on the third day, or, as Matthew has it, "after three days" —an expression which means the same thing, though not strictly identical in form. Obtaining authority, therefore, they placed a guard by the tomb and sealed up the stone.

"He Is Risen"

The subject of the resurrection is full of difficulty, less so intrinsically than is an attempt to fill up the gaps in our knowledge of what happened on the first Easter Sunday and the forty days following. But, as the late Lord Salisbury once said, there is no event in history better attested than the fact that Jesus Christ rose from the dead, for without this fact the existence of Christianity itself is absolutely unexplainable. However we are to view it, it is certain that something tremendous, something overwhelmingly convincing, must have taken place in order to transform our Lord's dismayed followers into the intrepid spiritual forces they afterwards became. What was it?

All the gospels are agreed that it was Mary Magdalene who played the principal part in the discovery of the empty tomb. Whether there was any one with her to begin with is not quite so certain. Mark names several others as being present, John mentions Mary alone, Matthew two Marys, Luke adds Joanna and the other woman who had belonged to the Galilean fellowship. They expected to be baffled by the sealed stone, especially as it was much too heavy for their frail hands to move. They may or may not have known of the guard that had been placed there. But, to their astonishment, they found the stone rolled away, the tomb empty, and no one to be seen. Matthew's special source says that there had been an earthquake shock, which is not unlikely, seeing that there had been indications of the kind on the Friday afternoon while the crucifixion was going on. From this version of events we should gather that a severe storm accompanied the shaking of the earth's surface, for we are next told of the appearance of a heavenly being whose visage was like lightning and who wore a vesture of dazzling brightness. The narrative states that it was he who rolled away the stone and sat upon it, to the extreme terror of the men who had been left on guard. These fled into the city with their tale and were forthwith bribed to silence, or, rather, to avow that the body of Jesus was stolen while they slept. It is not said that any one actually saw Jesus emerge from the tomb, but all the accounts testify

to at least one supernatural visitor on the scene
when Mary and her friends arrived; Luke and John
say two. Mark speaks of a young man arrayed
in a white robe, and Luke of two in shining garments, but they evidently refer to beings not of
this world. It was these who gave the first intimation to the women that Jesus was risen. Matthew
and Mark say no more of any Jerusalem appearance. Mark's story of the stupendous event stops
abruptly at this point. It tells us that the women
were instructed by the supernatural watcher to go
and tell Peter and the rest of the disciples that Jesus
would appear to them in Galilee. It adds that they
said nothing to any one because they were afraid.
The last twelve verses of the gospel are manifestly
a compilation from the others and may be neglected
for the purpose of our inquiry into the facts of
this marvelous occurrence.

Matthew and Luke agree that the women were
told to tell the apostles, but Luke omits what
Matthew relates that, as they were going, Jesus
Himself met them and confirmed the message they
were to deliver about the Galilean appearance.
Luke states that Peter went and examined the
tomb, but saw nothing, and that the rest of the
apostles regarded the women's reports as idle tales.

It is to John that we must look for a fuller and
more moving recital of the first sequences of events,
and he writes as one sure of his ground. It was
Mary Magdalene who first came upon the empty
tomb, "early, while it was yet dark." She went at
once to tell Peter and John, and these both came

in haste to inspect the scene. John got there first, as being younger he was the fleeter of foot, but he did not enter the tomb. Stooping down he saw that the body was gone, for he could discern the linen clothes in which it had been wrapped lying by themselves. Peter, on the other hand, did not hesitate; on arriving he went straight in and saw for himself that the body was not there. John followed, and both noted that the cerements lay, as Dr. Latham points out,[36] as though the body had risen through them instead of shaking them off, for the linen cloth that was about the head lay apart from the rest on the raised slab on which the head had rested. Satisfied that what they had heard was true, they went back home again. There is no mention of there having been any heavenly visitant.

But Mary did not go. She remained standing without the tomb weeping, and presently, like the two apostles, she stooped down and looked into the sepulcher, when, contrary to aught she could have expected considering the examination of the tomb a few moments before, she saw two persons sitting, one at the head and the other at the foot, where the body of Jesus had lain. Apparently she did not suspect that they were other than human, though she might have wondered why Peter and John had not referred to them. They asked her why she wept and she replied, "Because they have taken away my Lord, and I know not where they have laid Him." [37] They appear to have said

[36] *The Risen Master*, chap. i.   [37] John xx. 13.

no more just then, and she was turning away disconsolate when she saw Jesus Himself standing near her amid the breaking shadows of the morning. He put the same question, and she, thinking Him to be the man who kept Joseph of Arimathæa's garden, asked to be told whither he had conveyed her Master's body. "Mary!" came the answer, tenderly spoken in the old familiar accents she had thought never to hear again. In swift revulsion of feeling she flung herself at His feet with the glad cry, "Rabboni," and would have clutched Him in her agony of delight, as though never again to be parted from Him. In St. John's mention of this striking detail we have an undesigned correspondence with Matthew's statement that the women rushing from the tomb met Jesus and held Him by His feet and worshiped Him. "Take not hold on me" was the gentle remonstrance; "for I am not yet ascended to my Father; but go to my brethren, and say unto them, I ascend unto my Father, and your Father; and to my God, and your God." [38] They were not to seek to detain Him here or expect to resume the old relationship on exactly the same footing; a new, and higher, and closer relationship would begin from this time forth. They may not yet have known what ascension meant, but it was not long before they did. The risen and ascended Lord was henceforth to be a closer, dearer, more intimate companion than the earthly teacher whose words had been spirit and life to them.

Several striking post-resurrection appearances

[38] *Ibid.* 17.

are recorded in Jerusalem and the neighborhood, as described not only by the third and fourth evangelists, but by St. Paul. From Paul's words, which are the earliest record of the facts, we gather what was universally believed in the primitive Church in regard to the matter. Incidentally, he confirms by anticipation both the synoptics and the fourth gospel.

One of the most impressive and significant of the appearances receives bare mention only, but is none the less touching for that. It is the appearance to Peter, the poor, discomfited braggart who had promised so well and behaved so ill and was now lurking somewhere in utter despair, feeling that he could never lift his head again. We have seen that Peter, in the company of John, had hastened to the tomb at the first intimation that it was empty, so it is clear that these two had forsaken all unworthy rivalries in presence of their common sorrow. John, too, had something to reproach himself with. Like the rest, he had fled from Gethsemane even if he had afterwards returned and stood by the cross at Calvary. He would understand Peter's defection and be well aware of the true loyalty and devotion to Jesus' person which, nevertheless, underlay it, and which now filled the poor fisherman's heart with inconsolable grief. How much these two must have had to say to each other in John's lodging, wherever it was, to which they had betaken themselves, and where, be it remembered, the virgin mother had also been sheltered by the Lord's own command! To whom did Jesus first appear? Was

it to His mother? What passed between these twain
was not for mortal ears to hear. St. Paul mentions
first the appearance to Peter, and Luke incidentally confirms this by the report of the excited testimony of the eleven to two disciples: "The Lord is
risen indeed, and hath appeared to Simon." [39] To
Simon! Again not a word is told us of what passed
between the humble and penitent apostle and the
risen Master. How could there be? With tender-
est delicacy and compassion, Jesus came to comfort
His poor follower and restore him to His fellowship, a fellowship never again to be broken. Peter
was a changed man from that hour. He had no
more earthly rewards to ask for and no more dan-
gers to fear; henceforth he lived for Jesus and Jesus
alone. What he may have said to Jesus or Jesus
to him forms no part of the gospel tradition; it remained sealed within the hearts of both, a mutual
confidence too sacred and intimate to be disclosed
to the rest of the world. A public evidence of the
renewed understanding had yet to be made,
but what happened at this first interview when
the erstwhile crucified Savior came in private
to talk with the man who had been the first to recognize His true Messiahship and yet denied Him in
the hour of His passion is their own secret. We
are told no more than that the interview took place,
but that is enough to suggest a whole range of beautiful things. Perhaps the meeting was in the house
where John and the Virgin dwelt, and Jesus may
have seen all three separately and then conversed

[39] Luke xxiv. 34.

with them together in that abode but recently so
full of woe and now of a joy the like of which surely
earth had never known before; for in deed and truth
the incredible had taken place, and henceforth to
these privileged ones death had no terrors as earth
had no glamours.

John tells how this same evening Jesus came
through closed doors to the disciples in the upper
room or perhaps in the house of Mark's mother.
"Then were the disciples glad when they saw the
Lord" [40] is the simple and restrained comment which
the evangelist makes upon the awe-inspiring scene.
Doubtless this is the experience which Paul mentions as having been to the twelve, as it certainly is
the one described by St. Luke in terms so different
as to show that the two sources are quite independent of each other, though mutually consistent. It
is the third evangelist also who relates the winsome
episode of the appearance to a disciple named
Cleopas on the way to Emmaus some time between
the morning and the evening of that wonderful
first Easter day. Paul adds that after that "He
was seen of above five hundred brethren at once." [41]
Where this meeting took place is not indicated; perhaps it was in Galilee, which is rather more likely
than Jerusalem; but that it was no vague tradition,
but an authentic event, is proved by the apostle's
accompanying statement that the greater number
of those so privileged were still alive at the moment
of writing. Luke and John hardly leave room for

[40] John xx. 20.   [41] I Cor. xv. 6.

Galilean appearances, especially the former, but they contain nothing inconsistent with the testimony of Matthew and Mark—if Mark can be cited in this connection—that there were such appearances. The statement that the apostles met Jesus in Galilee as well as in Jerusalem rests upon Matthew's authority only, but it is quite definite. The only difficulty about it is that of accounting for a journey of the eleven to Jerusalem again afterwards, for it is said to have been from Jerusalem that the Master's final departure took place. The addendum to St. John's gospel, chapter xxi, is additional testimony, however, that the journey north must actually have been made, for it describes an appearance to a few of the apostolic band at the lake of Tiberias as they were engaged in their former avocation of fishing. John calls this the third appearance to the disciples, but it does not follow that it was the third appearance in all. There is the special appearance to James the Lord's brother, which Paul says took place after these previously mentioned events. Henceforth James and the rest of the family are associated with the company of disciples in Jerusalem, and James appears from the first as head of the Church there. On the whole, the most reasonable supposition is that during the forty days intervening between the resurrection and ascension our Lord, first in Jerusalem and then in Galilee, explained to His followers all that was necessary concerning the foundation of the Church, and advised them to go home to Galilee and settle their affairs there as a necessary preliminary to beginning their new work as missionaries to their nation and the world. Jerusalem was the natural center from which to begin, not Galilee, but as the majority of them came from Galilee they had to return thither after this tragical Passover with its astounding sequel before coming south again to the capital to await their Master's will.

There may have been a few other appearances in Jerusalem and neighborhood during the first Easter week. Cleopas and the unnamed friend who journeyed with him to Emmaus—perhaps Luke himself—were not of the innermost circle of disciples, so it is not too much to infer that others may have been similarly privileged. On this occasion Jesus is said to have been recognized by them in the solemn act of the breaking of bread. This can hardly have been an allusion to the Last Supper, for as these men were not apostles they would not be present thereat. Perhaps it was characteristic of Jesus to bless a meal before partaking of it, or what is more probable, the expression may simply mean that while He was in the act of pronouncing a blessing on this occasion He had momentarily resumed the form and feature to which they had previously been accustomed and they instantly knew Him. The whole story is one of singular attractiveness as well as authenticity. John says that it was as much as eight days after this before the further appearance of Jesus in the upper room at which Thomas was present; so we may conclude that for at least that time the Galilean followers of the Master had remained in Jerusalem before obeying the direction sent to them through the women that they should meet Jesus in Galilee. Mark's story that He was going before them into Galilee is no contradiction of this fact. He was; perhaps Peter and the more intimate circle had already gone, for they are not mentioned as having been present on this occasion. This special appearance appears to have been for the benefit of Thomas who had not been able hitherto to believe the good news unless he were allowed personally to verify it.

John's story of the appearance to Peter, Thomas, Nathanael, and James and John by the lake of Galilee at a later stage is memorable for the conversation which ensued between Jesus and Peter. Three times Peter had denied his Lord in Pilate's hall; three times he is now asked to affirm his loyalty. He had claimed to be more faithful than the others, so the first question was, "Lovest thou me more than these?" [42] Peter was in no mood for boasting now or for asserting his own superiority to the rest in personal fidelity or anything else, so he merely answered in simple terms, "Yea, Lord, thou knowest that I love thee." [43] Thereupon he received the solemn commission to feed the flock of Christ; he was now ready by his very humility to take up the office which had been designed for him from the first. A second time the same question was put, and the same answer given; and yet a third. We are told that Peter was grieved because the question was put a third time, but the reason of his morti-

[42] John xxi. 15.　　　[43] *Ibid.*

fication is not apparent in the English version of the text. It was not the iteration but the form of the question which wounded him. There is a play here on the English word "love." Two words are employed in the Greek original which are translated into our tongue by this one term, thus missing the main point. In the first two questions Jesus employed one word and Peter answered with another. The former was a loftier word than the latter, expressive of the highest form of love $(\dot{\alpha}\gamma\dot{\alpha}\pi\eta)$; Peter's word was the humbler term, expressive of a heart's fellowship, unpretentious and individual $(\omega\iota\lambda\dot{\iota}\alpha)$, the word which is the root of our "philanthropy." The third time Jesus put His searching question He came down to Peter's term, and it was this which hurt Peter; it seemed as though the Master doubted his sincerity, hence the disciple's shamed remonstrance which was in effect this: "Surely, dear Lord, you who know all things, including the human heart, are well aware that despite all my cowardice and treachery to my vows, despite my abandonment of you in your hour of direst need, I loved you all along. Neither shall I boast nor claim precedence of any one; I but love you as a child might love a mother, as one who has everything to gain and nothing to give. O, believe it; I make no higher pretension." This was all Jesus wanted, and He closed the impressive colloquy with another definite allusion to Peter's former hopes of reward and honor. His greatest honor in this world was to be that in time to come he should die for his Lord. Tradition says that this prophecy was exactly fulfilled, for Peter was crucified in Rome head downward as a martyr in the cause of Jesus and His Church.

The resurrection body of Jesus is said to have behaved in supernormal ways and to have been possessed of powers unknown to ordinary human flesh. He could appear and disappear at will, could pass through walls and doors as though they were nonexistent, and finally He was devitated from the midst of the wondering disciples and vanished from their view. Nevertheless, it was no phantom Christ who ate and drank before His friends, not, perhaps, because He needed such sustenance, but to convince them that His body was real, was, in fact, the very same body that had hung on Calvary and been laid in the tomb. [44] It was for this reason also, doubtless, that He invited Thomas to place his finger on the print of the nails. To the modern mind such phenomena seem incredible, and so they might be were there no context for them, no category to which to relate them nearer to our own time. That the resurrection of Jesus is unique goes without saying, but the fact of the passage of matter through matter is not unique. [45] As Frederick Myers says in his *Human Personality and Its Survival of Bodily Death*:

[44] Oskar Holtzmann's view that "the reanimation of Jesus' earthly body could only have been important if He was to continue His life on earth" (*Life of Jesus*, p. 500) misses the purpose of that reanimation as most of the modern negative criticisms of the traditional belief do.

[45] *Vide* Zöllner: *Transcendental Physics.* chap. vii. and many other testimonies.

RESURRECTION AND ASCENSION

On a basis of observed facts Christianity, the youngest of the great types of religion, does assuredly rest. Assuredly those facts, so far as tradition has made them known to us, do tend to prove the superhuman character of its Founder, and His triumph over death; and thus the existence and influence of a spiritual world, where men's true citizenship lies. . . . I venture now on a bold saying; for I predict that, in consequence of the new evidence, all reasonable men, a century hence, will believe the Resurrection of Christ, whereas, in default of the new evidence, no reasonable men, a century hence, would have believed it. . . . There is nothing to hinder the reverent faith that, though we be all "the Children of the Most Highest," He came nearer than we, by some space by us immeasurable, to that which is infinitely far. There is nothing to hinder the devout conviction that He of His own act "took upon Him the form of a servant," and was made flesh for our salvation, foreseeing the earthly travail and the eternal crown.[46]

The fact is that we do not know anything about the ultimate relation of matter to spirit. Matter is the language of spirit. Living our lives, as we do, under the conditions of a three-dimensional world, our bodies are our means of expression and of communication one with another. But if once we could be freed from the limitations of our three-dimensional experience of life, many things which now appear to us impossible, or at least abnormal, would become normal and reasonable. After the resurrection, our Lord was a being no longer subject to physical limitations, but used His physical

[46] Vol. II, pp. 286, 289.

body for a time as the very best kind of language
He could employ wherewith to assure those who
loved Him that He had triumphed over sin and
death and in spirit was with them evermore. The
ascension was not the carrying up of a physical
body to another plane of existence above the sky,
but its withdrawal into and assimilation to its spiritual background, like the melting of a white cloud
into the fathomless blue of the firmament out of
which it arose. The whole story is literally and exactly true.

Jesus is forever the one Master of the human
race. Other masters may come and go; a few are
not unworthy to stand beside Him; but He only
has given us God. The creeds may fail to explain
the relationship of the Father and the Son, but
they testify to the discovery Jesus brought to mankind: we have found God in Him: to Him we owe
all we know or are able to understand of the spiritual order: He is in very deed the Way, the Truth,
and the Life. It is really Jesus we worship when
we name the name of God. It is not that we have
exalted Jesus to share God's throne, but that our
very conceptions of God have become exalted by
being associated with the person of Jesus. And yet
He is of ourselves; only once has the world seen
perfect man, and that was in Jesus. The divinely
human, the humanly divine, He has revealed to us
our own possibilities, made us to glimpse a little of
the glory that shall be when we know as we are
known. In no forensic sense, but in simple and un-

escapable fact, He is Lord of all; our source, our goal; our Savior, our Judge; our hope of ultimate victory over all the ills of our present lot and of entrance into everlasting habitations.

Amen.

One is Better for reading a Book like this, yet it is a pity there are so many of the author's peculiar suppositions in it, the lack of accepting Miracle is greatly to Be deplored, a great Book for all this But it cannot take the place of Farrar's, Geikie's, Edersheim's & such others Lives of Him whose Life after all cannot Be written for He is Eternal

N.S.

Read Feb. 1922

APPENDIX—NOTE A

PERSONAL APPEARANCE OF JESUS

It is remarkable that in the gospels we have so little reference to a subject on which modern readers would greatly desire information. What was Jesus like in appearance? Was He tall or short, robust or frail, handsome or the reverse? Did He resemble in any degree the conventional portrait of Him which has now become all but universal in Christendom? How did He dress; and what characteristic features, if any, did He possess—what sort of voice, look, gesture, such as we are wont to associate with those dear to us, would those who knew Him always remember as specially His?

On all these points the evangelists are strangely silent. All we can gather from them is—and they are impressively at one in regard thereto—that He carried with Him a suggestion of great personal force and at the same time of wonderful winsomeness. He created awe in His hearers, and in His case familiarity did not breed contempt, for we read that the disciples were very conscious of this quality in Him up to the last. Thus Mark says (x. 32): "And they were in the way going up to Jerusalem; and Jesus was going before them: and they were amazed; and they that followed were afraid." Evidently something in the Master's demeanor, the solemn resolve to go to meet suffering and death, the lonely majesty, the spirit not of this world, the suggestion of unearthliness that clung to His every movement filled these simple men with a feeling akin to fear. They could not understand Him, but His very presence cast a spell upon them such as none other ever did. It must have been a personality of extraordinary loftiness and power that could produce this effect in those who lived within its immediate influence from day to day. On another occasion (Mark ix. 32), we read: "They understood not that saying, and were afraid to ask Him."

Even His enemies were conscious of this to some extent. Again and again we are told that no man after a certain episode "durst ask Him any question" (Matt. xxii. 46; Mark xii. 34; Luke xx. 40). After the resurrection, as we might expect, the feeling was intensified on the part of the disciples (John xxi. 12). Everywhere and at all times throughout the earthly ministry the disciples are represented as treating Jesus with the utmost reverence as a being infinitely superior to themselves—and yet He was but a young man! Priests, Pharisees, and scribes did not find it easy to challenge Him openly. They scowled, and murmured, and intrigued against Him, but it was not until He was actually a prisoner in the hands of His foes that they dared openly to show Him any violence. How otherwise are we to account for the fact that more than once when violence was actually threatened He was able to go away unscathed? "He, passing through the midst of them, went His way" (Luke iv. 30). (*Cf.* John viii. 59 and x. 39). Why was it that the rulers of the Temple dared not lay hands on Him when He swept out the money changers? Why did they slink abashed from His presence? Why but for the same reason, that the overwhelming moral force which radiated from Him made it impossible to do otherwise? Is not this the explanation also of the remarkable passage (John xviii. 6) in which it is stated that those who came to arrest Him in Gethsemane "went backward, and fell to the ground"? No one liked to be the first to touch Him, and as He advanced they retreated, stumbling over one another, until at length they summed up courage enough to seize their unarmed victim.

On the other hand, note the readiness with which little children came to Him. There is one incident which illustrates this even more than the saying "Suffer little children to come unto me," which finds a place in all the synoptics, and that is the placing of a little child in the midst of the wondering circle of quarreling men and bidding them imitate him if they would attain to membership in the Kingdom of God (Matt. xviii. 2; Mark ix. 36; Luke ix. 46, 47). This child must have been well content to stand between Jesus' knees with Jesus' arms around him; no hint is offered to the contrary. And where did He find the child? The suggestion is that he was there already, standing looking up into the Master's face, and that Jesus had simply drawn him to His side to point His discourse. Children could have felt no fear of Jesus. Evidently, therefore, there must have been something attractive and kind in His very look when it rested on a little one, something tender and winning.

The erring and the downtrodden discerned this also. The woman taken in adultery remained near Him when her accusers fled discomfited (John viii. 1-11); the woman that was a sinner washed His feet with her tears, regardless of the opinion of those about her (Luke vii. 38); little Zacchaeus blurted out his promise of amendment in the presence of a company that scorned him, sure of the Master's sympathy and understanding (Luke xix. 8)—all that was good in him rose up and found expression under the serene gaze of those kind eyes.

And what eyes Jesus must have had! All of the evangelists repeatedly draw attention to the way in which He looked at people. Evidently they were struck by this. Those who listened to Jesus habitually must often have spoken about it—that look at Peter in the judgment hall, for instance (Luke xxii. 61); the look that He gave to the churlish Pharisees before the act of healing in the synagogue (Mark iii. 5) ; most of all, perhaps, the smiling sympathy with which He regarded the rich young ruler (Mark x. 21). As to His voice, we are told that "the common people heard Him gladly" (Mark xii. 37), which they would not have done if there had not been a certain charm in the cadences of the voice that uttered the words of eternal life. "Never man spake like this man" (John vii. 46) was the testimony of the officers of the Sanhedrin sent to arrest Him. In their absorption in what He was saying and in His way of saying it they forgot their commission and later felt they could not carry it out.

His dress, His demeanor, His walk would all be in keeping. There would be a dignity and simplicity about these which accorded with the rest of what we are told about Jesus. He was not rich, so His garments must have been those of the ordinary person of His class in that day. He may have worn the praying shawl of white with colored edges which was common in that day as at present, principally in the synagogue, but also outside. The long, straight undergarment worn by natives of Palestine by night and day, and extending from the neck to the ankles, no doubt formed part of Jesus' costume. This, too, may have been white, and was probably fastened with a girdle. On His head would be a large white or colored napkin, folded diagonally. A sleeveless cloak or coat of goats' or camels' hair or wool, for outdoor use, and sandals for the feet would complete the wearing apparel as in Tissot's realistic pictures.

Authentic portraits of the Master we have none. But the Rev. J. R. Aitken says in his admirable volume, *The Christ of the Men of Art* (T. & T. Clark) chap. i, that there is more to be said for the authenticity of the traditional face than has been generally admitted. There is a tradition that St. Luke was not only a physician but a painter, and a portrait of Jesus attributed to him is treasured in the Vatican. It cannot be supposed authentic, but is very early, and it is interesting to note that in outline it is the traditional face which is presented therein. The present writer remembers seeing many years ago a remarkable portrait of Jesus which had been discovered in the wall of the church of San Silvestro in Capite at Rome. It was believed to date from the 6th century, and had been built into the wall to save it from destruction at the hands of marauding invaders. The colors were quite fresh. This also was a representation of the traditional face.

But the whole subject is one with an interest and a literature of its own. In addition to Mr. Aitken's book, mentioned above, the reader might consult Dean Farrar's *Life of Christ in Art* and Sir Wyke Bayliss' *Rex Regum*. Dean Farrar takes the view that the traditional face of Christ is conventional only, and that we have no means of knowing what He was really like; Sir Wyke Bayliss argues for the contrary view.

APPENDIX—NOTE B

THE KIND OF HOME IN WHICH JESUS LIVED

In a country like Palestine, where so much life is spent in the open air, dwellings tend to be simpler than with us, at any rate among all classes except the very wealthy. As Jesus did not belong to the latter it is probable that the house which sheltered Him, in Capernaum as well as in Nazareth, would be comparatively small and rudely built. The Capernaum house would be larger if Jesus intended to make it a kind of community headquarters, which may have been the fact; it is not at all probable that the house in which He spent His early years at Nazareth could have accommodated an audience. It would be built of clay, or clay and stone, and roofed with clay and wattles. It might contain two or three rooms, but hardly more. There would not be much furniture—a low table for meals, a few rude kitchen utensils, a small, open, oil lamp, vessels to contain water, corn, and oil or perhaps wine, would be about all except a few pallets for sleeping on. The Capernaum house may have been arranged around a courtyard after the Græco-Roman fashion, as shown in the excavations at Ostia and Pompeii. Life was much simpler in Palestine in Jesus' day than in the modern western world, and still is; but due allowance should be made for the fact that Galilee then was much more fertile and prosperous than the same district is now.

Jewish home life was much superior to that of surrounding nations in so far as personal relationships were concerned. The mother held an honored position and was the child's principal teacher until He was old enough to go to the synagogue. Both at home and in the synagogue education had a definitely religious basis. In the school connected with the synagogue Jesus would be taught to read and write and cast accounts in addition to memorizing and reciting the Old Testament Scriptures; but it would be from His mother that he would first learn the great truths of religion as understood by the nation to which He belonged. That the atmosphere of this home was one of earnest piety and devotion may be gathered, not only from the utterances of the world's greatest religious genius, who was trained in it, but still more, perhaps, from the fact that a man like James the just was also an inmate thereof; for the one writing of his which we possess is redolent of the finest type of Old Testament piety and morals.

BIBLIOGRAPHY

ADDIS: *Hebrew Religion.*
AITKEN, J. R.: *The Christ of the Men of Art.*
ARMITAGE, ROBINSON: *The Study of the Gospels.*

BARRETT, SIR WILLIAM: *On the Threshold of the Unseen.*
BOUSSET: *Jesus.*
BOX: *The Virgin Birth of Jesus.*
BRUCE: *The Kingdom of God; The Parabolic Teaching of Christ; The Training of the Twelve; The Miraculous Element in the Gospels.*
BURKITT: *The Earliest Sources of the Life of Jesus; Jewish and Christian Apocalypses.*
BUSHNELL: *Nature and the Supernatural.*

CAMPBELL, LEWIS: *Religion in Greek Literature.*
CARPENTER, PRIN. ESTLIN: *The Historical Jesus and the Theological Christ; The First Three Gospels.*
CHARLES, R. H.: *Religious Development between the Old and New Testaments; Testaments of the Twelve Patriarchs.*
CHASE, BISHOP: *The Gospels in the Light of Historical Criticism.*
CONYBEARE: *The Historical Christ.*

DEISSMANN: *Bible Studies, Light from the Ancient East.*
DILL: *Roman Society from Nero to Marcus Aurelius.*
DREWS: *The Christ Myth.*

421

BIBLIOGRAPHY

DRUMMOND, PRIN.: *The Character and Authorship of the Fourth Gospel.*

EDERSHEIM: *Life and Times of Jesus the Messiah.*
ENCYCLOPAEDIA BIBLICA: Articles in.
ERSKINE OF LINLATHEN: *The Spiritual Order.*
EUCKEN: *The Life of the Spirit; Problems of Human Life* (for teaching of Jesus philosophically examined).
EXPOSITOR'S GREEK TESTAMENT, THE.

FAIRBAIRN, PRIN.: *Studies in the Life of Christ.*
FARRAR: *Christ in Art.*
FORREST: *Christ of History and of Experience.*
FRAZER: *Golden Bough* (sections).

GARDNER: *Exploratio Evangelica.*
GLOVER, T. R.: *Conflict of Religions in the Early Roman Empire; The Jesus of History.*
GORE: *Dissertations on Subjects Connected with the Incarnation; Prayer and the Lord's Prayer; The Sermon on the Mount.*

HAMILTON: *The People of God.*
HARNACK: *Expansion of Christianity* (Vol. I); *Luke the Physician; The Sayings of Jesus.*
HARRIS, RENDEL: *Sidelights on New Testament Research.*
HASTINGS DICTIONARY OF THE BIBLE: Articles in.
HAWKINS: *Horae Synopticae.*
HEADLAM: *The Miracles of the New Testament.*

KEIM: *Jesus of Nazara.*
KIRSOPP, LAKE: *The Resurrection of Christ.*

LATHAM: *Pastor Pastorum; The Risen Master.*
LECKY: *History of European Morals.*
LIDDON: *Bampton Lectures; Sermons on Some Words of Christ.*

BIBLIOGRAPHY

LOBSTEIN: *The Virgin Birth of Christ.*
LODGE, SIR OLIVER: *Survival of Man.*
LOISY: *The Religion of Israel.*

MARTI: *Religion of Old Testament.*
MILLIGAN: *The Resurrection of Our Lord.*
MOFFAT: *A New Translation of the New Testament.*
MONTEFIORE: *The Religious Teaching of Jesus; The Religion of the Ancient Hebrews; The Synoptic Gospels.*
MOULTON, J. H.: *Early Zoroastrianism* (for Magi).
MURRAY: *Jesus and His Parables.*
MURRAY, GILBERT: *Four Stages of Greek Religion.*
MYERS, F. W. H.: *Human Personality and Its Survival of Bodily Death.*

OESTERLEY: *Introduction to the Apocrypha.*

PEAKE, A. S.: *Critical Introduction to the New Testament.*
PETRIE, FLINDERS: *The Growth of the Gospels.*
PFLEIDERER: *Early Christian Conceptions of Christ.*

RAMSAY, SIR W. M.: *Education of Christ; The Church in the Roman Empire; Luke the Physician.*
RENAN: *Life of Christ.*
ROBERTSON, J. M.: *Pagan Christs.*
RYLE and JAMES: *The Psalms of Solomon.*

SADLER, GILBERT: *Behind the New Testament; The Inner Meaning of the Four Gospels* (regards Christ as an ideal only).
SANDAY: *The Criticism of the Fourth Gospel; Life of Christ in Recent Research; Outlines of the Life of Christ.*
SCHAFF: *History of the Church.*

BIBLIOGRAPHY

SCHMIEDEL: *The Johannine Writings* (over-emphasizes the allegorical character of the Gospel).

SCHÜRER: *The Jewish People in the Time of Jesus Christ.*

SCHWEITZER: *The Quest of the Historical Jesus.*

SCOTT, E. F.: *The Fourth Gospel.*

SEELEY: *Ecce Homo.*

SMITH, DAVID: *The Days of His Flesh.*

SMITH, GEORGE ADAM: *Historical Geography of the Holy Land.*

STANTON: *The Gospels as Historical Documents.*

STRAUSS: *Leben Jesu.*

SWETE: *The Holy Catholic Church; Studies in the Teaching of Our Lord.*

S. P. C. K.: Series of translations of Apocalyptic and other writings edited by Dr. Oesterley and Canon Box (most useful and helpful).

THOMPSON, J. M.: *The Synoptic Gospels.*

TYRRELL: *Christianity at the Cross Roads.*

VON HÜGEL: *Eternal Life.*

VON SODEN: *The History of Early Christian Literature.*

WALKER, W. L.: *The Teaching of Christ.*

WEISS, B.: *Life of Christ.*

WENDT: *The Teaching of Jesus.*

WRIGHT: *Synopsis of the Gospels* (attributes much importance to oral tradition).

ZÖLLNER: *Transcendental Physics.*

INDEX

Abgar, legend of, 91
Addis, note 7
Adulteress, Christ and an, 351
Aenon, near Salim, 176
Aitken, Rev. J. R., 416
Alabaster box of precious ointment, 368
Allegories. *See* Parables
Andrew, brother of Simon Peter, 153, 154
calling of, 184
Anna the prophetess, 67, 111
Annas sends Jesus to Caiaphas, 384
Annunciation, the, 105 *et seq.*
Antipas. *See* Herod Antipas
Apocalyptic, idea of the Messiah, 140, 141
importance of, 47 *et seq.*
Apocryphal gospels, the, 28, 90 *et seq.*, 115
Apostles, call and selection of the, 185
dispute for precedence, 327
powers granted to, 234
return from their mission, 236
sent out two and two, 185
their mission, 185
Apostolic story of life of Jesus, 24 *et seq.*

Aramaic language, the, 69, 70
Archelaus, son of Herod the Great, 115
Arimathæa, Joseph of. *See* Joseph
Ascension, the, 398
Auber, Harriet, a well-known hymn by, 255
Augustus, Emperor, 104

Baal worship, 6
Bahai movement, the, 331
Banias. *See* Cæsarea Philippi
Baptism, 242
an essential for admission of Gentiles into Judaism, 58
of Christ, 127
symbolic nature of, 126, 174
Barabbas, 387
Bar-jona. *See* Peter
Bartimæus, healing of, 363
Bauer, Bruno, and the gospel tradition, 41
Baur, F. C., 42
Bayliss, Sir Wyke, 417
Beatitudes, the versions of Matthew and Luke, 191, 195
Being, the two planes of, 7 *et seq.*
Benefactors, 341

INDEX

INDEX

INDEX

Eucken, 14 note

Eusebius, 69, 74, 192

Evangelists, the, gospels of, 69 *et seq.*

    their accounts of the transfiguration, 321, 322

Extra-canonical writings, 90 *et seq.*, 115

Fairbairn, Principal, on miracles, 258 note

Faith, Christ's insistence on necessity of, 290

the perfect, 325

Farrar, Dean, 417

Fasting, Christ's answer to John's disciples regarding, 224

Fayum fragment, the, 90

Feast, an unnamed, in John v., 205

Fig-tree, parable of, 356

"Fishers of men," 185

Fishes, miraculous draught of, 185

Fitzgerald, Edward, 66

Five thousand, feeding of the, 206, 267 *et seq.*

the miracle discussed, 270

Fool, parable of the rich, 334

Forgiveness, Jesus' insistence on necessity of, 301

Forgiveness of sins by Christ, 188, 209, 210

Four thousand, feeding of the, 308

Francis of Assisi, St., 86, 214

Gadarene demoniac, healing of, 260

swine, episode of, 205, 261

Galilean ministry of Christ, 181

Christ's disappointment at spiritual results of, 303

Galilee, Christ's final retirement from, 305

Hellenization of, 55, 56

Sea of, sudden tempests in, 257 note. *See also* Gennesaret

the settlement in, 114

Genealogies, the, 100 *et seq.*

Gennesaret, Lake of, sudden storms on, 280

Gerizim, Mount, 55

German criticism on the gospels, 40 *et seq.*

Gethsemane, Garden of, 380

our Lord's threefold prayer in, 381, 382

Gladstone, W. E., 16

Glover, Dr., 4 note, 138

on the Jewish people, 65

Gnosticism and the pseudo-gospels, 92

God, Jewish conception of, 7

Good Samaritan, parable of, 356

Gore, 132, 147 note, 200, 291 note

Gospel, origin of name, 27

Gospel tradition, sequence of, 41

Gospels, the, and the apostolic story, 26

canonical and uncanonical, 68 *et seq.*

earliest writing of, 68 *et seq.*

origin of, 25

Greek civilization, classical, 4

influence on apostolic Christians, 54

INDEX

language, and the Gospels, 69

Grenfell and Hunt, Messrs., and the Oxyrhyncus sayings, 90

Hamilton, Prof., 5 note, 7 note, 191 note

Harnack, Adolf von, 44, 92 note, 192, 193

Harris, Rendel, 14 note, 54 note, 84, 94 note, 330

Healing, Christ's works of, 186 *et seq.*

Hebrew Gospel, the, 69

Hebrews, Gospel according to the, 90, 92, 93, 94, 122, 336 note

Herod Antipas, Christ sent by Pilate to, 386
desires to see Christ, 245
orders execution of John the Baptist, 245
rebuked by John the Baptist, 176

Herod Philip, 311

Herod the Great, 112, 113
death of, 115

Herodians, 230, 231, 303

Herodias, 245

Higher criticism, theories of, 32 *et seq.*
misleading results of, 21

Hill, J. Arthur, on miracles, 186 note

Hillel, law of, 59

Hinnom, valley of, 299

Holtzmann, H. J., 320 note
and the synoptic problem, 43

Holtzmann, Oskar, 248 note, 408 note

Home, D. D., 280 note

Houses, Oriental, 418

Hügel, Baron von, 15

Immaculate Conception, dogma of the, 97

Impotent man healed at pool of Bethesda, 206, 228

Ireland, 66

Iscariot. *See* Judas

Israelitish prophets, rise of, 5

Jacob's well, 177

Jairus' daughter, raising of, 359

James, the Lord's brother, 121, 122, 404
head of the church at Jerusalem, 80, 117, 121, 404

James the Just, 419

James the Less, calling of, 184
Christ's post-resurrection appearance to, 406
intimacy with Christ, 340, 341
rebuked by Christ, 329, 333
sleeps in Gethsemane, 381
witnesses the transfiguration, 320

Jehovah, Jewish conception of, 6

Jerusalem, Christ's lamentation over, 354, 355
Christ's post-resurrection appearances in, 400 *et seq.*
Christ's triumphant entry into, 364
examination of Christ's discourses at, 180
Feast of the Passover at, 118, 165
Temple at, 55; veil of, rent, 395

INDEX

INDEX

INDEX

205 *et seq.*, 228 *et seq.*, 239, 279, 307, 308, 311, 325, 351, 358, 359. *See also* Nature miracles

Mob psychology, problem of, 390

Mohammedanism, birth of, 52

Mons, the angels of, 14

Montefiore, Mr., 7 note, 59, 64
  on the Pharisees, 51

Mosaic Law, Jewish allegiance to the, 56

Moses at Christ's transfiguration, 321

Mount Gerizim, 55

Mount, Sermon on the, 78, 190

Mountain, Christ retires for prayer to a, 274

Murray, Prof. Gilbert, 4 note

Myers, F. W. H., 264 note
  on the resurrection of Christ, 408

Nain, raising of widow's son at, 359

Nathanael of Cana in Galilee, 67

Nathanael, the Apostle, calling of, 156, 157
  Christ's post-resurrection appearance to, 406

Nativity and childhood of Jesus, 80, 96 *et seq.*

Nativity of Mary, Gospel of, 91, 120 note

Natural order, the, 8 *et seq.*
  invasion of, by supernatural, 13

Nature miracles, Christ's, 256 *et seq.*
  modern-day, 258

spiritual significance of, 259, 269
  See also Miracles

Nazareth, Christ reads and expounds the scripture at, 183
  Jesus' home at, 418
  the holy family settle in, 115

Necromancy discouraged by the Church, 263

New Testament criticism, 32 *et seq.*
  of what composed, 25
  the apostolic story and, 24 *et seq.*
  the Church and, 19
  the Epistles and Gospels of, 25

Nicodemus, 60
  at Christ's burial, 175, 395
  Christ's interview with, 172
  Gospel of, 91
  mentioned in the Talmud, 173
  speaks in defence of Christ, 175

Nobleman's son, healing of, 182

Non-resistance to evil, Jesus' teaching on, 296

O'Brien, Smith, 66

Open-air preaching of Christ, 203, 204

Origen, 94, 120 note

Oxyrhyncus, sayings of Jesus from, 90

Palestine and the world-empire, 53 *et seq.*
  houses in, 418
  population of, 66

Palm Sunday, 365

INDEX

Papias, 69, 192
and Petrine origin of
Mark's Gospel, 73, 74
Parables, Christ's teaching
in, 198, 218, 220 *et seq.*,
256, 355, 356, 362, 373
Paradise, 393
Paralytic healed on the Sab-
bath day, 205, 209
Parousia, the, defined, 237
Passion week, 371
Passover, Feast of, 165
Passover, was the Last Sup-
per a? 374
Paul, St., 79, 98, 198, 199
Pauline epistles, the, 25, 26,
42
origin of the Gospels, 79
People, the state of, in time
of Jesus, 63 *et seq.*
Perea, Christ's stay in, 354,
355
Personal appearance of
Jesus, 413 *et seq.*
Peter, St., 73 *et seq.*, 171
at Christ's grave, 401
at Christ's walking on the
sea, 275
Christ's last charge to,
402, 407
Christ's post-resurrection
appearance to, 402
denies Christ, 385
Gospel of, 90, 94
his bearing at the Last
Supper, 377
his position among the
Apostles, 312
his profession of belief,
156, 278, 283, 312
rebukes Jesus, 315
sleeps at Gethsemane, 381
traditional crucifixion of,
76, 407
warned by Christ, 378, 379

witnesses the transfiguration, 320
wounds servant of high
priest, 383
Petrine origin of the Gospels, 73 *et seq.*
Pharisee and publican, parable of, 363
Pharisees, the, 57, 64
and baptism, 243
as Nonconformists of their
age, 57
Christ's denunciation of,
243, 309, 371
conspire with Herodians,
230, 231
demand a sign from
heaven, 309
disciples warned against,
310
seek to kill Jesus, 359
the leaven of, 310
their hostility to Christ,
176, 188, 203, 204, 222,
224 *et seq.*, 303 *et seq.*
Philo of Alexandria, 85
Philip, Gospel of, 90
Philip the Apostle, 156
Phœnicia, Christ in retirement in, 305
Photism, 323
Pilate, cowardice of, 386,
387
Jesus before, 386
presentiments of, 387, 389
washes his hands, 388
Post-resurrection appear-
ances of Christ, 400 *et
seq.*
Pounds, parable of the, 363,
373
Prayer, Christian classic on
subject of, 356
importance attached by
Christ to, 291

435

INDEX

INDEX

437

INDEX